GARDEN STYLE

GARDEN
Style

A practical Australian guide to creating your ideal garden

CHERYL MADDOCKS

DOUBLEDAY
Sydney   Auckland   New York   Toronto   London

ACKNOWLEDGMENTS

I would like to thank the following people for allowing me to photograph their beautiful gardens.

Honeysuckle Cottage (Bowen Mountain, NSW), Chris Wallace, Mark Way, Manuela Darling, Lyle and Dorothy Davis, Tony and Inga Morphett, B. Reid, Mary Davis (Colonial Cottage, Kenthurst, NSW), Mr and Mrs F. Charnock, Sarah Crawford, Heide Park and Art Gallery (Heidelberg, Victoria), P. Fowell, Joseph Sontrop, David Putnam, Mrs Genner, Mr and Mrs Beecham, Everglades (Leura, NSW), Steven Dean, Steven Melas, Bruce and Elizabeth Forbes, Penny Coleing, Poppy McDonald, Ian McCorknichal, Reg Livermore, Annie Wordsworth, Robyn Widdy, Duane Norris Garden Designers (Woollahra, NSW), Bronwyn and Colin Bachali, C. and R. Sullivan, Jenny Smith, (Jenny Smith Landscapes, Melbourne), Sue Duval, Sandra and Paul Ferman, Brian Moore, Margaret Fink, Tom and Robin Naylor, Mike and Jenny Davis, Ivor and Jenny Kants, Mr and Mrs Fowell, Colonel and Mrs Hughes, Joe and Wendy Bertony, Heronswood, Cherry Cottage (Mt Wilson, NSW), Pam and Jim George, Mr and Mrs Rob-Brown, Ethel Knight, Honeysuckle Garden Centre (Double Bay, NSW).

Special thanks to John, Celeste and Nicholas.

First published in Australia and New Zealand in 1990 by Doubleday, a division of Transworld Publishers (Aust.) Pty Limited, 15-25 Helles Avenue, Moorebank, NSW 2170 and Transworld Publishers (NZ) Limited, Cnr Moselle and Waipareira Avenues Henderson, Auckland.

© Cheryl Maddocks, 1990

All rights reserved. No part of this publication may be reproduced, stored in a retrieval system, or transmitted, in any form or by any means, electronic, mechanical, photocopying, recording or otherwise, without the prior permission of the publisher.

National Library of Australia
Cataloguing-in-Publication Data

Maddocks, Cheryl
Garden Style: a practical Australian guide to creating your ideal garden

Includes index
ISBN 0 86824 421 X

1. Gardening — Australia. 2. Landscape gardening — Australia. I. Title

635.0994

THIS BOOK WAS PRODUCED BY CHERYL MADDOCKS

Designed by Steven Dunbar
Edited by John Maddocks
Illustrations by Mary Forbes
Photography by Cheryl Maddocks
Jacket background by Crump and Stubbs, Sydney
Type output by Everysize Typeart Services, Sydney
Printed by Tien Wah Press, Singapore

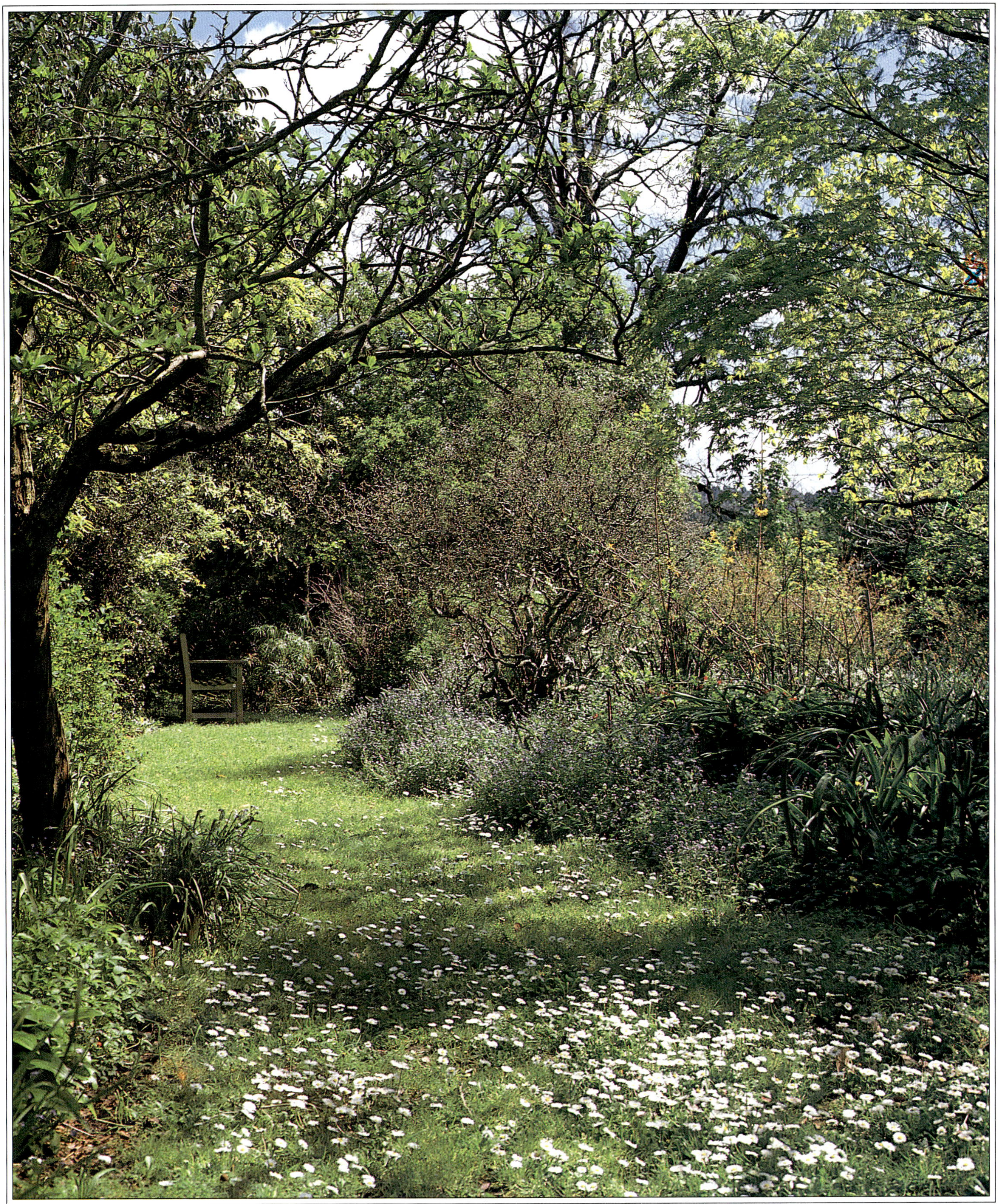

Contents

Garden Styles

An Inner-city Courtyard 10
Restful Areas
  of the Garden 12
An Elegant Garden Bed 15
Italian Style 17
An Impressionist Scene 20
A Green and White
  Garden 23
The Wild Garden 26
Shades of Blue 29
The Summerhouse 32
The Perennial Garden 34
A Courtyard Wall 36
Entrance Steps 38
Colour Drifts 40
A Shaded Pathway 43
The Spring Garden 44
The Kitchen Garden 46
A Garden Retreat 50
A Natural Swimming Pool 53
A Perfumed Garden 54
A Woodland Grove 57

A Charming Entrance 58
Planting Around a
  Birdbath 60
A Sylvan Glade 62
The Charm of Yesteryear 64
A Tropical Courtyard 68
Along the Side of a Path 71
Autumn Colour 75
A Romantic Rose Garden 76
The Garden Shed 79
A Garden Picture 80
A Garden of Day
  and Evening Fragrances 82
A Walled City Garden 86
A Paved Courtyard 88
Garden Enchantment 90

Creating your Ideal Garden

Creating a Garden Style 94
Aspect and site 94
Micro-climates 94
Garden planning 99
Garden design 102

Within the Garden 105
Steps 105
Pathways and paving 108
Internal walls and fences 112
Garden accessories 114
Garden structures 118
Water 120

Garden Boundaries 124
Fences 124
Hedges: a living boundary 125
Gates 126

Colour Design 128
Use of colour 128
Colour themes 129
Colour combinations 130

Garden Restructuring 135
Structure 135
Redesigning 135
Underplanting 137

Perennials 138
Designing a perennial border 138
Perennial maintenance 141
A selection list 143

OLD–FASHIONED ROSES 150
Landscaping with roses 150
Care and maintenance 152
A selection list 153

CLIMBERS 160
Landscaping with climbers 160
Selecting climbers 162
A selection list 165

GROUNDCOVERS 170
Landscaping with groundcovers 170
Choosing groundcovers 172
Planting 173
A selection list 174

BULBS 176
Types of bulbs 176
Landscaping with bulbs 176
Bulb care 177
A selection list 179

ANNUALS 182
Landscaping with annuals 182
Care of annuals 185
A selection list 186

BIRD–ATTRACTING GARDENS 190
Bird-attracting plants 192

A BUTTERFLY GARDEN 194
Butterfly–attracting plants 195

SHRUBS 196
Landscaping with shrubs 196
Hedges within the garden 199
Topiary 200
Knot gardens 201
Parterre gardens 201
Standard shrubs 202
Planting shrubs 202
A selection list 203

TREES 208
Using trees in the landscape 208
Tree shapes 211
Pleaching 212
Espalier 213
Pruning 213
General maintenance 213
A selection list 214

THE HERB GARDEN 218
A formal herb garden 218
An informal approach 218
Cultivation of herbs 220
Harvesting and preserving herbs 221
A selection list 225

THE PRODUCTIVE GARDEN 228
The art of vegetable cultivation 228
Garden layout 230
Companion planting
   with vegetables 231
Maintaining the
   vegetable garden 232
Fruit and berries 235

PRACTICALITIES

MAINTAINING THE EFFECT 240
Soil 240
Regenerating the soil 241
Mulching 242
Compost — natural recycling 242
Feeding 245
Watering 246

CREATING NEW PLANTS 248
Growing from seed 248
Cuttings 250
Division 252

INDEX 253

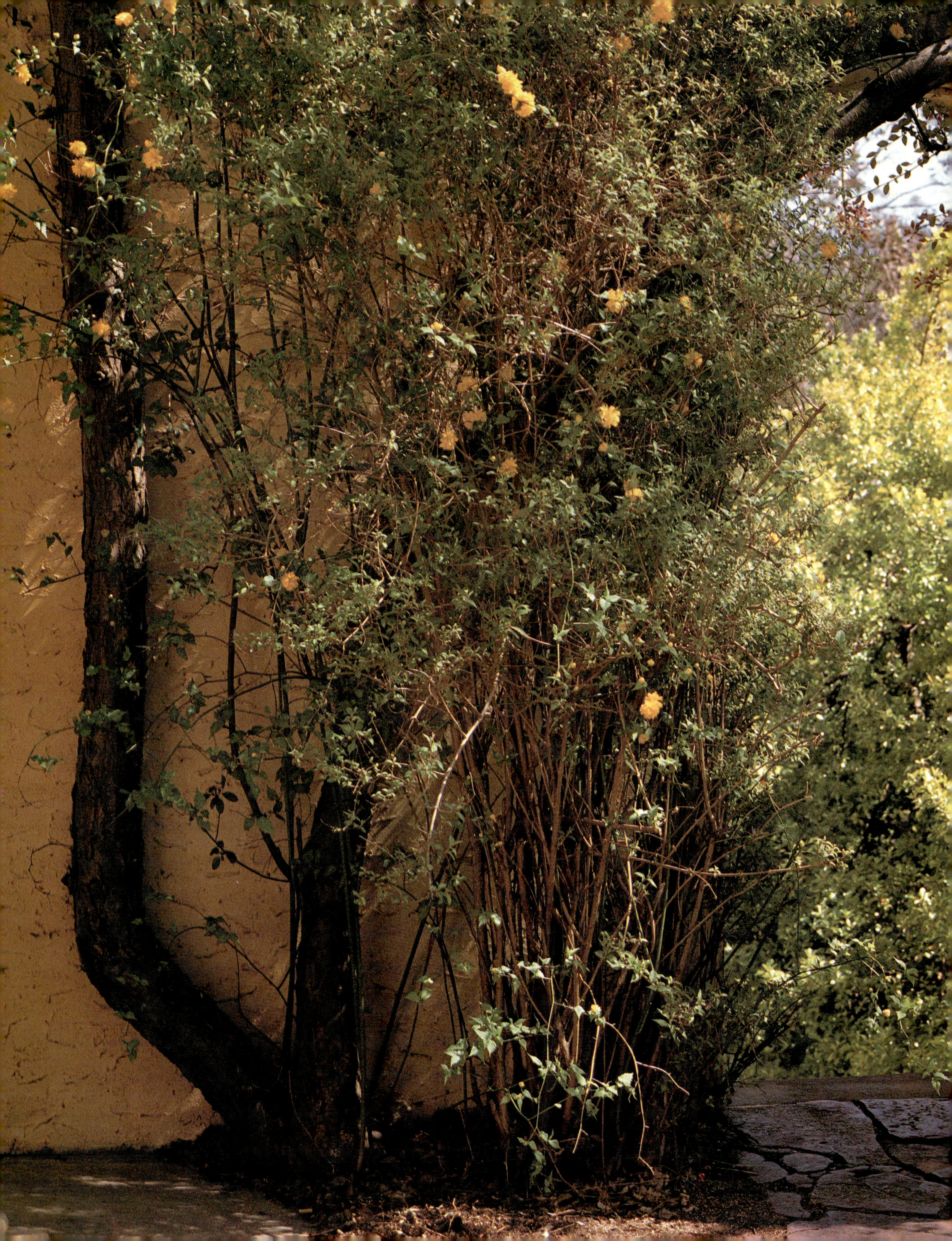

GARDEN STYLES

An Inner-city Courtyard

This very small courtyard garden is full of charm and style. The structure is simple and the garden looks wonderful when observed from any window. The lines are straight and stark but the selected plant material has a softening effect. The whole garden has a feeling of utter freshness and simplicity.

The garden receives considerable shade from adjoining buildings as well as the large cotoneaster hanging over the courtyard. The main aim of this garden was to create a low maintenance area in which the owner could relax.

The trellis wall draws your eye immediately. It is a feature of the garden which was built for a practical reason — to disguise the brick wall of the adjoining garage.

Blue and white with a touch of pink are the main colours in the garden. The small range of plants has been selected for durability and differences in leaf types. The strap-like leaves of blue agapanthus are a rich dark green throughout the year and produce an abundance of flowers during summer. Box (*Buxus sempervirens*) provides a border for the bed of agapanthus and also highlights the change of level in the garden. The different shades of green and the varied leaf types of the agapanthus and box stand out immediately. Busy Lizzie (*Impatiens wallerana*) in shades of white and pink is the other main plant used in this garden. Tolerant of shade and a lover of heat, its self-seeding habit ensures that it will remain in the garden.

The large terracotta urn gives architectural form to the garden, creating an instant garden design. Pots are used extensively in Mediterranean countries and are at last filtering into Australian garden design. Choose several large pots for visual impression and fill smaller ones with flowers. Behind the large pot the foliage of *Pittosporum* species softens the wall, providing a perfect backdrop.

Ivy trained to grow up the side walls will eventually cover the brick with its dark leaves and give the garden a cool, fresh feeling.

Opposite Simplicity is the main theme in this courtyard. Careful selection of plants creates visual appeal.

GARDEN STYLES 11

Restful Areas of the Garden

Every garden needs a quiet area where one can sit and contemplate, read or just enjoy the ambience of the garden. For centuries people have enjoyed sitting in their gardens to savour the fragrance, the different seasons, flowers and the fruits of their labour.

A seat may be positioned in a sheltered, shady, quiet corner of the garden or it can be situated to overlook the entire garden.

These two seating areas are vastly different but both are perfect settings in their own right.

The simple wood and cast-iron garden seat is tucked away in a corner of the garden. It is carefully placed under a deciduous tree so that one may receive the benefits of the winter sun and be cool in summer.

In spring the soft, light pink and white flowers of *Clematis montana* create a magical effect. The clematis has been allowed to ramble romantically through the hydrangea and the pink flowering *Weigela florida*.

White or soft-pink flowers planted in areas of the garden where the contrasting leaf colours are deep greens create a very tranquil feeling.

The whole effect is enchanting and the colours are soft to avoid sharp contrasts.

A completely different but equally romantic setting has been achieved with the use of wooden seats enclosed by large open trellis. The use of blue-grey paint has made the trellis a feature of the garden, contrasting perfectly with the dark green foliage.

Two terracotta pots containing *Buxus sempervirens* frame this elegant but restful setting. Chinese star jasmine (*Trachelospermum jasminoides*) entwines its way through the trellis. The striking, dense, dark green, glossy leaves are veiled with a lacy canopy of fragrant, ivory-white flowers from late spring to early summer. The seat is positioned to view the rest of the garden. A perfect spot for thinking, reading or spending time with friends.

Opposite Solitary splendour; a wooden seat placed in a quiet, romantic setting.

Right Wooden seats in a trellis setting are placed to enjoy the garden, while ensuring that the area will be a focal point.

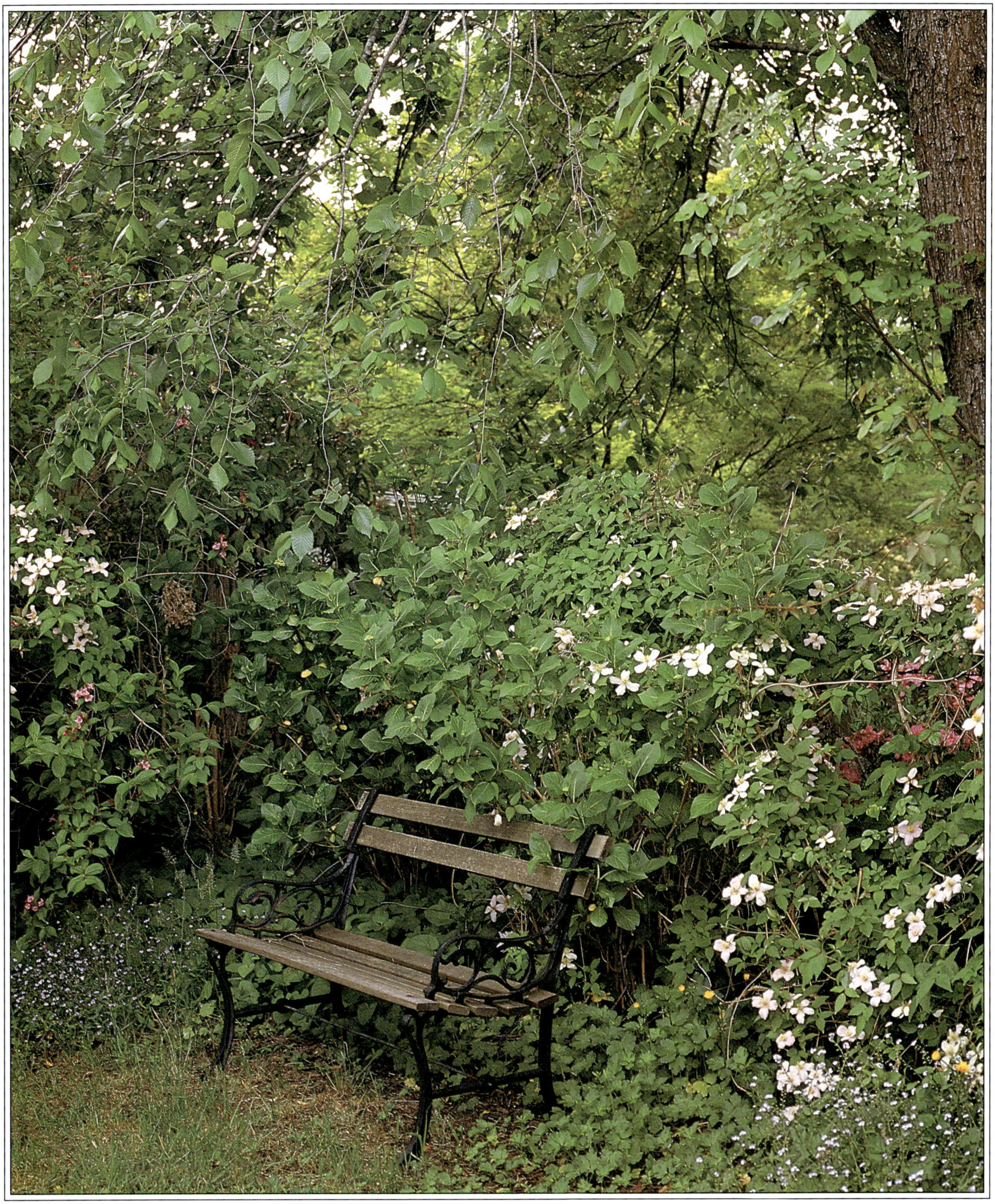

14 Garden Styles

AN ELEGANT GARDEN BED

This rather flat garden was originally an expanse of grass dotted with a number of large trees. To break the monotony but to keep the effect simple and stylish, a garden bed was created and filled with an interesting mixture of shrubs, annuals and bulbs. There are seasonal shows of colour among the smaller plants. But the form, colour and texture of the shrubs hold interest even when there is nothing in flower.

The garden bed is comprised mainly of shrubs, including a variety of Japanese maples, a grey-leaved juniper (*Juniperus* 'Grey Owl') and a yellow-leaved juniper (*Juniperus communis* 'Depressa Aurea'). The twisted stems of a standard tortured hazelnut (*Corylus*

This elegant garden bed provides variety and introduces a slight change of level. The architectural structure of the garden's evergreens ensures year-round interest and provides a perfect foil for seasonal plantings.

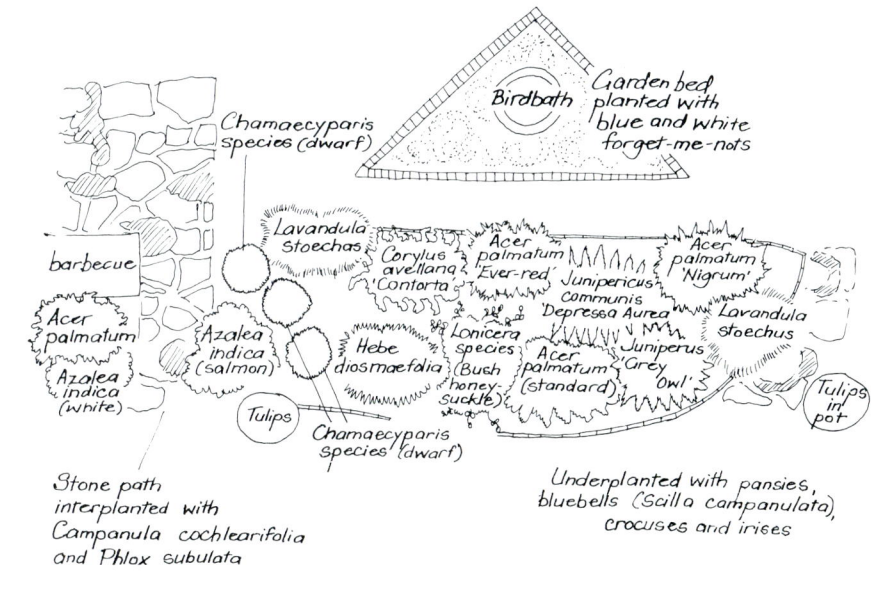

The garden bed viewed from the rear of the garden. A small simple triangular bed bordered with bricks frames the birdbath.

avellana 'Contorta') hold interest even in winter when the shrub loses its leaves. Fragrance is achieved by including Italian lavender (*Lavandula stoechas*), a bush honeysuckle (*Lonicera* species) and the small flowers of *Hebe diosmaefolia* 'Variegata'. The bed is underplanted with pansies, bluebells (*Scilla campanulata*), crocus and blue and white forget-me-nots.

A pink and a white azalea frame the stone step leading to the barbecue and contrast beautifully with alpine phlox (*Phlox subulata*) and (*Campanula carpatica*) wandering through the stone.

An elegant arch leads to the rear of the garden bed where there is a stone birdbath in the middle of a triangular bed filled with blue and white forget-me-nots.

Italian Style

This beautiful Italianate garden adjoins an early Australian sandstone house and the two styles complement each other perfectly. The pathway leads from the front door to a large urn (the focal point of the garden) and continues past this to the garden gate.

The narrow variety of plants used in the garden gives it a simple but elegant atmosphere. The colour scheme is comprised mainly of shades of blue and purple with a touch of white. Irises are featured heavily in this garden. In spring the rich blues and purples of Louisiana iris combine perfectly with the blue-violet flowers of a large jacaranda tree growing near the house. These are followed by Japanese irises (*Iris kaempferi*) which start flowering in early summer and bring the main iris season to a spectacular conclusion. The grey-green, strap-like leaves of iris look good even when the plant is not in flower and provide magnificent contrast with the dark green leaved plants.

Box (*Buxus sempervirens*) has been placed at the beginning of the pathway and also in strategic spots along the side of the path and around the urn. Babies' tears (*Erigeron karvinsckianus*) tumbles down on to the pathway and seeds readily through the stone path. Plants in a pathway certainly add charm and character and will give even a new pathway an aged appearance. Also included in this pathway are bugle weed (*Ajuga reptans*), thyme and snow-in-summer (*Cerastium tomentosum*).

During spring blue flowers are provided from *Campanula* species, the masses of self-sown forget-me-nots and columbines (*Aquilegia* species).

Standard 'Iceberg' roses provide height in the garden bed and their profusion of white flowers will reward you throughout spring and into summer.

Mondo grass (*Ophiopogon japonicus*) produces dense tufts of dark green, grass-like foliage and forms the outer border of the circle garden. This hardy groundcover soon multiplies to form a thick weed-resisting mat. Once established it is drought resistant and hardy. Sweet peas ramble among the irises and boxwood around the urn, softening the effect and supplying fragrance.

A large urn is the focal point of the garden.

18 GARDEN STYLES

Opposite *A stone path leads to the circular garden. Self-seeded plants soften the pathway giving it a romantic tone.*

GARDEN STYLES 19

An Impressionist Scene

Water tends to attract the eye more than any other feature of the garden. It has the unique attribute of reflecting light and patterns. Water has been used in garden design for centuries, becoming especially popular during the Renaissance period. In more recent times this type of garden has often been the subject of Impressionist art because of the combinations of colours and qualities of light.

As part of a large garden, this pond is simply but effectively planted with irises and the large leafed *Gunnera mannicata*. The blue and yellow bridge is a feature of the pond. It blends perfectly with the yellow and purple irises.

Waterlilies add substance to the reflective qualities of the water. The atmosphere is serene and still and provides a perfect habitat for wild ducks.

Pines (*Pinus radiata*) around the pond are underplanted with azaleas and rhododendrons (*Rhododendron* species).

Opposite *The blue and yellow bridge is a feature of the pond.*
Right *The still, clear water displays reflective qualities.*

GARDEN STYLES 21

22　Garden Styles

A Green and White Garden

The use of individual colours has great significance in the garden. The colour green, for example, has many associations and may signify freshness and regeneration. White is valued for its capacity to attract attention without being overpowering. The combination of green and white creates a visually arresting and versatile effect, especially in summer. White flowers make the garden appear cool during the day, while remaining visible at night. The tranquil tone of a green and white theme makes a relaxing garden environment.

The garden bed pictured is one of the most attractive green and white gardens I have seen and has the advantage of being the least complicated in design. The garden bed itself is surrounded by a box hedge (*Buxus sempervirens*) and height is provided by standard 'Iceberg' roses underplanted with white azal-

The combination of white flowers and green leaves provides a versatile, visually arresting effect.

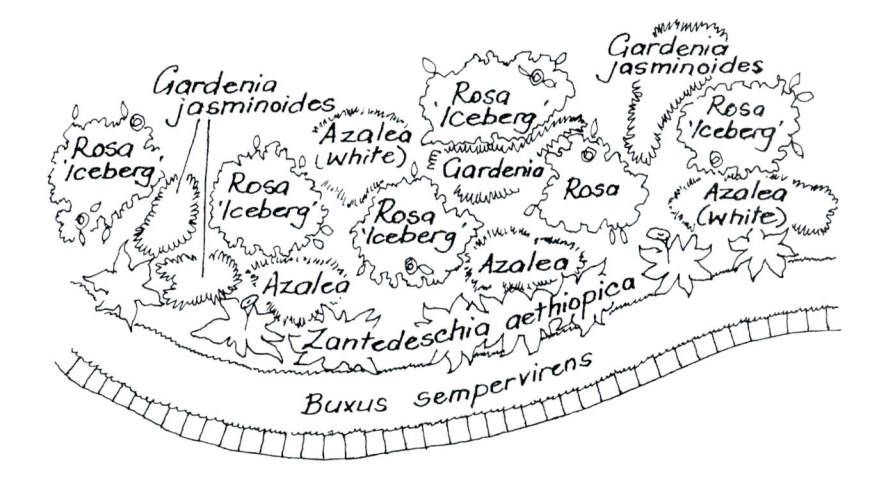

The large, glossy green leaves of arum lilies give a variation in leaf texture.

eas and gardenias. Arum lilies (*Zantedeschia aethiopica*) are planted behind the box hedge where their large, glossy green leaves provide a variation in leaf texture.

There are many other white flowering plants suitable for a white and green garden. White flowering shrubs are used to provide height in the garden. Ideal ones are to be found among the many varieties of camellia; Mexican orange blossom (*Choisya ternata*) which should be planted near a door, window or garden seat so its pervading perfume can be appreciated; white diosma (*Coleonema alba*), valued for its late winter to spring flowers; mock orange blossom (*Philadelphus coronarius*) whose scented flowers appear in late spring; *Prostanthera nivea*, a native plant admired for its abundance of flowers and mint-scented leaves and the various species of viburnum, many of which flower in late winter and early spring.

Buddleia davidii 'Wedding Day' produces a profusion of flowers similar to lilacs during summer which have a honey-like scent. Its capacity to attract large numbers of butterflies accounts for its common name of 'butterfly bush'. Another variety, 'Profusion', reaches a height of 3 m.

The Chinese angelica tree (*Aralia chinensis*) is a deciduous shrub with handsome, fern-like leaves and pure white panicles of flowers.

The white flowers of agapanthus always look striking against their dark green leaves. They flower in full sun or semi to dappled shade, making them most useful when planted under trees or large shrubs. Other bulbous plants include white watsonias which grow freely in all climates and have mid-green, strap-like leaves and tall spikes of flowers similar to gladiolus; *Freesia refracta* 'Alba' the fragrant, old-fashioned freesia which can be left to naturalise freely; the well-known white forms of liliums which are always eye-catching and chincherinchee (*Ornithogalum thyrsoides*) which has heads of white flowers and will last for over two weeks in a vase.

White bearded iris bloom at the end of spring during their first year if planted in autumn. They multiply three to four fold each year and can be divided every three years. Varieties include 'Frost Nymph', 'Heavenly Angels', 'Lacy Snowflake', 'Ice Sculpture' and 'Wedding Vow'.

For the shady corners of a white garden you should consider *Aquilegia vulgaris flore pleno*, the white flowering columbine loved for its short spurs and double flowers. White forget-me-nots form a carpet during spring and when planted with tall columbines create a spectacular contrast. Once in the garden both plants seed readily. For late spring Solomon's seal (*Polygonatum multifolium*) cannot be equalled. The long arching stems carry ribbed elliptical leaves held in wing-like fashion above them. These leaves display the pendulous clusters of waxy green tipped white bells

A neatly clipped box hedge surrounds the garden bed. A climbing 'Iceberg' rose has been encouraged to scramble over the door and the front of the house.

which are suspended from the leaf axils. White flowering impatiens — another shade-lover — can provide summer colour and the white Japanese anemone (*Anemone japonica*) produces outstanding autumn flowers.

A sunny position is suitable for numerous white flowering perennials. Fringed catchfly (*Silene fimbriata*) has airy panicles of fringed white flowers from late spring to autumn. An additional feature is its self-seeding habit. Shasta daisy (*Chrysanthemum maximum*) is a charming perennial with erect flowering stalks to almost 1 m. *Achillea ptarmica* 'The Pearl' has masses of small, pure white double flowers and provides colour from late spring through summer.

White sage (*Salvia coccinea* 'Alba') has soft green foliage and its prolific flowers are held on long stems. Other taller growing perennials include lavender shower (*Thalictrum dipterocarpum* 'Album') which looks like a white, misty cloud; *Penstemon* 'Swan Lake' which has stunning spikes of glistening, pure white, bell-like flowers and white gayfeather (*Liatris spicata* 'Floristan White') whose long spikes of flowers are ideal for the garden and last for ages when picked.

Queen Anne's lace is a pretty annual which develops large heads of small flowers in summer. *Gypsophila* 'Monarch White' also grows easily from seed, planted directly where it is going to grow. The flowers appear 10 weeks after sowing. *Cosmos* 'Purity' is a striking, tall annual which produces large numbers of long-lasting, ice-white blooms with yellow centres. The sheen of the petals creates a delightful glistening effect. Cosmos is easily sown from spring right through summer in the position in which it is to grow. A January sowing will ensure autumn flowers.

THE WILD GARDEN

The look in this wild garden is slightly unkempt but romantic. The aim of the owner has been to create an environment as naturally as possible. Things are allowed to happen rather than being thoroughly controlled. This allows one to be able to observe the garden and its changes, gaining a sense of the spirit of the place before intervening. It is a low maintenance garden which has been allowed to take on its own appearance with the use of self-seeding plants and clever planting.

The lawn, which also doubles as the pathway, is full of self-sown English daisies (*Bellis perennis*) adding a distinctive and romantic touch. These are the original ancestors of the modern double form of English daisy. The pretty white flowers can be mown but tend to appear in late winter and early spring before the mowing season starts. Sow them from seed in mid-winter or mix them with grass seed when sowing a new lawn.

A natural lawn requires much less attention than a formal lawn. Many flowers will thrive in a lawn, spreading of their own accord and becoming very eager in their bloom. Flowers worth considering are buttered eggs (*Lotus corniculatus*), blue speedwell (*Veronica persica*) and the dwarf variety of strawberry clover called 'Dwarf O'Connor's'.

Shrubs and trees are the main features in this garden and they have been heavily under-

This garden, with its slightly dishevelled appearance, looks as if it has been untouched by human hands and produces a natural tone.

GARDEN STYLES 27

A romantic place to sit: a wooden seat beside a small pond.

planted with drifts of bluebells, daffodils and snowdrops which thrive in the dappled shade cast from the mainly deciduous trees. In autumn the garden virtually dies, but this 'death' is allowable as one waits for the profusion of life which returns in spring.

Forget-me-nots are permitted to ramble and seed where they wish and once established in the garden never fail to return. Apart from blue forget-me-nots there are also pink and white varieties.

The large leaves of hostas add structure to the garden bed and thrive in the shade. These invaluable perennials die down each winter and there is a wide variety of different leaf types. Agapanthus will also thrive in these conditions and provide summer flowers. Their dark green, strap-like leaves remain throughout the year.

In spring the pretty flowers and rich leaves of polyanthus abound. These hardy perennials make a marvellous groundcover.

Climbing roses are allowed to climb trees in a wild garden. Choose a rose that flowers at a different period from its host tree.

Other self-seeding annual plants which thrive in the dappled shade of a wild garden include busy Lizzie (*Impatiens wallerana*), honesty (*Lunaria annua*), love-in-a-mist (*Nigella damascena*) and *Viscaria* species. The open-faced flowers of busy Lizzie remain throughout spring and summer. The colour range includes pink, white, lilac-blue, apricot and red. Honesty has either violet-pink or white flowers depending on the variety. The round, flat seed-pods can later be dried for indoor decoration. The delicate flowers of love-in-a-mist appear amid feathery, pale-green, soft, fine foliage. Flower colour is blue, pink or white and it will also grow in full sun. The small disc-shaped flowers of *Viscaria* species come in a colour range which includes mauve, blue and pastel pink. The more shade they receive, the richer the flower colour.

Shades of Blue

The recognition of the importance of colour and its role in creating atmosphere is to be found in the recent proliferation of single-colour gardens.

The colour blue has become a popular choice for such gardens. For many, blue flowers have become a passion to the point of addiction, possibly because of their comparative rarity. A blue garden demands visual attention.

Spatial illusions can be created by planting blue flowers at the rear of a small garden to make the yard seem larger. Spot plantings will have a similar effect, seemingly deepening a part of the yard or bringing it closer.

Generally, however, a cool colour like blue is good for a close viewing in which its impact can be emphasised. This grouping of potted plants in the corner of a courtyard has blue as the main colour with just a touch of white.

The combination of the blue flowers and the terracotta pots is perfect and further highlights the colour.

The grouping is simple and carefully chosen for the fairly long flowering period of each individual plant. The tiny white daisies of babies' tears (*Erigeron karvinsckianus*) at the back of the group will appear on the plant from early spring until autumn and will thrive in full sun or semi-shade. The white blotches on the small, exquisite blue flowers of trailing lobelia (*Lobelia erinus*) have a softening effect on the whole arrangement. Naturally, the dark violet-blue flowers of petunias need no introduction and the colour is perfect. White is supplied by the geranium and shade loving white impatiens tucked under the table.

Blue flowering shrubs could be included in the courtyard to extend the colour theme. Suitable shrubs include yesterday, today and tomorrow (*Brunfelsia latifolia*) whose open-faced, fragrant flowers open violet-blue, fade first to lavender blue and then to white, giving a three coloured effect; *Ceanothus burkwoodii* which is covered in blue flowers during summer and autumn; blue butterfly bush (*Clerodendrum ugandense*) which has four of its petals a clear blue while the others are royal blue to violet and *Plumbago capensis*, valued for its flowers which appear from late spring to late autumn.

Nearly all the shades of blue are found among the *Campanula* species. These perennial plants are available in tall growing species as well as mat-forming groundcovers.

Agapanthus provides strap-like leaves and is an invaluable plant because of its ability to flower in shade. There is a dwarf variety which only reaches a height of 45 cm. *Camassia cusickii* is another bulbous plant carrying large spikes of pale to deep blue, star-shaped flowers. It is a hardy plant that will grow in all soil types, even heavy clay ones.

Irises are among the more breathtaking bulbous plants. Plant them in clumps or around a large urn or waterbowl. Their long strap-like leaves provide a sense of structure even when they are not in flower.

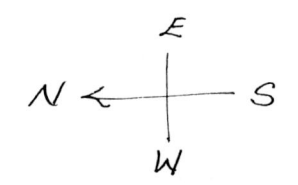

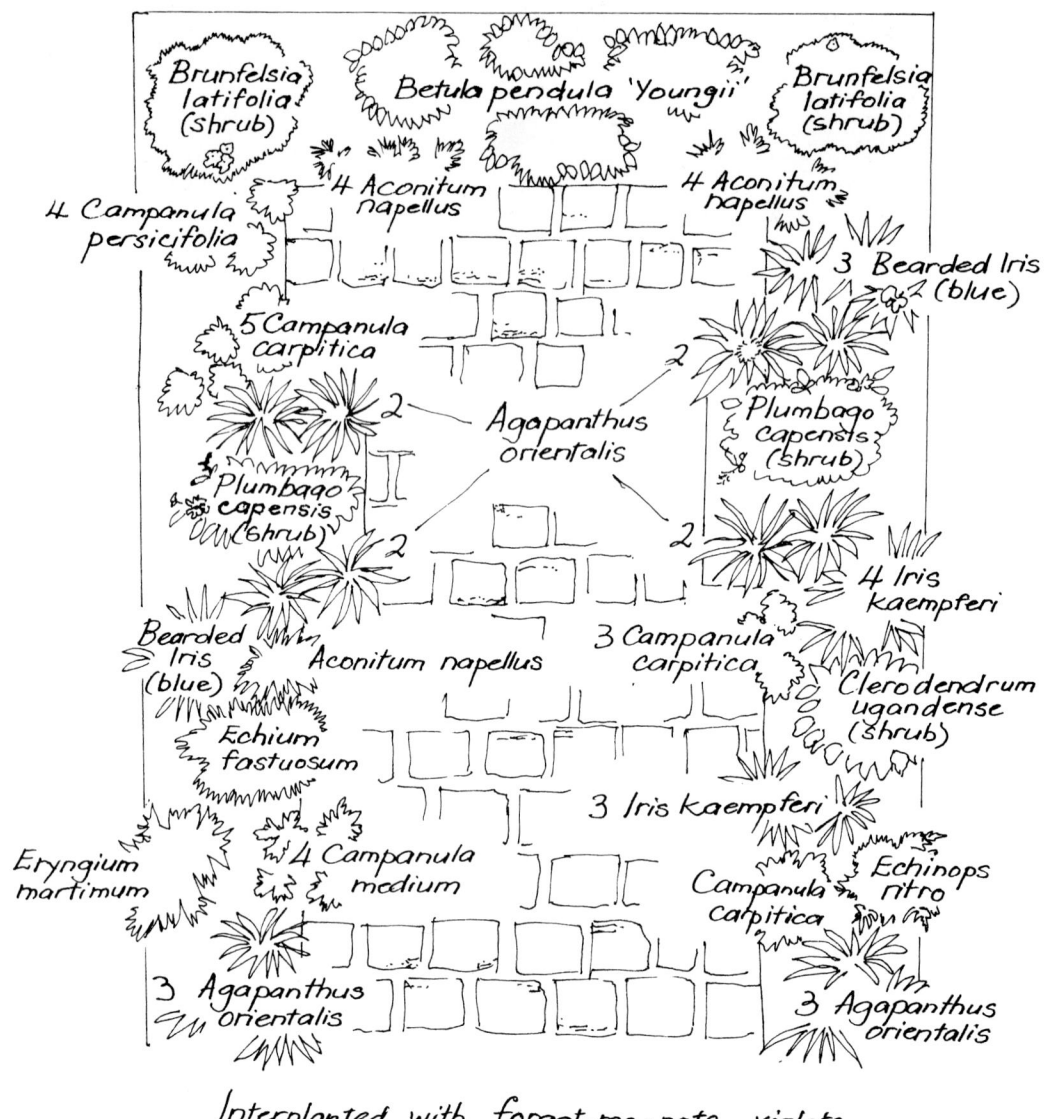

Blue Garden Theme for a Courtyard

(Compass: N ← → S, E above, W below)

- Brunfelsia latifolia (shrub)
- Betula pendula 'Youngii'
- Brunfelsia latifolia (shrub)
- 4 Campanula persicifolia
- 4 Aconitum napellus
- 4 Aconitum napellus
- 3 Bearded Iris (blue)
- 5 Campanula carpitica
- 2 Agapanthus orientalis
- Plumbago capensis (shrub)
- Plumbago capensis (shrub)
- 4 Iris kaempferi
- Bearded Iris (blue)
- Aconitum napellus
- 3 Campanula carpitica
- Clerodendrum ugandense (shrub)
- Echium fastuosum
- 3 Iris kaempferi
- Eryngium martimum
- 4 Campanula medium
- Campanula carpitica
- Echinops nitro
- 3 Agapanthus orientalis
- 3 Agapanthus orientalis

Interplanted with forget-me-nots, violets, love-in-a-mist (*Nigella damascena*), lobelia, bugle (*Ajuga reptans*), baboon flower (*Babiana stricta*).

Opposite An exquisite compilation of blue flowers with just a touch of white.

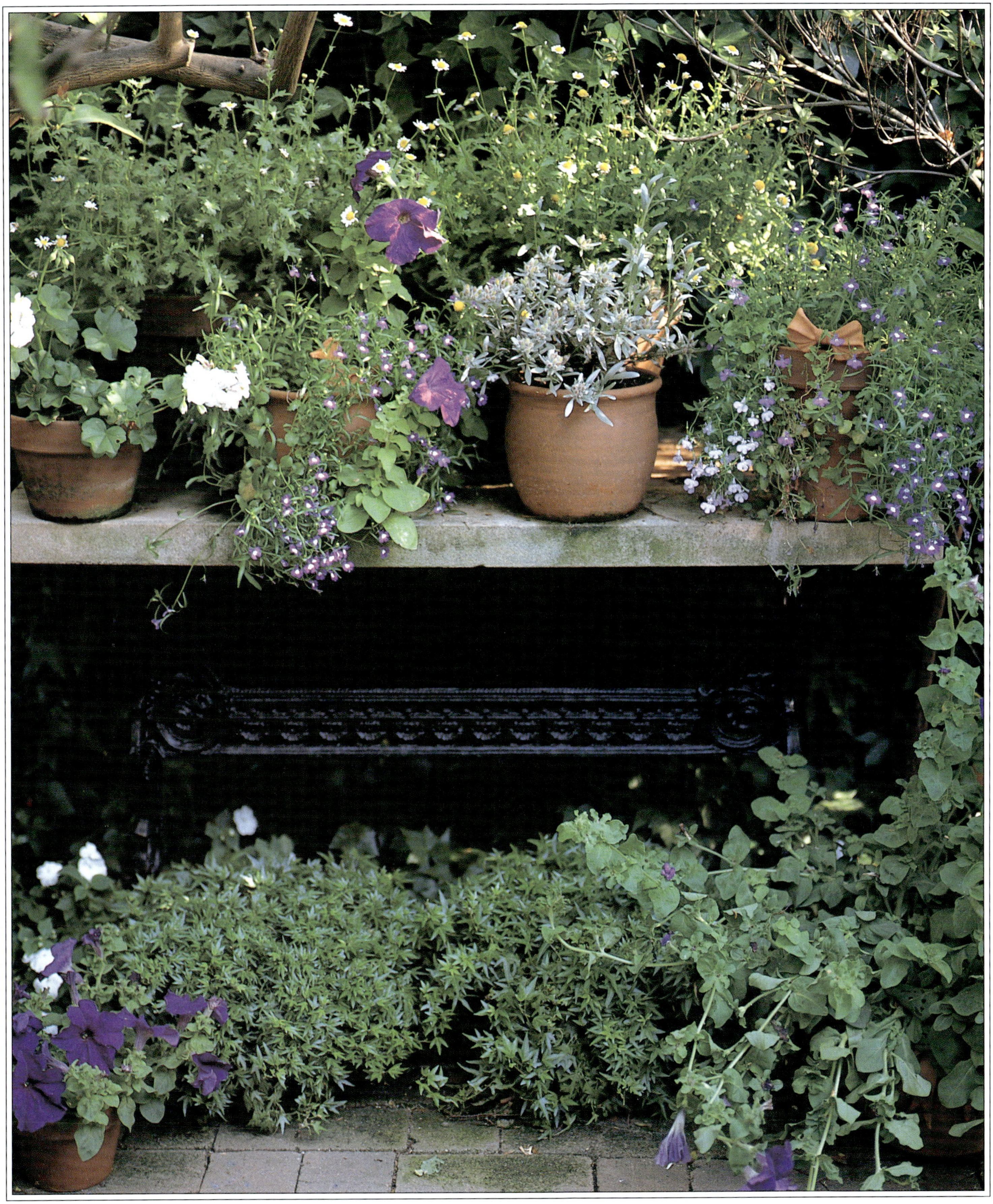

THE SUMMER-HOUSE

Australia has the perfect climate for summerhouses. These outdoor living areas are immensely practical especially in the heat of a summer's day. This large summerhouse is tucked away in a shady spot under deciduous trees in a large mountain garden, providing a breezy retreat on a hot day.

Jasmine rambles through the trellis providing a pervasive perfume in spring. Rhododendrons and azaleas provide a wealth of colour and may be viewed from any section of the summerhouse. Green from the surrounding foliage has a cooling effect during the hottest months of the year.

The siting of a summerhouse will be determined by the desire for sun or shade. Another point to consider is the overall design of the garden. You could make it a focal point at the end of a main path or it could be tucked away for peace and privacy in the quietest corner. But its main purpose will be as a place of repose during summer. It will be somewhere to sit to enjoy the tranquillity of your beloved garden.

This delightful shingle summerhouse receives shade from large trees, making it a perfect summer outdoor living area.

GARDEN STYLES 33

The Perennial Garden

The owner has observed this garden over several years and treated it like a painting by adding different colours as they were needed. The result is very enchanting. Although informality is the main theme, considerable thought has gone into the garden, the design and the overall effect to create an unplanned feeling. Because of this lack of formal structure the garden becomes a challenge rather than a place for the excessively neat and tidy person who would require every plant to be in its place. Self-seeding plants have been allowed to grow where they appear — often in unexpected places. The total look is evocative: a garden bed packed with flowers which are not in straight rows but jumbled together. There is perfect harmony as tall plants shelter low growing ones. The style is relaxed and pragmatic. It is very much a spring and summer garden, reaching its peak in early summer.

The look in this garden is evocative and slightly dishevelled. It is packed with flowers which are jumbled together rather than being in straight rows.

The Perennial Garden

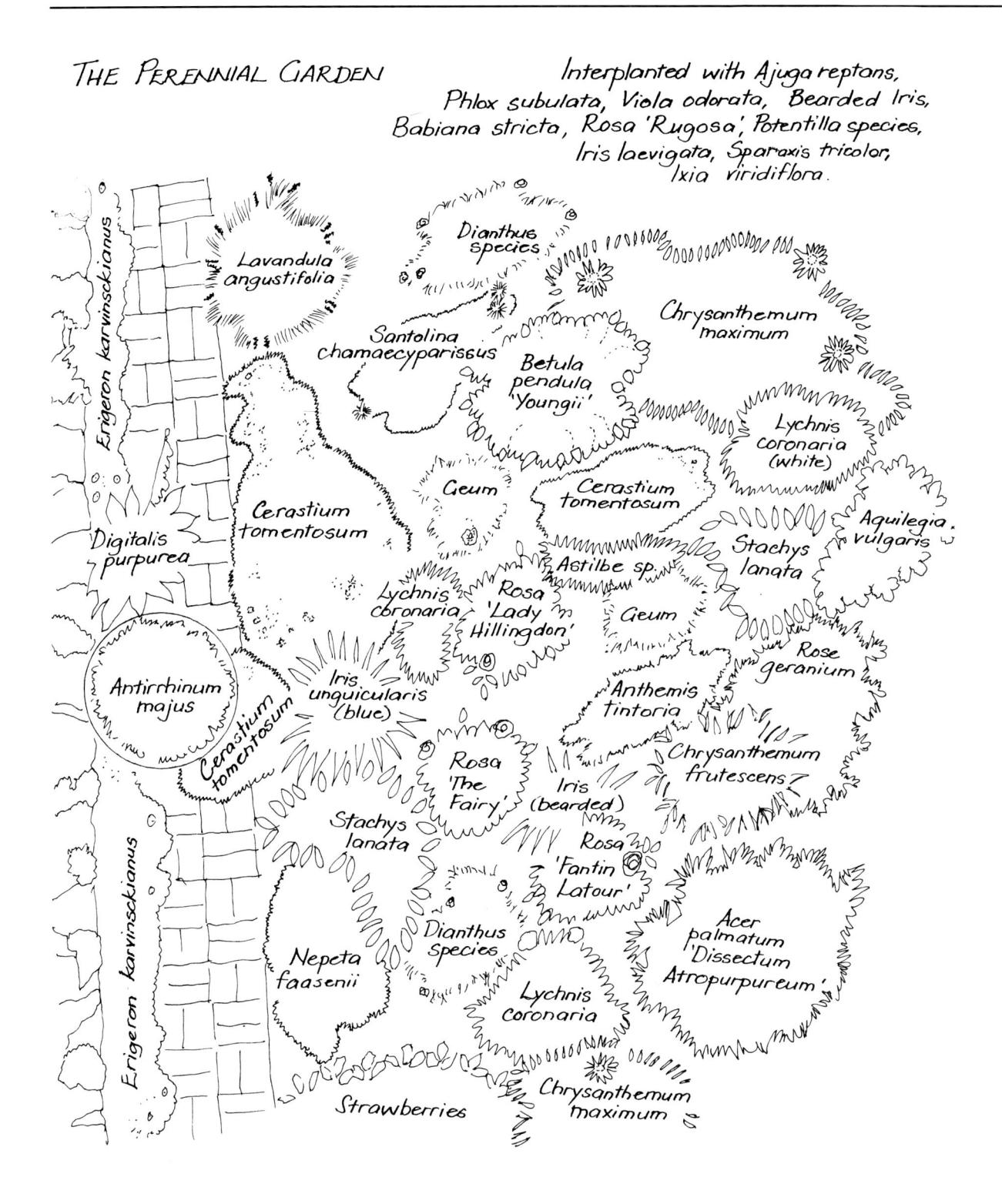

Interplanted with Ajuga reptans, Phlox subulata, Viola odorata, Bearded Iris, Babiana stricta, Rosa 'Rugosa', Potentilla species, Iris laevigata, Sparaxis tricolor, Ixia viridiflora.

Plants labelled in the diagram:
- Erigeron karvinsckianus
- Lavandula angustifolia
- Dianthus species
- Santolina chamaecyparissus
- Chrysanthemum maximum
- Betula pendula 'Youngii'
- Lychnis coronaria (white)
- Digitalis purpurea
- Cerastium tomentosum
- Geum
- Stachys lanata
- Aquilegia vulgaris
- Astilbe sp.
- Lychnis coronaria
- Rosa 'Lady Hillingdon'
- Geum
- Rose geranium
- Antirrhinum majus
- Cerastium tomentosum
- Iris unguicularis (blue)
- Anthemis tintoria
- Chrysanthemum frutescens
- Rosa 'The Fairy'
- Iris (bearded)
- Stachys lanata
- Rosa 'Fantin Latour'
- Acer palmatum 'Dissectum Atropurpureum'
- Nepeta faasenii
- Dianthus species
- Lychnis coronaria
- Strawberries
- Chrysanthemum maximum
- Erigeron karvinsckianus

The main colour theme is soft in shades of blue, pink and white combined with the odd splash of red. Grey leaved plants soften this effect even further. Old-fashioned roses are planted throughout the garden to supply fragrance and add structure to the bed as they reach full height. Many old-fashioned roses are repeat flowering to ensure a supply of flowers throughout spring and into summer.

This is a garden where herbaceous plants are allowed to run riot and jostle each other for space. The result is delightful.

A Courtyard Wall

This classic fountain completely transforms an otherwise plain wall in a small city courtyard. It gives instant warmth and style to what would otherwise be a bare area. The rich terracotta colour blends perfectly with the dark green leaves of the gardenias. During summer the fountain acts as a cooling agent and creates a delightful setting for *al fresco* eating.

Courtyard walls can also be transformed by the use of climbing plants. Some climbers are capable of clinging on to a wall with the aid of sucker discs. These include creeping fig (*Ficus pumila*) which has small, dense, leathery foliage; ivy (*Hedera* species) of which there are also variegated varieties and Boston ivy (*Parthenocissus quinquefolia*) having a deciduous habit and beautiful leaves which open purple in spring, change to green throughout summer and become a brilliant red in autumn.

Other climbers generally need the support of a trellis or wire to help them climb. Perfumed climbers are excellent for courtyard walls as their aroma will pervade the house and garden. Perfumed climbers include *Jasminium polyanthum* with its tinted rose-pink and white spring flowers; Chilean jasmine (*Mandevilla laxa*) which is loved for its milky-white summer flowers and quick growth and snail flower (*Phaseolus caracalla*) which has unusual light purple and yellow flowers with a sweet heavy perfume. For plants that provide instant perfume and a long flowering period I strongly recommend sweet peas (*Lathyrus odoratus*).

For a shady courtyard wall you could include kangaroo vine (*Cissus antarctica*), *Cissus discolor* or *Clematis aristata*.

The combination of colours and the refined sense of proportion create a near perfect wall setting.

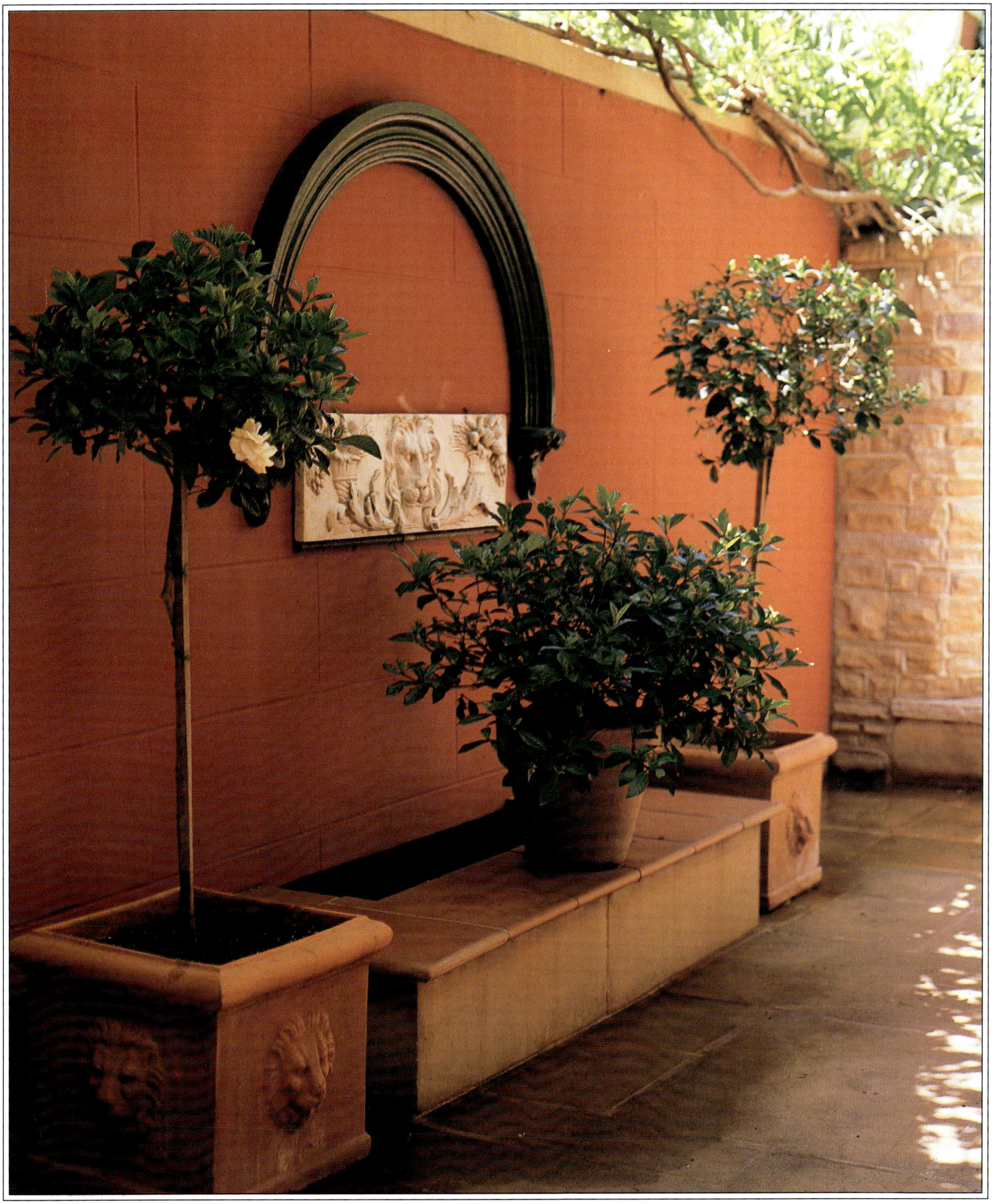

ENTRANCE STEPS

After opening the gate of this early Australian cottage the garden style that greets you is romantic and inviting. A wooden support for climbers surrounds the picket fence and gate. The prolific potato vine (*Solanum jasminoides*) has almost completely covered the support. Its small, dainty, white, potato-like flowers have central yellow stamens and appear in abundance during summer but also spasmodically throughout the year. Planted each side of the support next to the potato vine are old-fashioned roses 'Francis E. Lester' and 'Apple Blossom'. Having been allowed to ramble through the potato vine, their soft-pink, single flowers provide soft colour in spring.

The wide concrete steps invite you to walk down them. The steps, which were only constructed a year ago, have a timeless quality. The sides are softened by babies' tears (*Erigeron karvinsckianus*) and spaces were deliberately left in the concrete for more babies' tears, thyme and any other self-seeding plant that will fill gaps.

English daisies (*Bellis perennis*), forget-me-nots (*Myosotis species*) and pansies provide a low border behind the babies' tears. Foxgloves (*Digitalis purpurea*) flank the steps providing height and a nostalgic, English feeling. Interplanted with the foxgloves are tall pink and white flowering cosmos (*Cosmos bipinnatus*) which commence flowering after the foxgloves have finished. The pink flowers of Marguerite daisies (*Chrysanthemum frutescans*) are perfect for this cottage garden scheme and flower dependably from early spring until the end of summer. The shiny green leaves of a camellia in a large terracotta pot look appealing even when flowers are absent. You can assess how successfully this entrance has been designed by imagining the plain concrete steps without the imaginative planting of the garden border.

Opposite The wide, thoughtfully designed steps explore further the delights of a romantic garden.

GARDEN STYLES 39

Colour Drifts

A combination of blue and clear yellow was one of French Impressionist painter Claude Monet's favourite colour schemes and one which he used extensively in his famous garden at Giverny. Monet loved the colour scheme so much that he even designed china in blue, yellow and white to be used in a yellow dining room which he decorated with blue accents.

The large drift of daffodils and bluebells evokes a feeling of spring. This bold planting creates a carpet of blue and yellow in wild but elegant abandon. The colours glisten and glow, warming the garden throughout the day.

You do not need a large area to create a drift of spring colour. Daffodils and bluebells may be planted in the corner of a lawn, in a wooded glade or allowed to spill over a country fence. They can also be planted with other perennials as a border lining a pathway. When the bulbs stop flowering, perennials push their way through to provide summer colour.

An enchanting spring carpet of blue and yellow daffodils provide elegance through simplicity.

GARDEN STYLES 41

42 *Garden Styles*

A Shaded Pathway

Shady areas of the garden are always difficult to deal with especially under large trees where competition for food and water is fierce. However this mass planting of helleborus is perfect for such a situation. I have seen helleborus thriving under large conifers where often nothing else will grow. If the soil around them is kept well-mulched they will readily self-seed to eventually form a thick groundcover. The beautiful subtle flowers start appearing in winter and remain on the plant for a long period. The common names Lenten rose and Christmas rose originated in the northern hemisphere.

There are many forms of the Lenten rose (*Helleborus orientalis*) and these produce greenish-white, rose or dull purple flowers which are often spotted or marbled with darker shades. The Christmas rose (*Helleborus niger*) has leathery dark green leaves and large, saucer-shaped, white or tinged rose flowers with golden anthers. *Helleborus corsicus* has light green leaves and cup-shaped, yellow-green flowers.

The well-known *Agapanthus orientalis* is another plant that will thrive in shaded conditions. My feeling is that because this plant is so common its merits are often overlooked. Its long, arching evergreen leaves have a bold appearance and during summer the blue or white flowers are produced on metre high stems. There is also a dwarf species (*Agapanthus pumila*).

Because competition for food and water is the main problem for plants trying to grow under trees, keep the soil well mulched with cow manure or compost and place grass clippings or leaf mould on top of this.

Dappled sunlight highlights the subtle colours of the helleborus flowers.

The Spring Garden

Spring has always been a time of celebration and renewal. The onset of spring is represented in European myths as a period of fecundity that will lead, in the natural cycle of things, to new life and fruitfulness. In the garden, spring produces an almost magical transformation as the apparent winter lifelessness of trees and shrubs gives way to a new world of colour and scent.

Gardeners become aware of an air of expectation accompanying this gradual re-awakening. Many feel, as I do, that the first sighting of spring daffodils or prunus blossoms is a wonderful relief from the sense of barrenness associated with long winter months.

This beautiful garden exudes the beauty of spring. The flowering cherry is about to burst into blossom. The contrast of the soft pink flowers and the dark grey bark creates an exquisite effect. The more formal lines of the background conifers form a sharp contrast against the loose, open appearance of the prunus and the combination is perfect.

Daffodils and jonquils have been randomly placed in bold clumps and this loose flowing style gives the appearance of plants drifting into each other in a natural way. Clumps of *Polyanthus* species help form the spring carpet but start flowering in late winter before the daffodils.

The leaves from autumn have been left on the ground, forming a mulch for the coming hot summer months. This is a low maintenance garden that gains its charm from its beautiful trees and its natural, open, woodland appearance.

Spring produces a magical transformation as new flower buds burst into blossom.

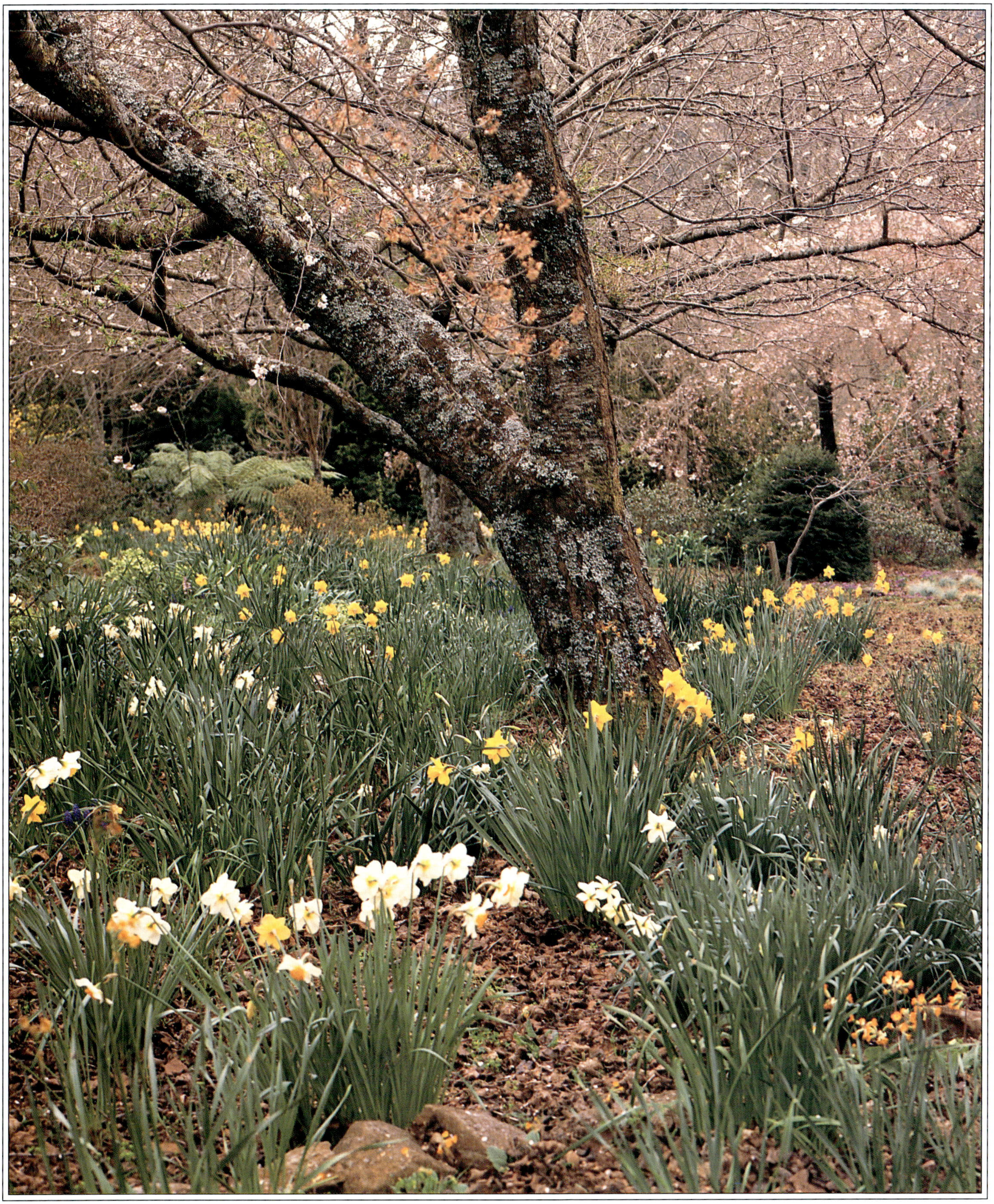

The Kitchen Garden

Kitchen gardens are enjoying a revival as people realise the decorative potential of growing flowers, herbs and vegetables in the one garden bed. Kitchen gardens originated in the sixteenth century, when they were part of knot and parterre gardens. However, this tradition died out at the end of the seventeenth century as gardening ideas changed and herbs and vegetables came to be grown in separate beds. The designs were either elaborate or based on simple geometric shapes with interconnecting systems of paths. Fruit trees. which were part of the design, were either planted out in circles around the garden or used as features of the garden bed.

This beautiful kitchen garden is in the Heide Park and Art Gallery in Victoria. This wondrous creation is crammed full of vegetables, herbs, old-fashioned roses and perfumed plants and the whole effect is a sensual delight. It is certainly a work of art created by an artist without the use of a palette.

The kitchen garden is enclosed by a wooden fence covered in a profusion of jasmine and old-fashioned climbing roses. The fence provides protection from wind and gives the garden a warm micro-climate. A kitchen garden could also be surrounded by a low hedge of lavender, boxwood or yew.

Because of the vast range of plant material and different leaf textures, the garden looks

A variety of different leaf textures and plant materials gives this kitchen garden charm.

GARDEN STYLES 47

Structural Plants in Heide Kitchen Garden

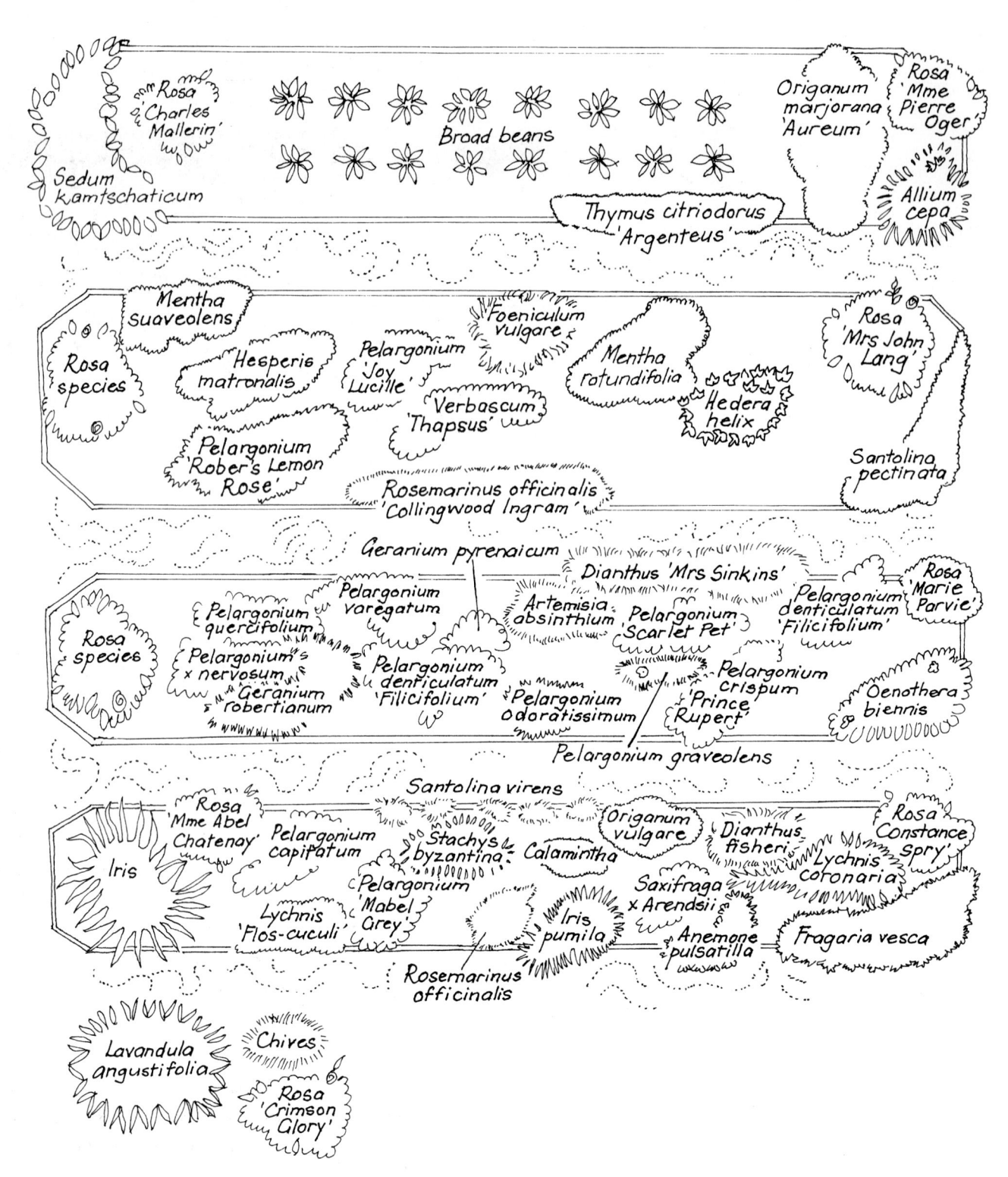

Bed 1 (top):
- Sedum kamtschaticum
- Rosa 'Charles Mallerin'
- Broad beans
- Thymus citriodorus 'Argenteus'
- Origanum marjorana 'Aureum'
- Allium cepa
- Rosa 'Mme Pierre Oger'

Bed 2:
- Rosa species
- Mentha suaveolens
- Hesperis matronalis
- Pelargonium 'Joy Lucille'
- Foeniculum vulgare
- Verbascum 'Thapsus'
- Mentha rotundifolia
- Hedera helix
- Rosa 'Mrs John Lang'
- Pelargonium 'Rober's Lemon Rose'
- Rosemarinus officinalis 'Collingwood Ingram'
- Santolina pectinata

Bed 3:
- Rosa species
- Pelargonium quercifolium
- Pelargonium varegatum
- Geranium pyrenaicum
- Dianthus 'Mrs Sinkins'
- Artemisia absinthium
- Pelargonium 'Scarlet Pet'
- Pelargonium denticulatum 'Filicifolium'
- Rosa 'Marie Parvie'
- Pelargonium × nervosum
- Geranium robertianum
- Pelargonium denticulatum 'Filicifolium'
- Pelargonium odoratissimum
- Pelargonium crispum 'Prince Rupert'
- Oenothera biennis
- Pelargonium graveolens

Bed 4:
- Iris
- Rosa 'Mme Abel Chatenay'
- Pelargonium capitatum
- Santolina virens
- Stachys byzantina
- Calamintha
- Origanum vulgare
- Dianthus fisheri
- Rosa 'Constance spry'
- Lychnis 'Flos-cuculi'
- Pelargonium 'Mabel Grey'
- Iris pumila
- Saxifraga × Arendsii
- Lychnis coronaria
- Anemone pulsatilla
- Fragaria vesca
- Rosemarinus officinalis

Lower:
- Lavandula angustifolia
- Chives
- Rosa 'Crimson Glory'

interesting even when not in flower. Grey leaved plants are used extensively, especially irises with their strap-like leaves which provide a sharp colour contrast even when not in flower. Lavender, rosemary, lychnis and artemisia give softer contrasts in grey.

Forget-me-nots (*Myosotis* species), rose campion (*Lychnis coronaria*), silene (*Silene dioacae*), violets (*Viola odorata*), tansy and fennel are among the self-seeding plants given the freedom to grow where they fall.

An arch draped with a climbing rose provides a focal point and lower-growing roses dotted through the garden add form to the beds. Simple bamboo structures support climbing peas or beans, while the mixture of vegetables and herbs provides a tapestry at ground level.

The kitchen garden changes slightly from year to year and with the seasons as new vegetables are planted and perennials die back but the main structure remains.

Garden beds filled with mixtures of herbs, flowers and vegetables.

A Garden Retreat

This idyllic setting is tucked away in a corner of a large cool-climate garden. A forest of pines is the perfect backdrop for an artist's studio which looks out onto a large pond. Pink, red and white rhododendrons have been planted close to the studio and thrive in the cool mountain climate. They never fail to produce beautiful spring flowers.

Clematis and jasmine run riot through the trellis and their perfume pervades the studio and garden.

Standard flowering cherries flank the front of the studio, forming a line alongside a timber pathway beside the pond.

Several species of iris thrive near or in water. The English water iris (*Iris pseudacorus*) makes a beautiful accent plant. It reaches a height of 2 m and has yellow flowers. *Iris laevigata* has wide, smooth foliage and will grow in sun or partial shade. Varieties include 'Alba' (white flowers), 'Semperflorens' (rosy-magenta flowers) and 'Royal Cartwheel' (navy-blue-purple flowers with a white slash down the centre of each petal). *Iris versicolor* will grow in ordinary garden conditions or in water. Flower colours include pink, violet, light and dark purple, white and shades of blue.

With such a spectacular setting and the changing moods of the pond one would not have to leave the garden to seek inspiration.

Flowering shrubs and climbers create an inspiring visual link between studio and garden.

GARDEN STYLES 51

52 *Garden Styles*

A Natural Swimming Pool

Swimming pools can become too dominant in the garden. The aim of this garden design was to make the swimming pool blend with the rest of the garden.

This small plunge pool surrounded by large rocks and pretty perennials has the appearance of an ornamental pool. Babies' tears (*Erigeron karvinsckianus*), with its pretty little daisy flowers, is a dominant planting around the pool. It flowers just as well in sun or shade from early spring until late summer. The grey leaves of snow-in-summer (*Cerastium tomentosum*) soften the appearance of the rocks. The leaves positively glisten in the sun.

The large white flowers and dark green leaves of the arum lily (*Zantedeschia aethiopica*) provide a striking contrast and make this a stunning feature plant. This handsome plant requires a moist situation with plenty of summer water.

Forget-me-nots, a potted standard lemon tree and cyclamen complete the picture.

Opposite A profusion of perennials and bulbs surround the pool to give it a very natural appearance.

Left A view of the whole garden with the pool tucked discreetly away in the corner.

A Perfumed Garden

There is something enchanting about being able to walk through a garden and smell the distinctive perfumes of fragrant plants. As soon as you enter the gatehouse of this delightful garden you can smell the captivating scents of perfumed plants.

A red standard azalea greets you and although it is not perfumed its colour complements the grey-blue gatehouse. Brick steps and a brick path lead you through the arch which is covered in a sweetly perfumed old-fashioned rose.

A birdbath tucked away in the shrubbery catches your interest. The birdbath is perfectly framed by the arch as you look from the courtyard. Tall flowering tobacco plants (*Nicotiana* species) surround the birdbath. The perfume is strong, especially at night, and the flower colour range includes white, lime green, lilac and maroon. *Nicotiana langsdorfii* is an exceedingly charming plant with delicate lime-green tubular flowers that hang down like candelabra. It will flower from spring until winter and reaches a height of 1.5 m.

Agapanthus form a border beside the pathway and their shiny leaves create a bold effect. Soft-pink and white old-fashioned roses fill the garden bed behind them.

Groundcovers include phlox (*Phlox subulata*), babies' tears (*Erigeron karvinsckianus*) and snow-in-summer (*Cerastium tomentosum*).

An elegant gatehouse invites you to walk into the garden.

GARDEN STYLES 55

Two gardenias flank the bottom of the steps and their sweet perfume does not detract from the more subtle fragrance of the roses and the potted lavender.

Apart from old-fashioned roses there are many climbing plants with strong perfume. Planting two with different flowering times on the same support will provide perfume for a long period. Carolina jasmine (*Gelsemium sempervirens*) has 5 cm long yellow flowers during late winter and early spring, and the evergreen foliage looks most attractive even when the plant is not in flower. It will grow in sun or semi-shade. *Clematis henyri* has ethereal white flowers measuring 20 cm across which appear after the flowers of Carolina jasmine have finished.

The beautiful climbing wax plant (*Hoya carnosa*) can be grown in warm and tropical climates although it does love a partially shaded area. Don't cut the flowers, as the same spurs continue to flower for several years.

Other perfumed climbing plants include pink jasmine (*Jasminum polyanthum*), star jasmine (*Trachelospermum jasminoides*) with its creamy-white flowers and Madagascar jasmine (*Stephanotis floribunda*), which is covered in clusters of large, waxy-white bells during spring and summer.

Fragrant groundcovers can be substituted for grass lawns in small gardens, eradicating the boring task of mowing and rewarding you with a delightful smell every time you walk upon it. They can be interspersed between stone, brick and the gravel of pathways and courtyards. Suitable groundcovers include the many varieties of thyme (*Thymus* species), camomile (*Anthemis nobilis*) and pennyroyal (*Mentha pulegium*).

The black locust tree (*Robinia pseudoacacia*) has a beautiful fragrance and will grow in cool or temperate climates, including the dry inland. The 20 cm long pendulous racemes of white pea-like flowers occur in spring.

The native frangipani (*Hymenosporum flavum*) gives tubular flowers about 3 cm across which appear in branched clusters above the foliage in spring. They open creamy-white then deepen through yellow to deep mustard, giving a three-toned effect. Native frangipani is fast growing, loves humid conditions and is suitable for a small garden.

Trees of the *Magnolia* species need no introduction as they have always been favourites in a perfumed garden.

Among the shrubs, the night-scented jasmine (*Cestrum nocturnum*) has greenish-white flowers that ensure it lives up to its common name. Grow it near a pool or courtyard where its fragrance can be appreciated on a balmy summer evening.

A favourite for hot climates is yesterday, today and tomorrow (*Brunfelsia latifolia*), whose interesting flowers open to violet-blue then fade to lavender and eventually white.

The great advantage of *Luculia gratissima*, a large shrub, is that its pink blossoms appear in early winter when other fragrant flowers are scarce. These may be followed later in the winter by the brown and gold, bell-shaped flowers of *Boronia megastigma* and the sweetly scented pink and red flowers of *Daphne odora*.

There are many fast growing perennials, bulbs and annuals which have powerful fragrances, like the fairy-tale lily of the valley, freesia, sweet peas, violets and garden phlox. All of these are grown without difficulty. There are literally dozens of different varieties of scented-leaved geraniums ranging from apple cider to lemon and rose. The leaves are usually very attractive, often smelling stronger than the flowers.

A Woodland Grove

This grove of silver birch (*Betula pendula*) makes an arresting scene. These graceful, slender trees with their silver bark and straight, tall trunks look even more stunning in autumn when their leaves turn a golden-yellow. During winter their silhouettes produce an interesting effect.

This grove of trees makes a perfect low maintenance but nevertheless fascinating front entrance. Its simplicity is its style. The magnificent terrace house with its iron lace makes a perfect backdrop.

For a stand of native trees you can't surpass *Eucalyptus scoparia*. The trunk is straight and tall, and the grey bark peels off to reveal a soft, cream colour. The narrow-leafed peppermint (*Eucalyptus nicholii*) is suitable for large gardens. The trunk is straight and the leaves have a willow-like habit. Its flowers are white, it is indigenous to cold, windswept areas and it thrives in poor soils.

This grove of silver birch (Betula pendula) *creates an uncomplicated but arresting garden style.*

A Charming Entrance

First impressions are usually the most memorable. While this is true of gardens, the entrance to your home is also particularly important in creating the impression you want visitors to receive.

I have found that a front entrance will be enhanced by the use of a few potted plants, which can achieve a variety of effects. This impressive entrance is enhanced by a standard marguerite daisy (*Chrysanthemum frutescans*). This is a good choice as it produces flowers from spring until autumn. The pure white flowers of cyclamen contrast perfectly with the tiled floor. The other pot is filled with daphne and during late winter visitors are greeted by its magnificent perfume.

Pandorea pandorana 'Snowbells', a pretty evergreen climbing plant, covers a wall alongside the front path. Its clusters of creamy-white, tubular flowers appear in abundance in spring. It is a good climber for a bare wall as its foliage is dense and attractive throughout the year. Give it some help to climb by using either trellis or wire.

Standard shrubs are becoming very popular and two flanking a doorway or placed at the bottom of steps look most elegant. The choice of standard plants available is immense — the only real limit to their use is your imagination. Among the most spectacular are fuchsias, citrus trees, azaleas, camellias, box, yew, grevilleas — especially *Grevillea rosmarinifolia* which responds well to clipping — pittosporum and hibiscus.

Citrus trees, well suited to pot culture, make interesting and impressive entrance plants. Any type may be used. Small citrus trees require tubs at least 40 cm across and large ones require at least 60 cm.

Meyer lemons hold their fruit for months, which makes them a visual delight to look at for most of the year. The fruit of oranges and mandarins look impressive against their shiny green leaves, while the weight of grapefruit gives the tree a pendulous appearance.

Shaded entrances need not be bare — they can be alive with greenery if the correct plants are chosen. A number of ferns thrive in pots, including *Angiopteris evecta*, a large tropical fern with fronds reaching up to 250 cm; mother spleenwort (*Asplenium bulbiferum*), which has soft, finely divided fronds; hare's foot fern (*Davallia pyxidata*), with its shiny, leathery fronds; soft tree fern (*Dicksonia antarctica*) and king fern (*Todea barbara*), both of which have beautiful, large fronds.

GARDEN STYLES 59

An archetypal terrace house with a climber weaving through the iron lace to add a romantic touch. A standard marguerite daisy flanks the entrance providing a profusion of flowers from spring to late summer.

Planting Around a Birdbath

It is hard to decide which is the feature — the birdbath or the selection of perennials and bulbs planted around it. This delightful planting creates an exquisite garden picture. Birdbaths will fit into any sized garden but should always be tucked into shrubbery or among tall plants so they don't look isolated. If possible place them near a window so the activities of the birds can be observed.

This simple but effective selection of plants provides flower colour and different hues of green and grey leaves. The blue, bell-like flowers of *Scilla campanulata* combine perfectly with the dark pink flowers of cosmos. The grey leaved perennial *Lychnis coronaria* has flowers nearly the same colour as cosmos but also produces pure white flowers and white ones with pink centres.

Geraniums have been reappearing frequently in gardens. The leaves and flowers of the pink geranium are perfumed. There are many varieties, some with large flowers and some with extremely scented leaves but small flowers. The leaves and flowers make an excellent addition to potpourri.

The slender leaves and white bell-shaped flowers of spring snowflake make a pretty spring show. These hardy plants will grow in almost any position from sun to shade.

Overall the effect is soft, natural and reminiscent of spring.

This delightful planting of perennials and bulbs is a perfect setting for a concrete birdbath.

Garden Styles 61

Callistemon
'Reeves Pink'

Grevillea sericea
(Pink Spider
Flower)

Grevillea
'Canberra
Gem'

Pimelea
ferruginea
(Rice flower)

Correa
reflexa
(Native
Fuchsia)

Dampiera linearis

Arum lillies
(Zantedeschia aethiopica)

Buxus sempervirens

A Sylvan Glade

The combination of deciduous trees, soft pink and white azaleas and the charming stone pathway produces a fairytale setting. When the spring flowers finish, the garden becomes an essay in green. But this does not mean it loses its charm, as the myriad shades of green and the different way light filters through the trees produces a very successful garden design. The green of deciduous trees changes throughout the year from the bright soft green of new unfolding foliage to the darker green of mature leaves. The leaves then colour once again before they wither and die.

The underplanting is very simple. Azaleas provide structure for the beds. The Christmas rose (*Helleborus niger*) forms a dense ground cover thriving in the dappled sunlight and is not disturbed by the competition from tree roots. Its dark green leaves are thick and leathery and the flowers which appear in winter when other flowers are scarce stay on the plant for weeks.

Bulbs form a strong part of the underplanting. Among the first to appear are snowflakes (*Leucojum vernum*) which are followed by jonquils and daffodils (*Narcissus* species) and bluebells (*Scilla campanulata*). Other bulbs that would thrive in these conditions include lily-of-the-valley (*Convallaria majalis*), *Freesia* species, true snowdrop (*Galanthus nivalis*) and grape hyacinth (*Muscari botryoides*) and *Sparaxis Tricolor*.

Forget-me-nots, lamium (*Lamium galeobdolon* 'Variegatum'), ivy and violets form a lower carpet and help to keep the weeds at bay. Lamium is a rapidly spreading ground cover which is very useful for shaded areas under trees, but because of its fast growth care

The combination of deciduous trees, soft pink and white flowers and the stone path produces an enchanting woodland setting.

must be taken that it does not become too invasive. It is generally best to plant it in areas where it is the only ground cover. Its leaves are evergreen and attractive throughout the year. In early summer whorled spikes of soft yellow flowers appear. The variegated form has silver edges.

The Charm of Yesteryear

Old-fashioned plants jostle for space in this cottage garden. Flowers reach their peak during early summer but there is usually something in flower throughout the year.

Cottage gardens are becoming increasingly popular. This popularity indicates a return to the gardening ideas of an earlier and more romantic era. The look is informal, abundant and relaxing with a random quality that gives the impression of being a little unkempt.

Cottage gardens are filled with an informal mixture of shrubs, bulbs, perennials, annuals, herbs and even the odd vegetable. Plants are crammed into garden beds to provide colourful mixtures, or are used in drifts through the garden to obtain the essentially casual look.

Although this may sound chaotic, there is a practical framework to this gardening style.

One of the main reasons cottage gardens are so popular is their low maintenance. With today's hectic lifestyle most people want to relax in their garden rather than spending all

Garden Styles 65

THE CHARM OF YESTERYEAR

Interplanted with pink, white and blue forget-me-nots, love-in-a-mist (Nigella damascena), Viola odorata, cream California poppies (Eschscholzia californica), Canterbury bells (Campanula medium), Cosmos and rose campion (Lychnis coronaria).

- Digitalis purpurea
- Cosmos
- Grevillea rosmarinifolia
- Chrysanthemum frutescans
- Erigeron karvinsckianus
- Cynoglossum amabile
- Papaver orientale (pink)
- Yellow Charles Austin Rose
- Rosa 'Belle Isis'
- Aquilegia (blue)
- Delphinium 'Pacific Hybrids'
- Chrysanthemum frutescans
- Cosmos bipinimatus
- Astrantia major
- Rose Scented Geranium
- Rose 'Perle d'ore'
- Gypsophila paniculata
- Aquilegia (blue)
- Papaver orientale (pink)
- Gypsophila paniculata
- Lychnis coronaria
- Digitalis purpurea
- Liatris spicata (pink)
- Rosa 'Cornelia'
- Aquilegia vulgaris
- Cynoglossum species
- Lychnis coronaria
- Hydrangea macrophylla
- Geranium pratense
- Digitalis purpurea
- Cosmos
- Erigeron karvinsckianus
- Agapanthus orientalis
- Liatris spicata (pink)
- Digitalis purpurea
- Chrysanthemum frutescans
- Digitalis purpurea
- Thalictrum dipterocarpum
- Cosmos
- Digitalis purpurea
- Rosa 'Cecile Brunner'
- Geranium pratense
- Stachys lanata
- Crocosmia masonorum
- Digitalis purpurea
- Geranium pratense 'Alba'
- Rugosa Rose (white)
- Agapanthus orientalis
- Rosa 'Belle Isis'

their time maintaining it. To this end weeds are kept to a minimum simply because of the abundance of plant material. Garden edges are not carefully defined and instead groundcovers are left to tumble over the edges.

Self-seeding annuals and perennials grow where they seed and the garden takes on an enchanting and natural feel.

This pretty cottage garden exudes charm. The soft colour scheme is in shades of blue, pink and white. Because it is in a cool region of Australia it starts to reach its peak in late spring and flowers abundantly through summer. Majestic foxgloves, cosmos, oriental poppies (*Papaver orientalis*), love-in-a-mist (*Nigella damascena*), columbines (*Aquilegia vulgaris*), old-fashioned roses, yarrow (*Achillea* species), gypsophila, delphiniums, rose campion (*Lychnis coronaria*) and forget-me-nots all jostle for space. The dense planting leaves no room for weeds.

Gravel paths meander throughout the garden and it is not surprising to find the odd self-seeded primula, strawberry, forget-me-not, silene or poppy among the gravel.

Groundcovers planted alongside the path and on the edges of the garden beds tumble over the edge. They include babies' tears (*Erigeron karvinsckianus*), snow-in-summer (*Cerastium tomentosum*), Swan river daisy (*Brachycome iberidifolia*) and *Arenaria montana*.

Daisies, which are perfect for a cottage garden, provide long lasting flowers which may also be cut for indoors. Marguerite and shasta daisies are used through this garden. Marguerite daisies (*Chrysanthemum frutescans*) have white to pale yellow flowers but there have been a number of varieties cultivated including those which produce shades of pink. The shasta daisy (*Chrysanthemum maximum*) has dark green foliage and strong stemmed, single white flowers with a golden eye, the flowers are produced in summer.

Perennials are among the mainstays of a cottage garden. These hardy plants add variety to the garden, filling the space between shrubs and groundcovers, but should not be planted in straight rows. Choose perennials of different heights, leaf textures and flower colours. Careful planning will ensure continuity of flowering throughout the seasons.

Some of the most popular cottage garden perennials include yarrow (*Achillea millefolium*), monkshood (*Aconitum napellus*), hollyhock (*Alcea rosea*), woodland anemone (*Anemone blanda*), Japanese windflower (*Anemone japonica*), columbines (*Aquilegia vulgaris*), English daisy (*Bellis perennis*), Canterbury bells (*Campanula medium*), *Delphinium* species, foxgloves (*Digitalis purpurea*), statice (*Limonium sinatum*), lupins (*Lupinus* species), oriental poppies (*Papaver orientale*), *Penstemon gloxinoides*, ornamental sage (*Salvia* species) and lavender shower (*Thalictrum dipterocarpum*).

Self-seeding annuals should be planted lavishly in a cottage garden. They include forget-me-nots in shades of blue, pink or white, sweet Alice (*Alyssum* species), busy Lizzie (*Impatiens wallerana*), honesty (*Lunaria annua*), tobacco plant (*Nicotiana* species), love-in-a-mist (*Nigella damascena*), poppies, pansies and *Viscaria* species.

An unexpected element in the cottage garden is the inclusion of vegetables among flowers. Lettuce can be planted as a border, while large plants like tomatoes can be planted at the back of flower beds. The bright green leaves of silverbeet make a pleasing contrast with white flowers. Ruby Chard is a variety of silverbeet with dark green leaves and bright crimson stalks.

Perennial sorrel has attractive leaves which die down during winter to appear in abundance the following spring. Globe artichoke is

An informal profusion of flowers which includes a yellow Charles Austin rose, cosmos and shasta daisies.

a tall perennial with large, silver-grey, Scotch thistle-type leaves. Planted at the back of the garden, the grey leaves add interest.

Accessories will add the finishing touch. A birdbath, sundial or simple statue adds charm, as do terracotta pots brimming with annuals. Carefully placed seats invite you to sit and relax.

A Tropical Courtyard

This small but well-designed city courtyard is mainly in shades of green with a few white flowers. Green is a restful and cool colour. It blends perfectly with the terracotta coloured walls of the house and the large terracotta pots. The garden, which is actually on three levels, is connected by sandstone steps. The paving is also sandstone.

Large palms provide instant character and give shade. They also produce delightful shadowed patterns on the paving. There are more than 200 genera and nearly 3000 species in the palm family and they range from mature miniatures of 45 cm to soaring giants of 30 m or more. Their leaf colours vary from yellow to deep green and blue-grey. There are numerous palms suitable for gardens and many of them thrive in shaded positions. Under these conditions palms always look good when grown with a variety of ferns.

The fishtail palm (*Caryota* species) has fronds that are ruffled at the ends and shaped like fishtails. *Chamaedorea* species will thrive in shaded gardens and include *C. elegans*, which is a graceful, relatively fast growing palm with dark green leathery leaves and *C. erumpens* which has bamboo-like stems and drooping leaves. The European fan palm (*Chamaerops humilis*) has a bushy appearance and forms stalks of various ages, so its stiff, fan-shaped leaves appear at several different levels. It looks wonderful when planted against a bare wall or background, as it forms a dramatic silhouette. Curly palm (*Howea belmoreana*) has an elegant appearance and very large fronds and can reach a height of 8 m. The Chinese fan palm (*Livistona chinensis*) has stunning, very large lustrous-green fan-shaped leaves which are cut halfway into many narrow, one-ribbed segments. These segments split again and the tips hang like a fringe.

Opposite Palms create stunning shadows on the paved middle-level courtyard of this small garden.

*Right The Bangalow palm (*Archontophoenix cunninghamiana*) shades the aviary and frames the steps leading to the carport on the third level.*

GARDEN STYLES 69

Wisteria rambles through a pergola giving summer shade. Its exquisite, fragrant flowers droop in spring to form a mauve carpet on the sandstone when their petals drop.

For a very tall palm you can't surpass the Canary Island date palm (*Phoenix canariensis*). It has a majestic appearance and as it ages the trunk is thickened by stems from the old leaves. The fronds are a dark glossy green while the stalks are a paler green. The Senegal date palm (*Phoenix reclinata*) has a feathery appearance because of its slender dark green leaflets precisely arranged on long arching fronds. A stunning effect can be achieved by the presence of petticoat palm (*Washingtonia filifera*). Its large, grey-green, fan-shaped leaves are divided into about twenty segments for at least half their spread. Fine fibres hang from the leaf divisions and the span of the leaves can be 60 cm or more. The bright green leaf segments of the thread palm (*Washingtonia robusta*) are stiffer and much less deeply cut than the petticoat palm. It is also thinner and faster growing.

A delightful aviary is a focal point in the garden and defines the side boundary on the middle level. The planting around the base of the palms is simple but effective. White agapanthus, irises, arum lilies (*Zantedeschia aethiopica*), gardenias (*Gardenia jasminoides*), and busy Lizzie (*Impatiens wallerana*) are the main plants. They have all been selected for their durability as well as their beauty.

Ivy (*Hedera* species) covers a brick wall near the steps leading to the carport. This hardy climber drapes the wall with greenery throughout the year.

The bottom level receives shade from a mauve wisteria during summer while allowing the winter sun to stream through.

The combination of the terracotta walls and the green foliage gives a feeling of utter freshness.

Along the Side of a Path

Paths divide the garden into different areas. They are both the framework upon which the garden is built and the means by which a garden is viewed. Paths establish mood and style and may be informal and winding or straight and formal. The planting alongside the path is as important as the path itself as it can soften the overall tone and provide contrasting textures. In a practical role they provide easy access to garden beds.

This enchanting pathway is part of a large cottage garden. It is partly shaded because of larger overhanging trees but in spring it becomes alive with colour. Camellias grow at the back of one bed to give a sense of height and create privacy. The lower-growing azaleas give structure to the beds. Columbines (*Aquilegia* species) and forget-me-nots provide a mass of spring colour in shades of deep blue, blue, pink and white. The common and botanical names of columbines are derived from two birds — the dove (columba) and the eagle (aquila). This combination was inspired by the shape of the flowers which are composed of plain petals intermixed with others that are hollow and horned, giving the overall impression of a dove with expanded wings. Another common name 'granny's bonnets' is derived from the columbine's bonnet-like appearance. These hardy perennials die down during winter but appear in abundance the following spring. The leaves have a fern-like appearance and produce flowers for a long period. Columbines also have the generous habit of self-seeding throughout the garden. There is a wide colour range which includes shades of blue, pink, white, cream or a combination of two colours on the one flower.

Blue and white forget-me-nots form a soft carpet appearing in early spring. The perennial Chinese forget-me-not (*Cynoglossum* species) has large leaves and intense sky-blue flowers and holds its flowers for a long period. It starts flowering after the annual forget-me-nots have finished. It is also available in pink.

Species geraniums were favourites of Gertrude Jekyll, the well-known English landscaper. These classic perennials make excellent groundcovers for pathway plantings. Included among the species are *Geranium anemonifolium* which has large anemone-like foliage and masses of soft purple flowers throughout spring and summer; *Geranium pratense* 'Mrs Kendall Clarke', with its large clear blue flowers; *Geranium pratense* 'Alba' which has pretty white flowers; *Geranium himalayense* which produces loose clusters of pure blue flowers and *Geranium sanguineum* which has very deeply cut leaves and attractive purplish-crimson flowers.

FERNS AND PALMS FOR A DAMP SHADED PATHWAY

- Dicksonia anartica
- Blechnum minus
- Phoenix roebelinii
- Adiantum formosum
- Todea barbara
- Todea barbara
- Nephrolepis cordifolia
- Phoenix roebelinii
- Adiantum formosum
- Chamaedorea costaricana
- Blechnum indicum
- 3 Howea forsteriana
- Adiantum aethiopicum
- Dicksonia antartica

SHRUBS AND PERENNIALS FOR A SEMI-SHADED PATHWAY

- Rhododendron species
- Acer palmatum 'Dissectum'
- Acanthus mollis
- Mahonia japonica
- Murraya exotica
- 3 Agapanthus orientalis
- Digitalis purpurea
- 2 Aquilegia vulgaris
- 5 Bergenia cordifolia
- Clivea miniata
- 5 Bergenia cordifolia
- Digitalis purpurea
- Aconitum napellus
- 2 Aquilegia vulgaris
- Azalea
- Azalea
- Clivea miniata
- Choisya ternata
- Azalea
- Liriope muscari (border)
- Rhododendron species
- 3 Agapanthus orientalis
- Osmanthus fragrans
- Digitalis purpurea

Underplanted with Ajuga reptans, viola odorata and Lamium

Opposite In spring the garden beds beside the path are alive with colour.

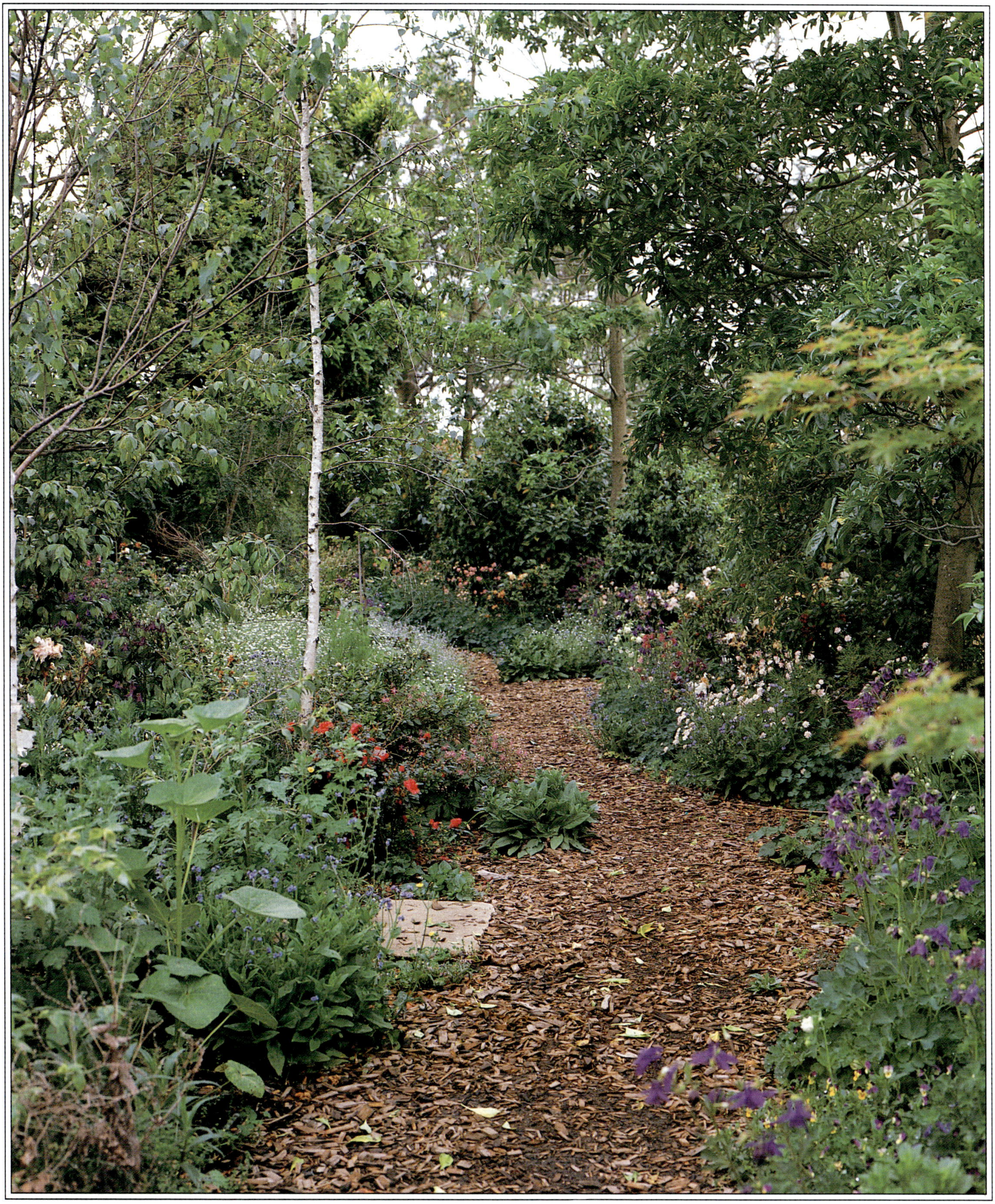

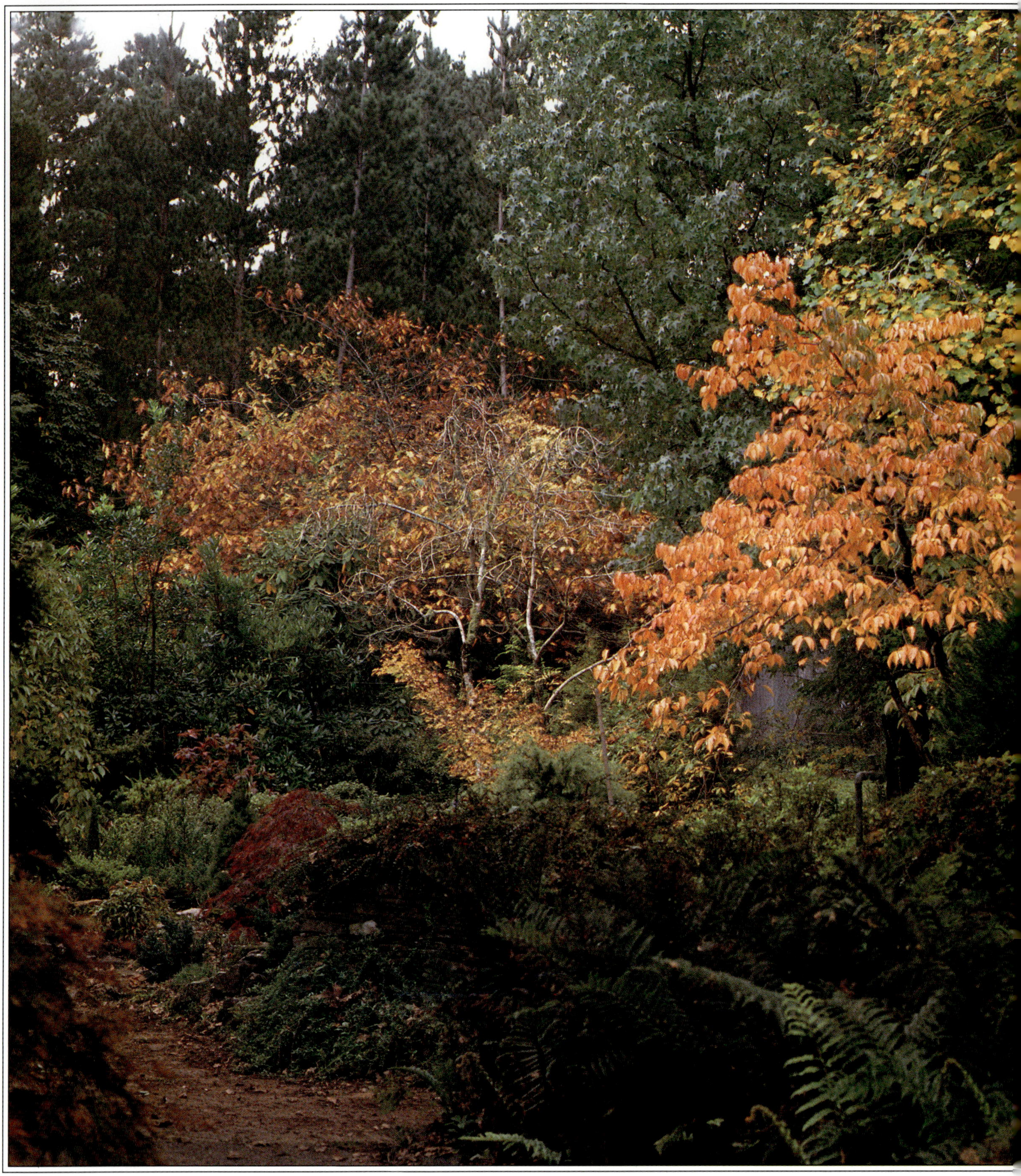

Autumn Colour

Trees are an exciting reminder of the changing seasons. Their changing canopies suddenly delight us with an announcement that a new season has begun. From the point of view of leaf colour, autumn is perhaps one of the most delightful seasons. The coloured leaves hang on the trees to give the impression that they are suspended in time. Once fallen they are an important part of the ecosystem. Their leaves are recycled to create food for the next season. Although deciduous trees are bare in winter, their strong silhouettes form interesting patterns and shapes.

Trees for autumn colour

Botanical name	Common name
Acer species	maple
Betula species	birch
Cornus species	dogwood
Cotinus coggygria	smoke tree
Diospyros kaki	persimmon
Fraxinus species	ash
Gingko biloba	maidenhair tree
Liquidamber styraciflua	American sweet gum
Metasequoia glyptostroboides	dawn redwood
Nyssa sylvatica	black tulepo
Parrotia persica	
Pistacia chinensis	Chinese pistachio
Populus species	poplar
Quercus species	oak
Robinia pseudoacacia	black locust or false acacia

During autumn this woodland garden turns into a kaleidoscope of colour.

A Romantic Rose Garden

I always love the sense of enchantment one feels when walking through a garden and smelling the heady perfumes of fragrant plants.

This particular country garden is filled with romance and perfume as it celebrates the beauty of the rose. Climbing roses hang in large groupings over arches and scrambling roses tumble down banks and line pathways. When one is captivated by such a profusion of roses it is easy to appreciate why the rose has always been the flower associated with romance and a sense of mystery.

A walk through any of the paths in the garden brings sensual pleasure. Every type of old-fashioned rose can be found in the garden — Tea, China, David Austin, Climbers, Musks and Rugosas. I find that old-fashioned roses can quickly become an obsession; they are so rich in history and their colours so soft. The colours of the newer hybrids are too fierce and bright, creating jarring contrasts in the gar-

'Cramoisi Superieur' is a China rose having masses of small double-cupped, deep-red blooms. The soft-grey leaves and flower spikes of the lavender tone down its dark-red flowers.

den. Roses are so hardy and easy to cultivate. There are very few gardens that will come to fruition as quickly as a rose garden. Combined with perennials and annuals a garden bed will look full and inviting after a couple of years.

Lavender and sweetly scented geraniums are planted in abundance throughout the garden. They form a perfect combination with the roses. The perfumes of all of these plants complement each other well, with none overpowering the other.

Climbing roses always need some type of structure on which to grow. This can be an arch, pergola, summerhouse or even an old fruit tree. If you are attempting to get a climbing rose to grow on a tree (and it won't do its host any harm), plant it at least 70 cm from the tree and on the side that receives the most sun. Help it to begin climbing with a chicken wire support placed loosely around the trunk. The wire should remain until the rose is large enough to scramble its way through the branches.

Banksia roses are ideal for planting over a

Swathes of roses flank the pathway.

An enchanting arch covered in the well-known climbing Rosa *'Albertine'. The arch frames the garden path and the sweet perfume encourages you to linger.*

pergola as they don't have any thorns. The double, white *Rosa banksia* is violet-scented, fast growing and comes into flower before the better-known yellow variety.

Many of the climbing roses have long flowering periods. *Rosa* 'Blackboy' has large, deep crimson velvety flowers, is mildew-proof and flowers profusely in spring followed by another flush later in the season and again in autumn. Red roses are beautiful but remember that you do not need many of them — one red rose goes a long way. Try to stay with the softer colours with perhaps a dash of red and whatever you do do not put a red rose against a brick wall as the result looks sickly. *Rosa* 'Cecile Brunner' has masses of small pink blooms through late spring and summer and *Rosa* 'Lady Hillingdon', a climbing form of one of the popular tea roses, has large golden flowers and blooms continuously from early spring. *Rosa* 'Clair Matin' is a low-growing climber which flowers endlessly. It has a clean, sweet, wild fragrance and the flowers are a pure, pale-pink with a central cluster of pale, golden stamens. The climbing form of 'Souvenir de la Malmaison' gives endless flushes of flowers with autumn usually being the most spectacular season. The huge, creamy, full-quartered flowers have a sweet spicy fragrance.

A fragrant rose useful for garden beds or borders is the Gallica variety. Old-fashioned Gallica roses were brought back from the East by the crusaders of the twelfth and thirteenth centuries and their petals were used for making perfume and medicines. They tend to be thicketing roses and do not grow more than a metre high. Hybrids of *Rosa gallica* include 'Belle Isis' which has soft-pink, double flowers that open flat; 'Cardinal de Richelieu' with its rich, purple blooms; 'Duchesse de Montebello', a shade-tolerant rose with soft-pink flowers; and 'Tuscany Superb', which has large, deep-red, very fragrant flowers.

Hybrid Perpetual roses are characteristic of nineteenth century Victorian and Edwardian gardens. The large flowers always have a strong perfume and they flower in several heavy flushes with great abundance and generosity. Included among these are 'Frau Karl Druschki' whose pure-white flowers emerge from carmine buds and 'La Reine' which has stunning globular buds which open to cupped, silvery-pink flowers. For a touch of red you cannot surpass 'Reine des Violettes' with its thornless branches and lovely violet-red flowers which age through rich lilac-purples and violet-greys.

The Garden Shed

Gardeners require space to store lawnmowers, seeds, potting mixtures, wheelbarrows and garden tools. In colder climates one needs a suitable area in which to store firewood. Garden sheds do not have to be elaborate but they should definitely not be a dominating structure in the garden. If you are lucky enough to have an old outhouse, it can always be converted into a shed. Australia is famous for its outbuildings. Old farms are often characterised by numerous buildings scattered on adjoining land. If, however, you do have to erect a shed, choose a simple structure that will fit into a corner of the garden or against a fence. You will be surprised how inconspicuous a utilitarian building can be.

A shed can always be screened from view by using trellis, climbing plants or large shrubs. Such screening is a must for metal sheds which, although functional, are often rather unsightly. The charm of a shed depends on how well it fits into the garden layout, its functional structure and effective complementary associated planting.

This typical Australian shed with a galvanised iron roof, thick wooden beams and slightly leaning angle is a feature in itself. As part of a large country garden it is surrounded by trees, shrubs and perennials. Although open to weather on three sides, it is adequate enough for storing garden tools and wood.

A Garden Picture

Opposite A perfect picture is framed by the arch.

Below This sweeping view can be observed upon passing through the arch. A large expanse of lawn frames the lake, which is a focal point of the garden.

Well-known English landscape designer Gertrude Jeckyll was a great believer in creating garden pictures. She designed her 'pictures' with the use of colour, plant combinations and light.

The use of colour for a garden picture does not necessarily involve a grouping of different colours. Different hues of one colour may be used, or simply two colours together.

A simple path with a group of silver birches or a large urn placed at the end can create a garden picture, as can a scene that catches your eye from a window or doorway.

The picture in this garden is framed by an arch covered with the sweetly perfumed, old-fashioned rose 'Albertine' and a white clematis. The vista opens up as soon as you walk through the arch. Looking through the arch your eye is led to a concrete birdbath nestled in a garden bed amid numerous sweet-smelling, gaily coloured perennials and annuals of every description — verbena, geums, iris, linaria, Californian poppies, foxgloves and Russell lupins. Old-fashioned roses are also planted in the garden bed, adding structure and perfume.

The arch entices you to walk through and explore the delights even further. A grassy slope leads you to a large lake which is the amalgamation of two medium-sized dams built to give the garden water during times of drought.

Water plays a vital part in this garden, reflecting both its changing moods and the surrounding plants. There is a small wooden jetty on which is a seat for quiet reflection.

Banks of azaleas are planted under pine trees growing at the rear of the pond. This garden has been well-designed, with separate areas creating their own pictures, moods and atmospheres. It is not a garden you hurry through but one that invites you to meander, look and discover.

GARDEN STYLES 81

A Garden of Day and Evening Fragrances

When the sun finally disappears, one can prolong pleasant experiences in the garden with the correct choice of plant material. It is a time when many plants produce nocturnal perfumes and when you can become aware of the influence that the fading evening light has on the colour of flowers — especially those which are white, lemon and soft pink.

From the moment you walk through the front gate of this garden you are charmed. Moonflower (*Calonyction aculeatum*) is draped over the front fence. This enchanting, night-flowering climber has huge 15 cm pure-white flowers which unfold at dusk to release a delicious, pervasive fragrance. It looks and smells so good that one would want to entertain so that one's guests would be able to appreciate it. A perennial climber, it reaches a height of 6 m and requires a warm, sunny position but likes its roots kept cool with a mulch.

The brick path is adorned with an arch covered in the white flowers of potato vine (*Solanum jasminoides*) and a climbing rose 'Cecile Brunner' which produces soft pink flowers. In garden beds alongside the path there are mass plantings of perennials, annuals and bulbs. Featured among these plantings is the flowering tobacco plant (*Nicotiana sylvestris*) — the largest of the flowering tobaccos. This evocative plant will flood the garden with a penetrating fragrance. The tobacco plant has been combined with evening primrose (*Oenothera biennis*), a cottage garden favourite with yellow, saucer-like flowers which awaken and open in the afternoon to pour forth a delicious fragrance. There are many different types of evening primrose and each species has pretty flowers and lovely perfume. Giant yellow evening primrose (*Oenothera hookeri*) is a magnificent perennial with greyish furry leaves and huge golden flowers on tall stems; *Oenothera caespitosa* forms a dense clump of dandelion-like leaves from which emerge huge pure white flowers which take on a pink blush as they age during summer; fragrant evening primrose (*Oenothera odorata*) has 5 cm wide golden flowers and pink evening primrose (*Oenothera rosea*) is a lovely perennial of extraordinary beauty that is smothered in large, saucer-shaped light-pink flowers that remain open during the day.

The shrub form of *Rosa* 'Cecile Brunner' is planted throughout the front garden. This sweetly perfumed, small, pretty rose appears continuously during summer.

The feature tree in the front garden is angel's trumpet (*Datura cornigera*) which displays its spectacular clusters of greenish white, prominently-ribbed, 25 cm long trumpets in late spring and summer. It is an ideal

Opposite An arch draped in potato vine (Solanum jasminoides) has been placed halfway along the brick path. Perfumed plants provide fragrance during the day and evening.

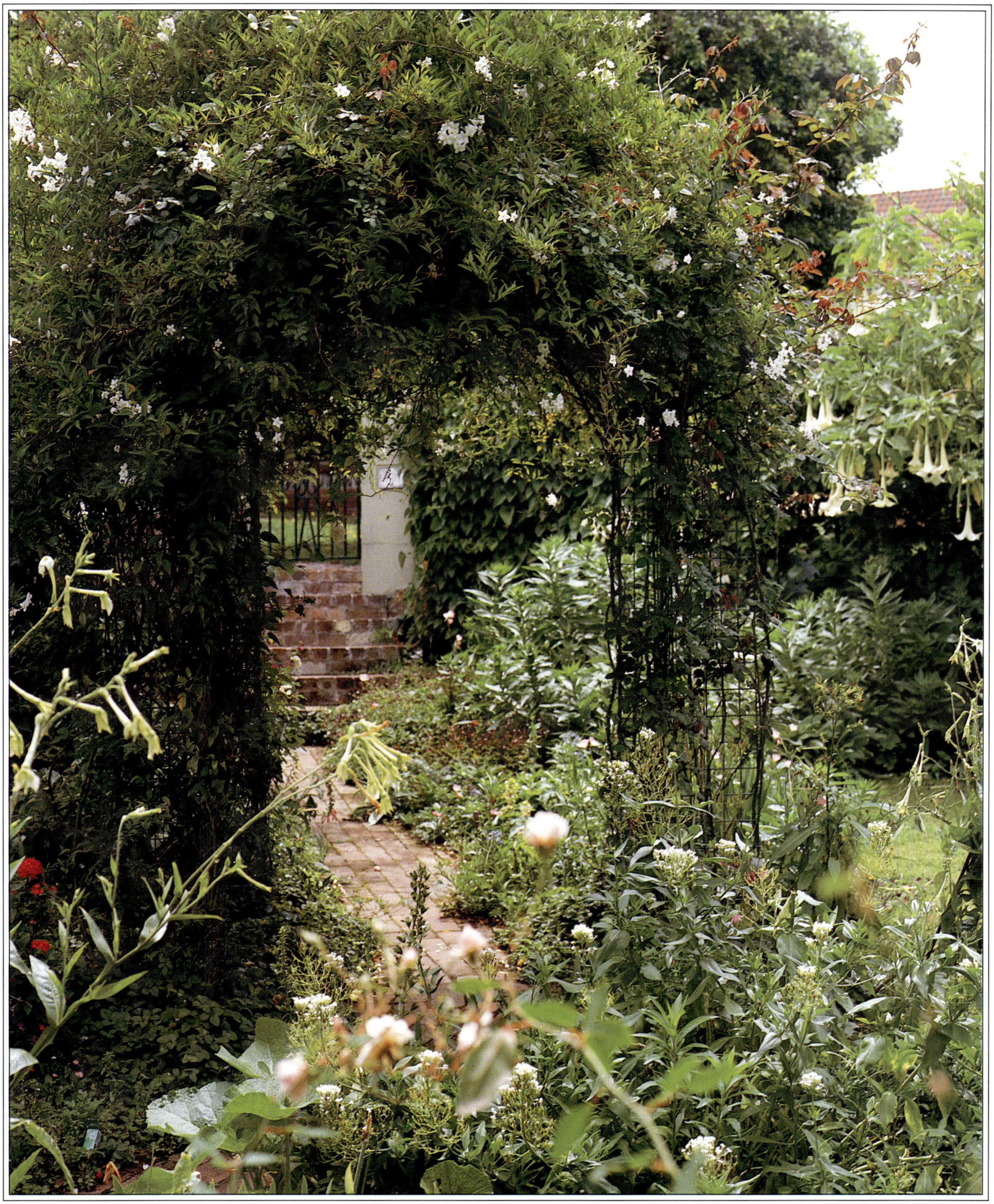

tree for a small garden reaching a height of 3 m and a width of 2 m. Its large flowers are visible at night.

The back garden has an evocative cottage garden touch with arches covered in old-fashioned climbing roses, a birdbath and an abundance of old-fashioned perennials and climbing plants. The look is soft and romantic. Apart from the many perfumed climbing roses there are also several other interesting climbers. These include the snail flower (*Phaseolus caracalla*) which, when given some support, will quickly clothe a wall in unusual light purple and yellow flowers. The flowers have a snail-like appearance, as the common name suggests. The perfume is heavy and sweet. The growth rate of the cup-and-saucer vine (*Cobaea scandens*) needs to be seen to be believed. Violet-purple flowers appear freely in spring and early summer among its dense green foliage. *Dolichos lignosus* is the perfect plant for areas requiring quick cover. The plant is almost engulfed in pea-shaped flowers during spring. Most situations will suit dolichos, but the flowers are more abundant in full sun.

Perennials include Queen Anne's lace (*Ammi majus*), poppies, foxgloves (*Digitalis purpurea*), love-in-a-mist (*Nigella damascena*), hollyhocks (*Alcea rosea*), columbines (*Aquilegia vulgaris*), species geraniums and babies' tears (*Erigeron karvinsckianus*). Annuals like larkspur (*Delphinium ajacis*), forget-me-nots and heartsease (*Viola tricolor*) grow among the perennials.

There are many other plants that release their fragrance at night. You will not need a watch if you are standing near the four o'clock plant (*Mirabilis jalapa*) because it does exactly what its name suggests and opens its flowers

A picture on the studio wall at the bottom of the garden is a pretty touch. Perennials and climbers surround the small courtyard and barbecue area.

about that time. They remain open at night and fade the following morning. Originating in tropical America, the four o'clock plant thrives in hot climates and the very fragrant, red, white and yellow or bi-coloured flowers appear from mid-summer to autumn.

Evening scented stock (*Mathiola bicornis*) is an annual with lilac summer flowers.

In early times Londoners used to plant common mignonette (*Reseda odorata*) in window planters to quell unpleasant street odours. The perfume of the heavily musk scented, yellowish-brown flowers will pervade a patio, especially on a warm, humid night.

Scented climbing plants are among my favourite garden inclusions. Some of these are noted solely for their night scent. The sweet and heavy fragrance of night-scented jasmine (*Cestrum nocturnum*) is particularly intense on humid summer nights. The mid-summer flowers are greenish-white. Because it is more of a sprawling shrub than a climber it needs to be manually attached to trellis or wire.

Honeysuckles will carry their perfume into the night. *Lonicera heckrottii* 'Gold Flame' has yellow flowers heavily flushed with deep rose. An evergreen plant, it will grow in most climates, reaching a height of 4 m. *Lonicera* 'Tellmanniana' is a spectacular hybrid with deep yellow-orange flowers which are red at the tips and just inside the trumpet. It will grow in complete shade and will make an interesting shrub if pruned to shape.

The main advantage of the fragrant perennial pea (*Lathyrus latifolius*), which has pink and white sweet pea-like flowers, is that it lasts right through the hot weather. Its coarse foliage will quickly scramble 3 m over a bank or wire fence or up a trellis.

A birdbath is a feature in the middle of the small back garden. Babies' tears (Erigeron karvinsckianus) softens the brick steps.

A Walled City Garden

A summerhouse is the dominating feature in the back garden of this small, stylish, city house. A generous scale and a bold, interesting outline are two of the successful ingredients in creating a garden like this. These ingredients, even in a small garden, can ensure that a building will become a splendid focal point. The summerhouse provides shelter from summer sun, in a quiet relaxing environment. The large trees surrounding the summerhouse are 'borrowed' from surrounding properties, giving an illusion of space.

Lawn bordered by gravel paths leads your eye straight to the summerhouse which was actually built to conceal a garage underneath. The soft blue walls give the garden a distinct Mediterranean feel. Blue flowering *Plumbago capensis* flank the entrance to the summerhouse. This evergreen shrub will flower from late spring to late autumn, peaking in late summer.

Wisteria rambles up through the trellis of the summerhouse to give the necessary shade in summer while allowing sun through in winter when the wisteria loses its leaves. *Cupressus sempervirens* 'Stricta' with their slender fastigiate habit are on each corner of the summerhouse to complete the exotic composition.

The summerhouse, decorated for Christmas, provides a focal point for this small garden.

GARDEN STYLES 87

A Paved Courtyard

This pretty paved courtyard is a vision of abundance in a minute area. The structure is simple, with a step leading from a small sitting area outside the back door to a larger paved area. A brick wall has been built around this area to provide a change of height and to create space for extra, well-stocked garden beds.

One immediately recognises that this is a garden lover's garden because of the great care and attention needed for the potted plants alone. Strategically placed pots may be used as points of emphasis in a garden in a formal or informal manner. A few well-placed pots can be arranged to look as if they are many. Potted plants are perfect for a small paved garden like this, turning an otherwise bare area of paving into a glorious display of flowers and foliage.

There is a huge range of plant containers in all shapes and sizes. Terracotta pots are among my favourites but their porous nature means that plants in them require constant watering. One method of avoiding the necessity for constant watering is to line the inside of the pot with black plastic. But do not line the

A glorious display of colourful plants in a garden where every inch of space is utilised. The native violet (Viola hederacea) forms a beautiful groundcover as it weaves its way around the potted plants.

bottom of the pot as this will impede drainage.

Large tree ferns have been planted near the fence and are underplanted with arum lilies (*Zantedeschia aethiopicum*), the striking leaves and flowers of which provide continual interest. Potted plants have been used to create seasonal shows of colour against a backdrop of permanent green. They fill the courtyard and hang from trees. The potted plants are so well-placed that they form garden pictures in their own right.

In the courtyard one's eye is drawn to a potted, standard, dark-pink, flowering bougainvillea. Surrounded mainly by white and yellow flowering plants the contrast makes the colour scheme bright and cheerful. Pots are filled with shrubs, annuals and perennials. Pots brimming with herbs add interest and variation to this collection. Herbs thrive in pots as they like the free drainage that potting mixtures allow.

The loveliest thing about this garden is that every available space is packed with plants. The garden beds which are raised up from the courtyard are filled with a wide variety of plants including busy Lizzie (*Impatiens wallerana*), irises, begonias, geraniums, native violets (*Viola hederacea*), fuchsias, poppies, forget-me-nots and old-fashioned roses. The bright yellow daisy-like flowers of *Euryops pectinatus* provide a soft glow through the garden. This evergreen shrub can reach a height of 2 m and is valued for a flowering period that lasts from spring to summer.

A group of well-placed pots soften the hard appearance of paving.

Garden Enchantment

Often you can walk into a garden that absolutely exudes charm and character. A number of components are responsible for creating these attributes. Such a component may simply be a well-placed selection of pots or ornaments, or perhaps it will be the style of the garden itself. This garden is characterised by a timeless quality and a slight look of abandonment.

The garden is surrounded by high walls and receives a considerable amount of shade during the day. An exuberant muddle of climbers has been encouraged to clamber up the walls, along the ground and up a dead tree in the

A small quantity of water can be used to great effect. This garden is enhanced by a simple fountain, the running water from which gives a tranquil feeling.

middle of the garden. The garden is virtually an essay in green. This garden demonstrates an appreciation of the use of myriad shades of green, an appreciation so fundamental to garden design.

The fountain is used as a central focal point. The sound of running water creates a peaceful environment. Brick paving fans out from the pool and through the rest of the garden. Plants grow happily in between the bricks to create an aged look. Ferns and palms add to this timeless quality. Ferns have flourished over the earth in some form for millions of years and vary in size from tiny moss-like plants to the large tree ferns. For stunning foliage in shaded or semi-shaded positions they cannot be surpassed.

This garden has a tone of the unexpected, with statues and plant-filled containers appearing in unusual corners. It is a garden with a sophisticated ambience and yet one in which the owners can relax and apprecite nature.

An arresting statue draws your eye to create a handsome focal point.

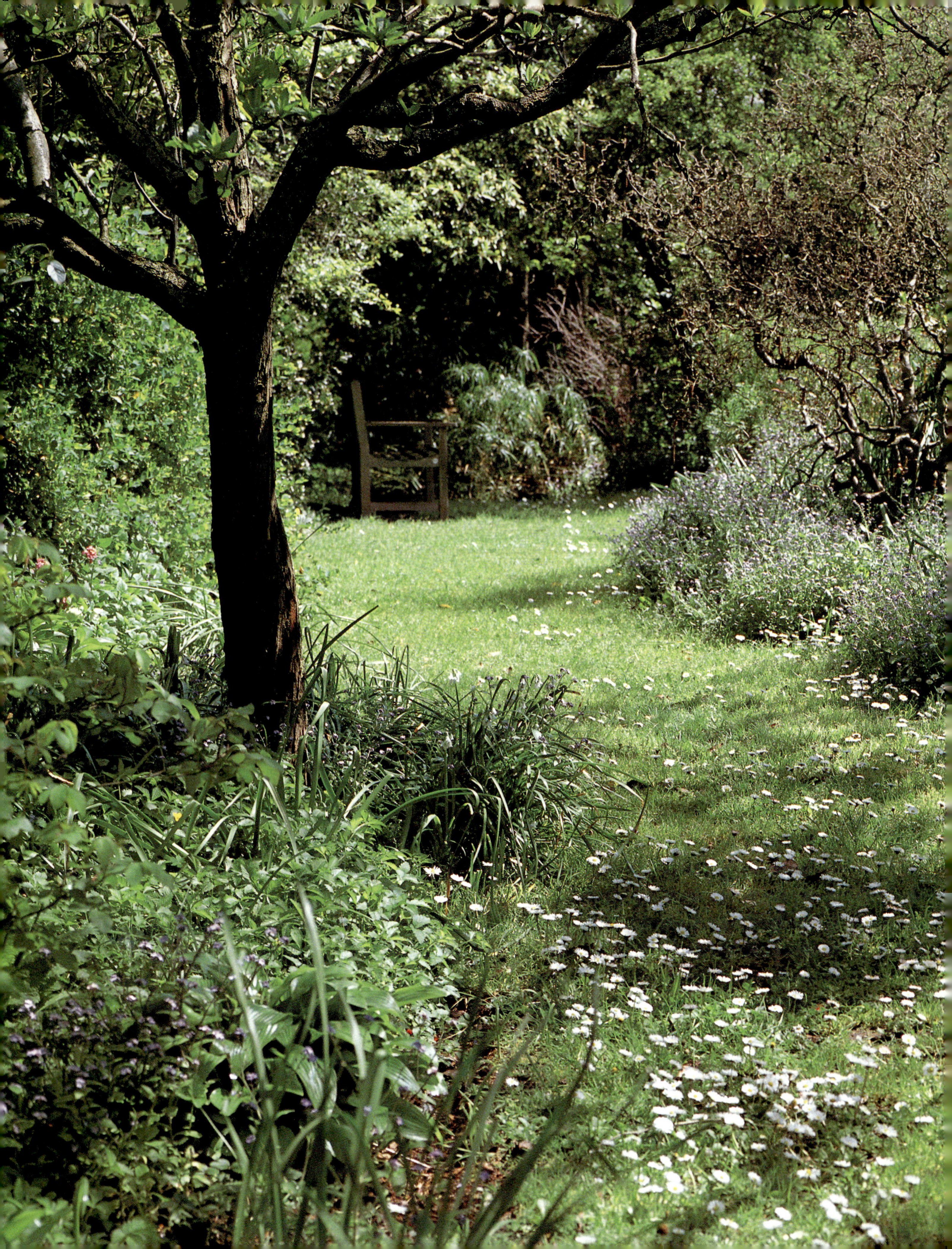

CREATING YOUR IDEAL GARDEN

CREATING A GARDEN STYLE

Planning a garden involves creative ability and is an interesting and rewarding challenge. A garden should be a place of beauty and tranquillity where one can relax with a sense of harmony. The ultimate result should be a low maintenance garden that can be enjoyed rather than becoming a weekend chore. The objective in creating a garden style is a landscape that is pleasing as well as functional and composed of plants that are suitable to the climate.

ASPECT AND SITE

Whatever your needs when planning a new garden, they will be conditioned to some extent by the site and its aspect. You may be lucky enough to have acquired an established garden but a new block is often covered in clay and rubble with every piece of plant material removed. Established gardens also have their problems as they have often been neglected and plants wrongly placed, but at least you will have something to work with.

It is important to examine the type of soil on your land, its depth and quality and to determine if it is adequately drained. A new garden may not have any topsoil at all, so you will have to bring in garden loam. Other considerations are exposure to wind, shade and sun. Also note if there are any objectionable views that need screening out.

A sloping block can cost you considerable amounts of money if retaining walls are required. Take a good look and see if you can work with the slope rather than trying to level it. Perhaps you will be able to level part of it and plant in the sloping areas.

The aspect of your house determines the amount of sun the garden receives. South-facing gardens receive little sun, while gardens to the north enjoy sun for the best part of the day. Understanding the aspect helps you decide the type of garden you can make. In hot climates shade is desirable but in cold or temperate climates large trees blocking the sun's path can cast shadows which restrict plant growth and give the garden a cold feeling.

MICRO-CLIMATES

The many climatic variations that occur in a garden are called micro-climates. Factors creating these micro-climates include exposure to the sun, proximity to ponds and pools, prevailing winds, building structures, plants, slopes and other topographical variations.

This uncomplicated but well-planned garden complements the style of the house.

A house built on a block of land is an obvious example of how micro-climates can be formed. A warm, sunny area facing north will be created, contrasting with the shady area on the south side of the house. Trees, walls or fences influence the distribution of sunlight and shade and the force of prevailing winds. The ground surface can absorb or reflect heat. Water in a pool reflects light and stabilises the temperature of the air around it. The degree to which this occurs varies according to the size of the pool.

By understanding the various micro-climates in the garden you will have the option of altering them and using them to your advantage. Mentioned below are four basic micro-climate factors which should be considered if you are to take the most advantage of your site.

WIND

A windy garden makes it difficult for plants to grow and is unpleasant to sit in. Contrary to popular opinion, a solid windbreak is not the most efficient. The most efficient windbreak has equal proportions of solid sections and voids. This causes the velocity of wind to be reduced but the turbulence created by the solid obstruction is avoided.

TEMPERATURE

Materials like bitumen, concrete, stone and brick absorb a great deal of heat during the day and release it at night.

The darker the surface the more heat that is absorbed. In cold climates brick walls facing the sun have been used for centuries to espalier semi-tropical fruit which otherwise could not possibly grow.

A large body of water like a swimming pool helps to maintain a fairly constant temperature and actually reduces the extremes of air temperature in its immediate vicinity. On the other hand a small ornamental garden pond will quickly absorb the heat of the sun.

SUN AND SHADE

The angles of the sun change throughout the year. Once you have established how the sun falls in relation to your garden then you will

Above A dense hedge provides a warm micro-climate for this exquisite perennial garden.

Left A sheltered garden allows for an abundance of plant growth.

A bed of Clivia miniata *thrives in the shade cast from a very old wisteria.*

have a much more accurate idea of how to design it. This is equally important for people and plants. For outdoor living you may want full sun in the early morning but you may require shade in the same spot for lunch. When siting a swimming pool the angle of the sun has to be given full consideration.

For summer shade and winter sun there is nothing better than deciduous vines or trees. These give precious shade in summer, especially over a pergola, but allow the winter sun through.

Shade

Shade occurs in every garden where there is a plant or structure and always deserves special consideration. Shade alters the air and soil temperature, especially in dry areas, and often results in a humidity increase. Shade also dictates the types of plants suitable for planting.

Although shade is a general word for any darkening effect, the discriminating gardener should become aware of different types of shade. One should understand differences in the quality of light, the reasons for such differences and the effects they have on the soil.

Shade cast from a building or wall is permanent and the most difficult to come to terms with as it is dense and solid. It is usually found in south-facing yards and passageways which have tall walls and fences. There is less plant material for this type of shade.

Dense shade caused by tree foliage is easy to change by altering or thinning the heads of the offending trees. Thus deep shade can become medium, light or dappled shade.

Dappled shade is the lightest shade category and is also the type of shade that provides the widest range of gardening possibilities.

There are two varieties of shade determined by location. Different micro-climates can exist side by side in gardens. Damp shade which generally receives no sun at all and always has moist soil can co-exist with dry shade which is found under eaves and close to buildings.

Working with shade

Damp, densely shaded soil can become dank and sour because the circulation of the air is restricted. This is easily corrected by turning the soil a couple of times. Allow a break of at least a week between each turn to allow air circulation. Shaded soil often becomes very acidic but is easy to check with a soil testing kit. The soil in shaded areas is often lacking in nutrients and needs supplements of fertiliser. Mulches of cow or chicken manure and compost are ideal as they attract earthworms which in turn help to aerate the soil. As the mulches break down they also add structure to the soil, encouraging better drainage. This is most important in dry shaded areas as organic matter will help to retain moisture.

If the shade is under a large tree it may be thinned to allow more sun through. But if the tree has a mass of surface roots which make it difficult to grow anything underneath you can always limit the plants to containers.

If shade is produced by a structure like a house or fence the situation is different from planting underneath trees. The amount of light such areas receive is different from the dappled sunlight caused by a canopy of leaves. Often areas like this receive some morning sun and then are in complete shade for the rest of the day. These areas can be turned into complete shade gardens. Keep in mind the old rule of thumb that a great many shade-loving plants will tolerate morning sun but not afternoon sun.

Landscaping in the Shade

An empty, damp, shady space can be transformed with ferns, palms and large-leafed plants into an exotic jungle — the mundane supplanted by the mysterious. In making this transformation, use ferns and foliage plants for structure and interest and palms to provide

An interesting pergola draped with wisteria provides welcome shade for this courtyard during the hot summer months.

If shade is cast from a large tree it may be thinned to let more sun through. This allows a larger choice of plant material.

variation in height and leaf texture.

Palms can grow on a single trunk or have a clumping effect similar to bamboo. For this clumping effect, nothing is nicer than the bamboo palm (*Chamaedorea costaricana*) which reaches a height of 3 m and the golden cane palm (*Chrysalidocarpus lutescens*). The dwarf date palm (*Phoenix roebelinii*) will even tolerate some sun. Its stunning fronds always create exquisite patterns of light and shade.

One of the most graceful is the kentia palm (*Howea forsteriana*), the dark green fronds of which are supported on slender stalks. Never plant palms alone, as they always look better *en masse*.

Ferns have flourished over the earth in myriad forms for millions of years and vary in size from tiny moss-like plants to large tree ferns. The foliage of ferns and palms has always been complementary and stunning effects can be achieved when the large fronds of tree ferns and palms intermingle. Cooper's tree fern (*Cyathea cooperi*) has fronds measuring 6 m in length and is extremely hardy. The thick trunk of the soft tree fern (*Dicksonia antarctica*) is densely covered with brown fibrous roots and is worth growing for these alone. New fronds are covered with brown hairs which are shed as the frond uncoils.

Lower-growing ferns are ideal understorey plants. Spectacular species include the king fern (*Todea barbara*), hen and chicken fern (*Asplenium bulbiferum*), bird's nest fern (*Asplenium australasicum*) and the hammock fern (*Blechnum occidentale*).

To really create a jungle effect attach ferns

which are epiphytes to tree trunks. Favourites are the elkhorn (*Platycerium bifurcatum*) and the staghorn (*Platycerium superbum*). Bromeliads and orchids may also nestle in the trees or be planted on the ground.

Plants with strap-like leaves and waxy coatings always look at home in this type of setting, including ginger lily (*Hedychium flavum*), *Aspidistra elatior*, the many varieties of hosta and *Philodendron* species. *Agapanthus orientalis* will also reward you with blue or white flowers depending on the species as will *Clivia miniata*, valued for its bright scarlet flowers with yellow throats.

Dry shaded areas often receive some sun for a small part of the day even if they are under eaves. Dry shade is also created under trees because trees absorb all the moisture. Dense, large trees can also prevent moisture reaching the ground and keep it bare and dry. If the soil is regularly built up with organic matter and watered frequently then there is a large choice of plant material for such a position.

Bamboos will thrive in these conditions as long as there is no wind. Among the shrubs there are the *Berberis* and *Mahonia* genus. Rhododendrons, azaleas and hydrangeas provide flower colour as do fuchsias and winter daphne (*Daphne odora*).

Good groundcovers include lamium which gives a low cover of silver and green variegated foliage; *Hibbertia scandens*, an Australian native, has flowers like huge buttercups; bugle flower (*Ajuga reptans*) has green or bronze leaves and blue flower spikes; *Bergenia cordifolia* is loved for its large leathery leaves and pink flowers in mid-winter; lily turf (*Liriope spicata*) which has tufts of strap-like leaves with mauve flowers; wandering jew (*Tradescantia* species) with its pretty white flowers and periwinkle (*Vinca major*), which has an abundance of blue flowers.

Colour can be provided by perennials and annuals. Perennials include lily-of-the-valley (*Convallaria majus*), oyster plant (*Acanthus mollis*), woodland anemone (*Anemone blanda*), windflower (*Anemone japonica*), bleeding heart (*Dicentra spectabilis*), *Helleborus corsicus*, Himalayan blue poppy (*Meconopsis betonicifolia*) and polyanthus and primulas.

Shade-loving annuals include cinerarias, honesty, lobelias, love-in-a-mist, nasturtiums, pansies, Virginia stock, violas, toadflax, viscaria and sweet Alice.

Garden planning

The easiest way to commence planning your garden is to draw a plan of the block of land. It does not need to be elaborate or of landscape architect quality but simply as accurate as possible. If you use a large sheet of graph paper you can let the side of each small square on the paper represent a uniform distance on the ground — for instance one square can equal 1 m. When measuring the land the measurements between points on the ground must be absolutely level and not taken on a slope.

Mark the position of the house on the plan and locate water and sewerage pipes and underground utility lines. The position of overhead wires should also be checked. Having completed these preliminaries, mark any existing pathways, gates, paved areas, trees and shrubs. The plan will now show all the relevant details existing on the land and provide you with a basis for a new design.

Don't draw your design ideas on this piece of paper. Instead, get a large piece of tracing paper and lay this over the top of the plan. This allows you to draw different ideas and try different garden concepts.

Major constructions, like fences, pergolas or gazebos should be drawn in at this stage. So should ponds, waterfalls or streams. This also

A narrow walkway can be transformed by the use of lattice and climbing plants.

The classical fountain provides a sophisticated centrepiece for this small pond.

applies to swimming pools which will be a focal point in the garden.

Adapt the garden to your lifestyle

A landscape plan should be adapted to suit your lifestyle. There is no point in planning a formal garden with tidy edges, great expanses of lawn and formal, clipped hedges if you do not have the time or inclination to tend it. A low maintenance garden is easy to establish by choosing the correct plant material in the beginning.

If you have children, you will need space for play areas. Much entertaining is done in Australian gardens in summer, so thought should be given to barbecue areas and gazebos.

A garden pattern

The character of a garden depends on its underlying pattern. The curves of garden paths and beds all help create this pattern. There are some important points to consider when designing this part of the garden. Your garden plan will show everything from a bird's-eye view, but you must also visualise the perspectives from eye-level. Often sweeping curves made on a graph will look too excessive when seen from eye-level and will need to be drawn less sharply. Curves should always flow smoothly with changes of direction and not look too obvious. Two important design rules when drawing paths are that lines which diverge as they run away from the eye lessen the sense of distance, while lines which converge make the path look even longer.

A practical method of overcoming this is that when you have the basic layout on paper, mark out the actual paths and garden beds with a length of string or hose. You can then stand back and get the feel of the path or garden bed from different points of view.

Large gardens can have considerable movement within them with sweeping paths and garden beds. This invites you to walk around the garden with the paths leading to a point of interest or view. On the other hand small gardens do not need as much movement and should attempt to keep the eye contained within the garden.

Do not put the plant material on the plan yet as it is most important to get the initial design and feel of the garden with its paths, steps and enclosures. Plant material is chosen last.

Privacy

Privacy is one of the most important aspects of gardening, especially in Australia where a great deal of time is spent outdoors either entertaining or relaxing. The way to gain privacy depends on the character of your land. You may need to build a fence or wall. If you need privacy from above when, for example, a neighbour's house is looking down on you an overhead screen like a pergola or trellis may be required.

A wall of trees and shrubs around a block is the cheapest method to provide privacy. But before planting consider the way in which the sun falls on the block and make sure trees do not block the sun. Large deciduous trees with evergreen shrubs underneath on the north side of the house can provide summer shade but during winter allow the sun's rays to penetrate. The lower-growing foliage of the evergreen shrubs will still provide the much needed privacy during winter.

If you have a paling fence around your garden a simple method of gaining privacy is to attach trellis to it and grow climbing plants on it. This is ideal for small gardens where you do not want large trees taking up space and casting too much shade.

Utility areas

Every garden needs space for a washing line, compost heap and dustbins. Often these areas are not given consideration initially. Washing lines need not be placed in the middle of the garden but can be concealed in a sunny position in a corner. Better still there are many types which can be taken out, used and tucked away at other times.

Garbage bins and compost heaps can be concealed by the use of trellis, fences or shrubbery. If you have a vegetable patch, a compost heap can be placed in a corner of it. A warm, shady spot is ideal for a compost heap as too much sun will keep the compost too dry.

Ideally, utility areas should be screened from view by careful initial planning. In large gardens a sweeping garden bed filled with a

Garden planning at a glance

- What are your privacy requirements? Where is privacy most needed?

- Are you using to best advantage what you already have in the garden?

- Is there sufficient lawn and play area allotted for your children?

- Do you need boundary fences and do they need to be built for privacy or to enclose the land?

- How much time do you wish to spend in the garden? What you plant in the garden and your design will determine how much time you will need to spend in it.

- Are paths wide enough to negotiate easily? Are they wide enough for lawnmowers and wheelbarrows?

- Do you want quiet areas in the garden? Often a simple seat placed in a corner of the garden is all that is required.

- How much time do you spend entertaining in the garden?

- Have you created garden scenes outside windows that may be viewed frequently? Have you successfully screened out ugly views?

- Do you need protection from the sun and wind?

- Are there any boggy or badly drained areas in the garden that require drainage, or can they be turned into a natural pond or bog garden?

- Future extensions, if any, should be planned at this stage so the garden can be designed accordingly.

The strong form and texture of these plants attract the eye's attention and hold it.

mixture of shrubs, perennial and annuals will provide a screen while not keeping out too much sun.

Garden design

Garden design is an art form. A well-designed garden can stimulate our senses but our response is a very personal thing. The shape of different plants may do something for one person but leave another person unmoved. Garden design also varies with the shape and size of land and the climate. Although everyone has individual ideas there are certainly some basic rules which should be adhered to if you want the garden to have shape, texture and be alluring. Most gardens will contain some focal point or areas of interest. After all, gardens exist to entice us to wander and observe.

A well-designed garden is planted in such a way that when you walk in the front gate or out the back door you do not see the whole garden at once. Foliage may sweep out from the side of the garden into the middle. Or perhaps you will place a formally shaped bed in the centre. Such a bed will have to be walked around, inviting you to see what is on the other side.

Structure and texture

The structure and texture of a garden is one of the most important aspects of garden design. The strong forms and textures of different plants attract the eye's attention and hold it. Garden beds filled with plants of similar texture and form always look boring and unappealing. But garden beds filled with plants having both strong architectural shapes and fine or soft foliage prevent the garden looking flat. Dense, shrubby plants with rich, dark green foliage look more outstanding against a backdrop of fine, feathery foliage.

In cold climates evergreen trees and shrubs

can be an important feature as the colour of the leaves prevents the garden looking too cold. On the other hand the silhouettes of deciduous trees in winter allow you to appreciate the tracery, shape and texture of their bare branches.

Structural plants usually take longer to grow than perennials, annuals and bulbs but are more permanent, so careful initial planning must be undertaken. An abundance of perennials and annuals may always be placed around structural plants to begin with so the garden will not look too bare and later moved to other areas or swapped with friends.

The texture of plants is also very important. A garden bed where leaves are virtually all the same shape and colour will look flat and uninteresting. There should be a variety of differently shaped and coloured leaves. Leaves reflect light in different ways and this causes contrasts within the garden. Shiny leaves next to flat, dull leaves will contrast with each other to create interest. Different hues of green add charm to the garden.

In small gardens you can create an illusion of space by using plants with small leaves of different textures. Large leaves tend to attract your attention, reducing the sense of space within the garden.

Spacing plants

When you are starting a garden the temptation to overplant is irresistible. The mature height and width of a tree or shrub must be given full consideration before planting. Even if you cannot visualise that the small tree or shrub you have in the pot will ever become the size it is meant to, do not be tempted to plant trees and shrubs too close together. The result of overly close planting will be removal at a later date. The bare ground between trees and shrub can always be filled with tall, fast-growing perennials and annuals.

Planning a garden bed

Now the interesting work can be undertaken on your initial garden plan. Of course what you plant is largely determined by the climate and the locality of the site. A hot seaside garden is very different from that of a mountain garden. If you are lucky enough to have saved much of the native landscape you may wish to keep your garden predominantly native. Or if you live near the sea in an exposed situation and wish to keep the view then garden beds full of plants that will withstand these conditions must be used. There is no point in using plants that will not grow in your climate. They will never look healthy.

The first plants to list on the plan are feature trees and shrubs. Thought should be given to correct balance, so they graduate in height and blend with one another. It is important to visualise how the garden bed will look in a few

Varieties of leaf colour, texture and shape provide visually interesting contrasts in this garden bed.

Olive trees, a bougainvillea scrambling up the stone wall and daisies tumbling onto the path give this narrow walkway charm and character. Pots of geraniums add to the effect.

years time when the trees and shrubs are beginning to reach their full height. If a plant has a long life span, considerable thought should be given to its placement.

Work out different ideas on the tracing paper until you have the correct balance. Using more than one of the same small shrub or feature plant will create a stronger feature. The next step is to consider lower-growing herbaceous perennials, annuals, bulbs and groundcovers. Also take into account the shade that will be cast from taller feature trees and shrubs.

Plants like perennials, annuals, bulbs and biennials are used to fill the spaces between trees and shrubs. These give the garden considerable interest and provide texture and colour. There is more room for experimentation as they can always be removed to a better position in the garden if necessary.

But most importantly have confidence in your garden design and choose the plants that you particularly appreciate. A successfully designed garden has a strong sense of identity. Everything looks like it should belong and form a picture. This is especially evident in small gardens where you cannot have a variety of moods.

Another important point in garden design is the view from within the house. This must be taken into account when deciding on a garden plan. Try to create a picture that can be seen from inside. This forms a link from within the house to the garden. If you are looking down onto the view then the perspective should be just as pleasing from above as from eye-level.

On the other hand think of the view from the garden to the house. Ask yourself if the appearance of the building might be enhanced by climbers, pergolas or espaliered shrubs.

Borrowed views

Take note of distant views or neighbours' trees which need to be considered in your landscape plan and possibly incorporated in it. By borrowing landscape in this way it leads the eye from the immediate garden area to the surrounding area and then back again. This has the psychological effect of counteracting boundaries, making even small gardens appear large.

Often a view can be framed by a group of trees or shrubs. Framing a view allows you to control the parts of it you wish to see. Pathways may also lead to views, creating an element of surprise at the end of a stroll. A seat or summerhouse encourages you to sit and enjoy it.

WITHIN THE GARDEN

I have always felt that gardens need a number of thoughtfully selected objects to provide stability in the ever-changing plant scene. Your preffered objects may be practical — walls, seats, summerhouses, steps, paths — or purely decorative.

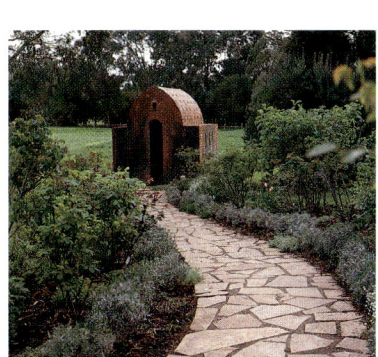

STEPS

Changes of level within a garden can occur through necessity or be used to break up an otherwise flat garden. For example, one step going from an area of lawn to a formal herb or rose garden will create a change of mood and garden scene. Steps may also lead to a garden ornament like a statue, sundial, or simply to a garden seat.

Steps don't usually exist in isolation, but as an extension of a path. It is thus essential that they are constructed of the same material as the path itself. Using the same material creates a unified effect rather than a disjointed one. This is most important next to a house, where steps should relate to the architecture and building materials.

If it is not possible to use the same material for both paths and steps, then attempt to have them constructed from ones that complement each other like wood and stone, gravel and wood or natural packed earth and stone. Where possible a path should lead into steps in a leisurely way to avoid the impression that they are an abrupt extension of it.

Steps should be used to make garden design more interesting. They can be incorporated in almost every garden, for no matter how flat the garden there is usually an opportunity to introduce a change of level. Two or three steps will break the monotony of what would otherwise be a flat and uninteresting area.

STEP WIDTH

Thought should be given to step width. A narrow group of steps looks less inviting than a wider set. A wide flight of steps looks gracious and encourages you to walk on it. It is nice to have steps which are wide enough for two people. Keep in mind that one is often carrying large things through the garden, and wide steps allow easy access.

TREADS AND RISERS

It is very important that steps are comfortable to walk on. Comfort is determined by the relationship of the rise and tread. The rise is the vertical face of the step and the tread is the

A stone path bordered with lavender leads to this unusual brick folly.

106 Creating your Ideal Garden

Above Self-seeded plants growing among the stones give these steps a timeless quality.

Stone Steps
Large bush stones
Gravel or packed earth

Wood & Gravel Steps
Sleeper
gravel

Stone Paths
Trench determined by size of stone

horizontal face. The correct relationship makes steps comfortable and easy to negotiate. Ideally, the height of the rise should be no more than 150 mm or 200 mm, while the depth of the tread should be no less than 375 mm.

Safety must also be taken into consideration when building steps. Treads which are on an unstable surface or which will wear too quickly to a smooth surface are dangerous. Treads which are set absolutely level will hold rainwater and create a hazard.

Grade

The grade of a flight of steps is an important consideration. A steep flight can be uninviting and make you quicken your pace. Steep steps are often difficult for old people to use and they detract from the relaxed feeling of the garden. The slope of the land will usually determine how steep or shallow the steps will be. A steep flight may be broken with a turning to the left or right. The turn can be broken with a landing.

Materials for steps

If a path leads to the steps then the steps should be constructed in the same material for a unified effect.

Stone is an ideal natural material for step construction. Stones can be laid overlapping or spaced with a filling of packed earth, gravel or bark in between. The appearance of stone steps is always improved by planting with small groundcovers on the sides or in between the stones.

Wood and gravel steps are easy to construct and blend perfectly with the garden. The wood forms the rise of the step and the gravel is laid on the tread. Roughcut hardwood or railway sleepers should be used.

Wooden rounds are also effective for the construction of steps. Wooden rounds are circles of timber which have been cut horizon-

Pink and white azaleas frame attractive stone steps.

tally from the trunk of a hardwood tree. They will last for about 15 years if treated properly. They have a natural appearance and merge well with the garden. The underside of the rounds, or any timber used in step or path construction, should be treated with creosote or a timber preservative of some kind. Sump oil is a cheap and efficient wood preservative.

Concrete slabs or pavers are available in tinted colours and are ideal for steps and courtyards. The colours are in soft shades of pink, grey and sandstone. Spaces should be left between the slabs and planted with small groundcovers. Concrete slabs should be bedded into sand on a firm rubble foundation or laid in a base of mortar. About 25 mm of mortar will be sufficient. A suitable mix is 1 part cement to 4 parts sand.

Steps can be made completely of bricks. Use either second-hand old bricks or rough-faced types. They are extremely strong and durable when laid in a base of mortar.

Plants for steps

Random planting in steps produces a magical effect. Spaces should be left when constructing steps for plants.

Perfumed plants exude fragrance when trodden upon. Thyme is ideal for step plantings. Mountain or alpine thyme (*Thymus pseudolanuginosus*) has minute, grey, woolly leaves and lilac-pink flowers during late spring and summer. It is one of the best matting plants for steps and paths. Creeping thyme (*Thymus serpyllum*) forms an attractive moss-green carpet of tiny leaves and has bright, rosy-lilac flowers in late spring and summer. There are many cultivars of this species. 'Albus' has white flowers, 'Coccineus' has crimson flowers and 'Magic Carpet' has lilac-pink flowers.

Other fragrant plants include camomile (*Anthemis nobilis*) and pennyroyal (*Mentha pulegium*).

Alpine strawberry (*Fragaria vesca*) has pretty leaves, edible fruit and a creeping habit. The flowers of alpine or moss phlox (*Phlox subulata*), a low-growing, mat-forming perennial, almost cover the plant in spring to early summer. Flower colour includes pale pink, lavender, blue, deep pink and magenta-red.

Low, wide steps invite you to walk to another part of the garden.

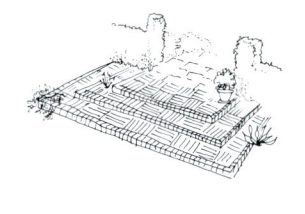

An arch placed at the top of circular steps provides a romantic tone.

Babies' tears (Erigeron karvinsckianus), *lambs' ear* (Stachys lanata) *and catmint tumble onto this enchanting brick pathway. Random planting in pathways creates a magical effect.*

ALONG THE SIDE OF PATHS AND STEPS

Plants grown along the sides of paths and steps can change their character completely. A straight path or flight of stairs can be made to look curved if plants are left to tumble over the sides. They also have the advantage of binding the soil and preventing it from disappearing. Choose plants that have a creeping or bushy habit.

Arenaria montana is an enchanting plant with green foliage and glistening white flowers in spring.

Snow-in-summer (*Cerastium tomentosum*) has small, silver leaves and white flowers through summer.

Little trumpet (*Convolvulus cneorum*) is a dwarf shrub with silvery, silky leaves and white trumpet-shaped flowers in spring and summer.

Swan River daisy (*Brachycome iberidifolia*) is loved for its blue flowers which appear from late spring to autumn. The foliage is fine and deeply divided.

A favourite for pathway and step plantings is babies' tears (*Erigeron karvinsckianus*). The tiny pink and white daisies appear from spring until early autumn. It readily self-seeds, springing up in any tiny crack on the steps or pathway.

PATHWAYS AND PAVING

Pathways should be a pleasure to walk on as well as a means of enjoying the garden. They should be used to break up the garden and to lead to points of interest. Do not make paths simply the shortest distance between two points but allow them to wander. This creates the impression that the garden is larger than it actually is.

Paths form the framework of the garden around which everything is built. They can be used to divide the garden into different areas, to lead you to places to sit, to allow easy access to garden beds and as focal points in themselves. The number of paths you have depends on the size of your garden and number of distinctive nooks and crannies you have in it. But don't overdo it as too many paths can make the garden look scattered.

Paths help create garden tone whether the garden is straight and formal or winding and informal. Formal gardens lend themselves to paths made from concrete blocks, pavers or bricks while informal ones may feature paths made from gravel, brick or even compressed dirt. The manner in which you use the paving materials sets the tone, no matter what type of garden design is used.

Paths will benefit from edging, which will give them a finished look. Reproduction terracotta and tile edging looks good in a formal or an informal garden. And bricks laid diagonally or upright can look as good as stone.

Thyme planted in between large stones on this pathway exudes a fragrance when trodden upon.

A packed earth path assumes a soft, natural look when groundcovers are allowed to flow over its sides.

When planning paths you must also give thought to their function. They should be wide enough for two people to walk on side by side in comfort and to take a wheelbarrow easily.

Try to have all the paths in the garden made from the same material, as this creates harmony in the garden. A mixture of too many materials looks fussy and restless.

When constructing a path, mark the site by line and pegs or by laying lengths of garden hose on the ground.

Paved areas

Paved areas are used for entertaining, as focal points or areas where one can simply sit and relax. It is important that paving materials used next to the house should be sympathetic in colour and materials. You can always bring a sample of the material home and place it *in situ*. It is often very hard to choose colours at the point of purchase as they often look completely different when placed in position.

Path and paving materials

Bricks laid in patterns can make a small paved area look most interesting. Experiment with different patterns on graph paper and you will find endless combinations. Many of the traditional patterns can always be expanded or contracted to suit your particular site.

Brick

Bricks used for paths or paving will last for years, are unobtrusive, versatile and can be laid in a variety of patterns. Second-hand bricks of the older type which come in subtle shades have the advantage of looking aged before they are laid. But these are becoming hard to find and expensive. If you are buying new bricks choose the softer shades and avoid the modern brown and dark red bricks.

Because bricks are small they can be used to make gradual changes of direction without showing large V-shaped joints which form when slabs or larger pavers are used.

Bricks can be laid in a number of patterns which will give style to a paved area or pathway.

Paving bricks

Paving bricks are denser and stronger than common house bricks and come in many different colours. The shape is usually rectangular, although some have curved ends that fit together to give a cobblestone effect. There are also some that interlock. Like ordinary bricks, paving bricks can be laid in a number of patterns.

Paving on a Sand Foundation

1. Mark out the area that is to be paved. If it is adjacent to a lawn keep in mind that mowing will be much easier if the paving is slightly lower than the lawn and that therefore some excavation will be necessary. Allow the depth of the pavers plus 75 mm for the sand and an additional 12 mm so that the pavers are slightly lower than the lawn level. In badly drained areas allow a further 50 mm of depth so that a layer of crushed gravel can be laid under the sand.

2. Use a spade to dig out the paved area, making sure that the base is firm and level and that there are no protruding tree roots or plant material. If there are any holes they can be filled with sand when it is spread over the surface. Try to make this dirt foundation as level as possible before you start.

3. Place a layer of sand 75 mm in depth over the excavated area and level it by drawing a flat board over the top. The board should be long and straight-edged to make the sand as smooth and level as possible. A spirit level is useful to check the levels.

4. Water the entire area thoroughly using a fine spray nozzle and leave it until it is completely dry. Some gaps may appear where the sand has sunk, and these will need to be refilled and levelled. Water it again thoroughly, then check that it is level after drying.

5. If you are paving with irregular sandstone, rocks or flagstone pavers lay the largest pieces first and fill in the gaps with smaller pieces so that the final spaces between the stones are not more than 25 cm wide. Keep the crevices between the stones as uniform as possible. Larger pieces should be laid along the edges as small pieces are not as stable.

6. Check regularly that the pavers are level. When all the pavers are level, fill between them with sand by spreading it over the surface and sweeping it into the gaps with a broom. Spray the pavers with a hose so that the sand can settle in between, then repeat the filling process. If you prefer a more solid filling between pavers, use a mixture of 3 parts sand to one part cement, brush this over the paving and hose down thoroughly.

Paving on a Mortar Base

A mortar base of at least 25 mm is required for pavers. If the ground underneath is not stable a hardcore base of 75 mm is required. The best mix is 1 part cement to 4 parts sand. Tap each paver firmly into the mortar. When the area is complete, brush a dry mixture of the same proportions between the joints. This mixture will gradually absorb moisture from the ground and set.

Brick Paving Patterns

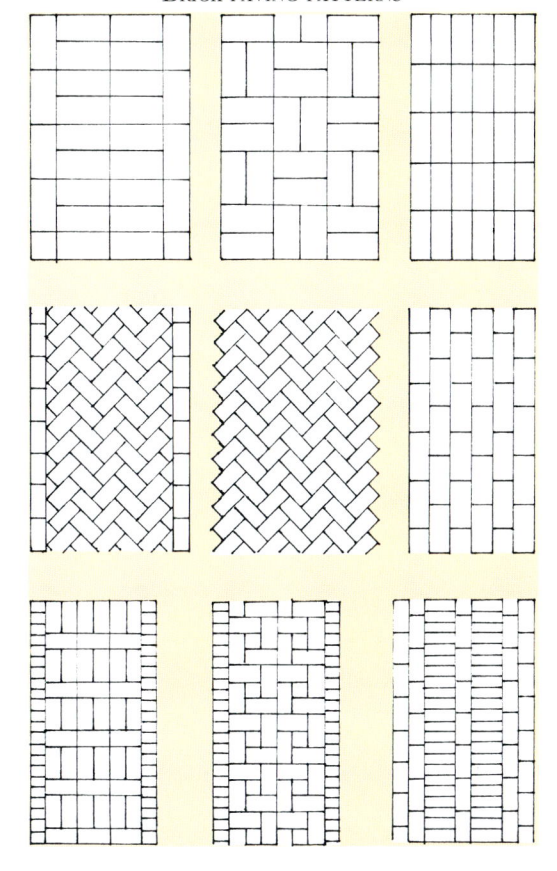

An elegant courtyard. Sandstone provides variation in this large expanse of brick paving.

Paving tiles

Paving tiles are thinner than paving bricks and come in a wide variety of colours and styles including terracotta. They are usually laid on a bed of mortar. Paving tiles can be used for courtyards and patios.

Concrete pavers

Although the idea of concrete paving may put some people off, there are many concrete pavers on the market in natural shades of pink, grey and sandstone that look very attractive in the garden. This type of paving is particularly strong and therefore ideal for driveways where considerable pressure is exerted on them.

Sandstone

Sandstone is ideal for paths, courtyards or patios which do not have to withstand heavy traffic. The colour is natural and sandstone comes in square or rectangular pieces for a formal look or irregular stones for a random appearance.

Packed earth

Packed earth paths assume a soft natural look, especially when groundcovers are allowed to flow onto their sides. To build a packed earth path, clear the area of all weeds and stones and then run a roller over the top. Once the earth has packed down weeds rarely appear and small, self-seeding plants can be encouraged along the sides.

Gravel

Gravel can be used for paths or courtyards. Gravel laid with railway sleeper or stone borders has a very natural appearance. If the garden beds are raised slightly on each side of the path, borders are unnecessary. The plant material from the garden beds can cascade onto the sides of the path, enhancing it further. Gravel in shades of terracotta, grey, white and brown is available. Gravel needs to be laid at least 25 mm thick for ease of walking and to prevent it washing away in wet weather. Areas of gravel paths can produce little surprises as plants will soon self-seed on the sides and in the path itself.

Grass paths

Paths made from grass often look stunning. But before embarking on such a venture you must be aware that grass paths will require continual maintenance with mowing and attention to edges. Choose the correct grass for the area you are going to plant — shade tolerant grass for shade and heat tolerant grass for hot, exposed areas — or you will never get the optimum looks and results.

Internal walls and fences

Walls and fences within the garden should not be mere dividing lines but should be used to add a decorative touch. Plants cascading over walls and around gateways give that 'secret garden' feeling, inviting you to walk around them to make new discoveries.

Walls and fences are often used as a backdrop to an herbaceous border where they provide contrasting texture and colour. Or higher screens might hide unsightly aspects of the garden like washing lines or compost

Smaller pavers form an interesting border around this paved courtyard.

heaps. Screens may give shelter or privacy to sitting areas or swimming pools. Gaps in the walls can be used to highlight views in the garden or beyond.

Picket fences, trellis, stone or brick may be used. The more simple the wall or fence in design the more effective it becomes when used as a backdrop to plants grown in conjunction with it.

Gates in the wall invite you to walk through to another part of the garden. They can lead to a courtyard, view, vegetable patch or another interesting area of the garden. A gate also gives the garden another dimension of space.

Stone walls

Many old country gardens contained traditional stone walls. They were often built to break the monotony of the garden or simply to sit upon when enjoying some peace and quiet. Soft climbers like clematis can be trained to grow over the walls or pockets can be left on the top of the wall for plant material.

Stone is becoming difficult to obtain and quite expensive but it is certainly an aesthetically appealing material. Traditionally each stone in the wall is so well placed that the whole structure is locked together without the help of mortar. To make such a wall requires considerable patience and trial and error as each rock must be painstakingly laid on top of the previous course.

The wall is usually commenced by excavating some of the soil at the base and laying a footing of concrete or large flat stones. The footing needs to be 7.5 cm below ground level. The stones are then laid on top of the footing in such a way that they tie the wall together. Large pieces are preferable and small stones should be kept to a minimum unless used as fillers on the inside of the wall. Where plants are to be grown in the wall a stone is left out and replaced with good soil. In this way plants can be incorporated as the wall is built.

If necessary mortar can be used as the wall is being built to bind it together but make sure the joints are deeply raked out so the mortar can't be seen. The sight of mortar can ruin the whole effect.

Left *This sandstone retaining wall is softened and enhanced by forget-me-nots and nasturtiums planted at the base.*

Below left *A romantic stone folly breaks up this large garden and provides a relaxing setting.*

Retaining walls

The building of a retaining wall is usually more specialised than that of a free standing brick wall used for decorative purposes. A check with your local council before building a retaining wall is often necessary, as many councils will not allow the home gardener to build a retaining wall over the height of 1 m. The essential purpose of a retaining wall is to prevent the lateral or downhill movement of a bank or slope. Try to incorporate plants into a retaining wall to soften the effect and add

When a fountain is tucked into an informal hedge it produces a mysteriously attractive effect.

colour when the flowers are in bloom. Alternatively, climbers can be grown from the bottom of the wall.

Adequate drainage is also important when constructing a retaining wall to allow water to escape from behind the wall. Weep holes must be left in the bottom of the wall to drain off excess water and drainage pipes should be laid behind the wall.

Plants for a stone wall

Stone walls should be covered with softly draping climbers and small herbaceous plants. Thyme, babies' tears (*Erigeron karvinsckianus*), *Arenaria montana*, *Cerastium tomentosum*, *Viola* species (especially *Viola hederacea*, the native violet), *Rosmarinus lavandulaceus* and *Lobelia* species can be planted in pockets.

Suitable climbers are *Clematis* species, climbing roses (*Rosa* species), *Dipladenia sanderi* 'Rosea', *Hardenbergia violacea*, *Hibbertia scandens*, *Hydrangea petiolaris*, *Maurandia barclaiana* and *Pandorea* species.

Living walls

Walls made from hedges naturally require more patience and waiting time than manmade ones but they are cheaper. Patience is required in waiting for the hedge to grow and in the training of the hedge. Draw design plans for the hedge before planting. Thoughtful planning can lead to interesting designs with the hedge forming piers, doorways, avenues or buttresses. Hedges can also be used to define beds and to divide them into geometric shapes. Hedge walls may be curved and broken up with featured topiary plants. Box and yew are most commonly used. Lavender, rosemary and santolina are fast growing and their grey-green leaves have a soft appearance.

Garden accessories

Accessories add charm and interest to a garden. Sculptural features may give a dramatic

Far left *An air of tranquility: the yellow flowers and the long, arching branches of yellow jasmine (Jasminum mesnyi) add the finishing touch.*

Left *An elegant iron seat is flanked by two urns to create a classical tone.*

Below *A cow constructed from corrugated iron makes a surprising and slightly bizarre garden accessory.*

effect or blend with the garden scene to create an impression of harmony. The type of accessory you have in the garden depends on the style of house and garden and the size of the garden. Ornaments should not be seen in isolation but should be part of a setting. They have to harmonise visually with the rest of the garden whether it be plant material or a paved area. When tucked in among plants, accessories can add an element of surprise and sophistication to the garden.

Sundials

Sundials have remained a popular ornament for centuries after ceasing to be of practical value. The conventional type of sundial is comprised of a simple dial and gnomon (or pointer) fixed to a plate and supported on a short column. Sundials are especially suited to cottage, formal or herb gardens.

Statuary

Nowadays statuary is used rather sparingly in comparison with its use in the classical era. Statuary can be used as a focal point in the garden or to create a balancing feature when placed next to, say, a large tree or shrub. Placed at the beginning of a pathway, it can have a welcoming effect. The main point to remember is that it should be placed in a position where it will be enhanced by, as well as enhancing, the surroundings. Statuary should look good from all angles at all times of the year.

Simple ornaments are often the most striking. Strong elementary shapes make beautiful accents when set among plants of contrasting colour and shape.

Scale is important. Statues should not be so small that they are easily overlooked or so large that they overwhelm surrounding plant material.

Use statuary sparingly, as often one piece is enough in a garden. If more than one piece is used spacing becomes important. Statues must be placed well apart so they don't detract from each another.

Urns and pots

Urns and pots lend themselves naturally to garden decoration because of their use in the cultivation of plants. Urns were used extensively during the romantic period of the eighteenth century when they became an important part of garden arrangement. Made of either lead or stone, they were placed on gate piers and walls, in alcoves and niches or used as individual features at the junction or termination of garden walks. Urns of today are generally constructed from concrete or terracotta. As with any garden ornament, careful placement is essential.

Simple terracotta, concrete or wooden pots placed thoughtfully throughout the garden create atmosphere and interest. They should be filled with flowers or greenery and tucked into unexpected places.

Seats

Seats placed throughout the garden are inviting and relaxing. Position them on the side of a path where they will tempt you to stop and sit, or in a sunny spot where you can enjoy the view. Seats can range from a piece of wood or large stone placed on stone or bricks to the classic English wooden garden seats popular in the late nineteenth and early twentieth centuries which are now being reproduced. Unpainted wooden seats are adaptable, readily available and blend well in the garden.

Because stone seats are so solid they need to be placed carefully. Strong background planting prevents them from looking too dominant.

Try to choose seats that relate to the garden's style. Seats may be framed in a setting. The appearance of a simple seat tucked into a shrub border can be transformed if a climbing rose or clematis is allowed to scramble around the back of it.

The positioning of seats is also important. Take into account where the sun falls during the day, the view and whether there is protection from the wind. You should consider whether the seat is going to be used for long periods or for brief periods only. If it is in a quiet area of the garden where you sit to read or ponder, then make sure it is comfortable.

Tables and chairs

Because of the wonderful Australian climate eating *al fresco* during warmer months is very popular. Wooden tables and chairs are the most durable and can be left outdoors throughout the year.

Cane, while aesthetically pleasing, needs to be stored from the elements when not in use.

Metal furniture often looks wonderful and is very comfortable if well designed. Like wood it is very durable and can be left outdoors throughout the year.

Antique cast iron is available but can be expensive. There are, however, many reproduction cast-iron seats and tables on the market at very competitive prices.

Birdbaths

Water in the garden will always attract wildlife especially birds and insects. Birdbaths are suited to any sized garden. They should not be placed too far out in the open as most birds feel safer when there is some shrubbery around. Tuck them into corners or place them among plants in an herbaceous border. Better still, place them near a window where the activities of the birds can be watched.

Birdbaths made of terracotta or stone have a natural appearance and will often grow moss around the edges. It is best to have them raised off the ground on a stem to minimise the attention of cats. Most birds prefer water about 25 mm deep.

Opposite This charming summerhouse secreted at the bottom of the garden provides a cool resting spot.

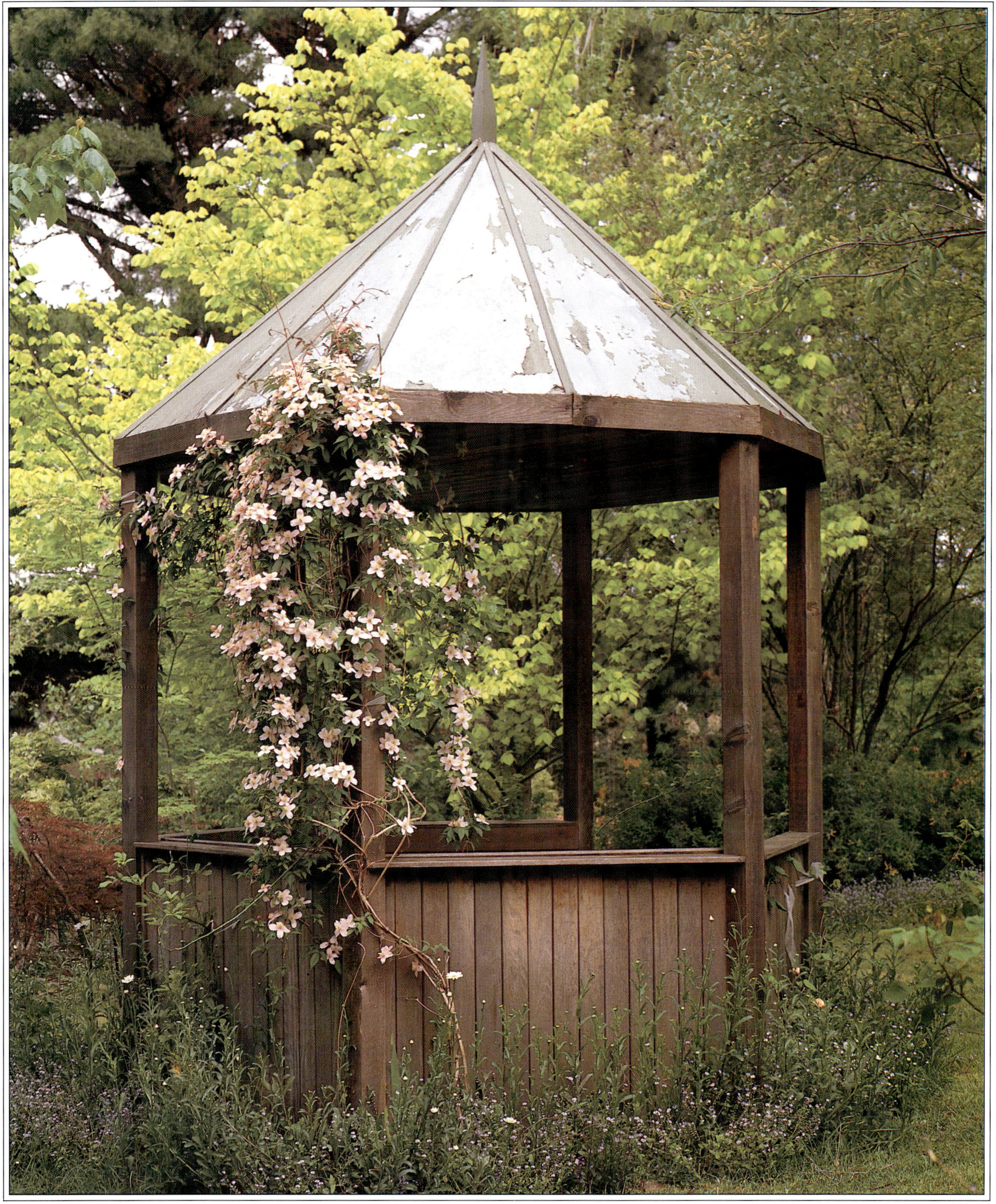

Garden structures

Gazebos, or summerhouses as they are often called, and pergolas are becoming part of the Australian way of life. They are used to provide shady resting places during the hotter months. Carefully placed deciduous climbers over pergolas or summerhouses add more shade during summer but allow the comfort of winter sun.

Gazebos or summerhouses

The charm of a summerhouse was that it was usually tucked away at the bottom of a large garden but many small gardens now appreciate the shelter produced by these structures. It is important that in a small garden the structure should match or complement the house because they will be in close proximity.

Gazebos or summerhouses are roofed structures which were originally sited at a corner or boundary wall with a good view of the surrounding countryside. They are generally constructed of timber, lattice or cast iron. The roofs were traditionally made from shingles or palings and did not have to be completely waterproof as their main purpose was to provide shade. Corrugated iron can be used and looks attractive if painted green, dark grey or a sandstone colour.

A simple gazebo can be constructed easily from wood and lattice. There are many which can be bought in kit form and erected in the garden without difficulty.

A wooden pergola draped with a yellow banksia rose creates summer shade.

Pergolas

Pergolas originated in Italy. In their simplest form they consisted of a series of rough poles which supported climbers, provided a shady walk and gave protection from the heat of the sun. In Australia they are often used as a covered way between the house and garden and for covering a patio or courtyard.

To be successful pergolas need to be carefully placed. They can be used to separate portions of the garden or as an extension of a walkway. The main point to remember is that if pergolas are to be used separately they should always lead somewhere.

In hot climates cover them with evergreen climbers. Choose a mixture of climbers including perfumed plants that flower at different periods. In cold climates pergolas can be covered with deciduous climbers to allow summer shade and winter sun.

Climbing roses planted over a pergola provide perfume and, if carefully chosen, also provide constant colour. 'Altissimo' produces masses of large, clear, rich red blooms throughout the season. The small pink flowers of 'Cecile Brunner' are borne in abundance and are also sweetly fragrant. 'Clair Matin' often known as 'Clear Morning' will flower endlessly. It is smothered in sweetly smelling, medium-sized, semi-double flowers of purest pale pink with a central cluster of pale golden stamens. Other recurrent flowering roses include 'Devoniensis' which has cream flowers; 'Dortmund' which is loved for its red, single flowers; 'Golden Showers' the flower colour of which is suggested by the name; 'Lady Hillingdon' with its golden tulip-shaped flowers and 'Titian' an Australian-bred climbing rose that bears large flat, deep cherry-pink flowers.

Pergolas are built out of lattice, timber or iron and some have brick or stone footings. The detailing of the pergola should match the period of your home and the structure should be in proportion.

Arbours

An arbour, as the name suggests, is a sitting place with a leafy canopy. This retreat is sheltered by trees or climbing plants. Arbours were built extensively by the ancient Egyptians, who made them by training vines over poles. They were used as summer living and dining rooms. Alternatively, they were formed en-

A wooden arch placed at the beginning of a pathway invites you to wander through this enchanting cottage garden.

tirely out of trees and shrubs by training the branches. Arbours can be built easily from wood and wire with climbers trained over them. Place a seat or table and chairs underneath.

Arches

Arches should always serve a definite purpose within the garden. They should be located to create a view, lead from one section of the garden to another or to form part of an entrance. They should draw your eye to the view within the arch and to the arch itself. They can be made from lattice, wood, cast iron, stone or brick. Living arches made from trained and clipped shrubs or trees are often the result of many years' work — training, tying and clipping the plants.

Arches may be formed at the beginning of a path, be free-standing over a path, or used to frame an object like a statue, birdbath or large urn. The last method is very successful when used in small gardens. A series of arches over a path makes an interesting walkway especially if the arches are planted with perfumed climbers. Choose climbers that flower in succession so that there is always a hint of perfume and something in flower.

Constructing a simple arch

A simple but effective arch can be constructed from reinforcing wire. The reinforcing wire is either cemented or dug into the ground on one side, curved to form an arch and secured in the same manner on the other side. The arch looks a little stark to begin with but once covered in climbers it takes on a soft appearance.

Water

Water in the garden brings life and movement and will add atmosphere to even the smallest area. Water has enchanting qualities, bringing

An exquisite fountain creates a focal point in this sophisticated courtyard.

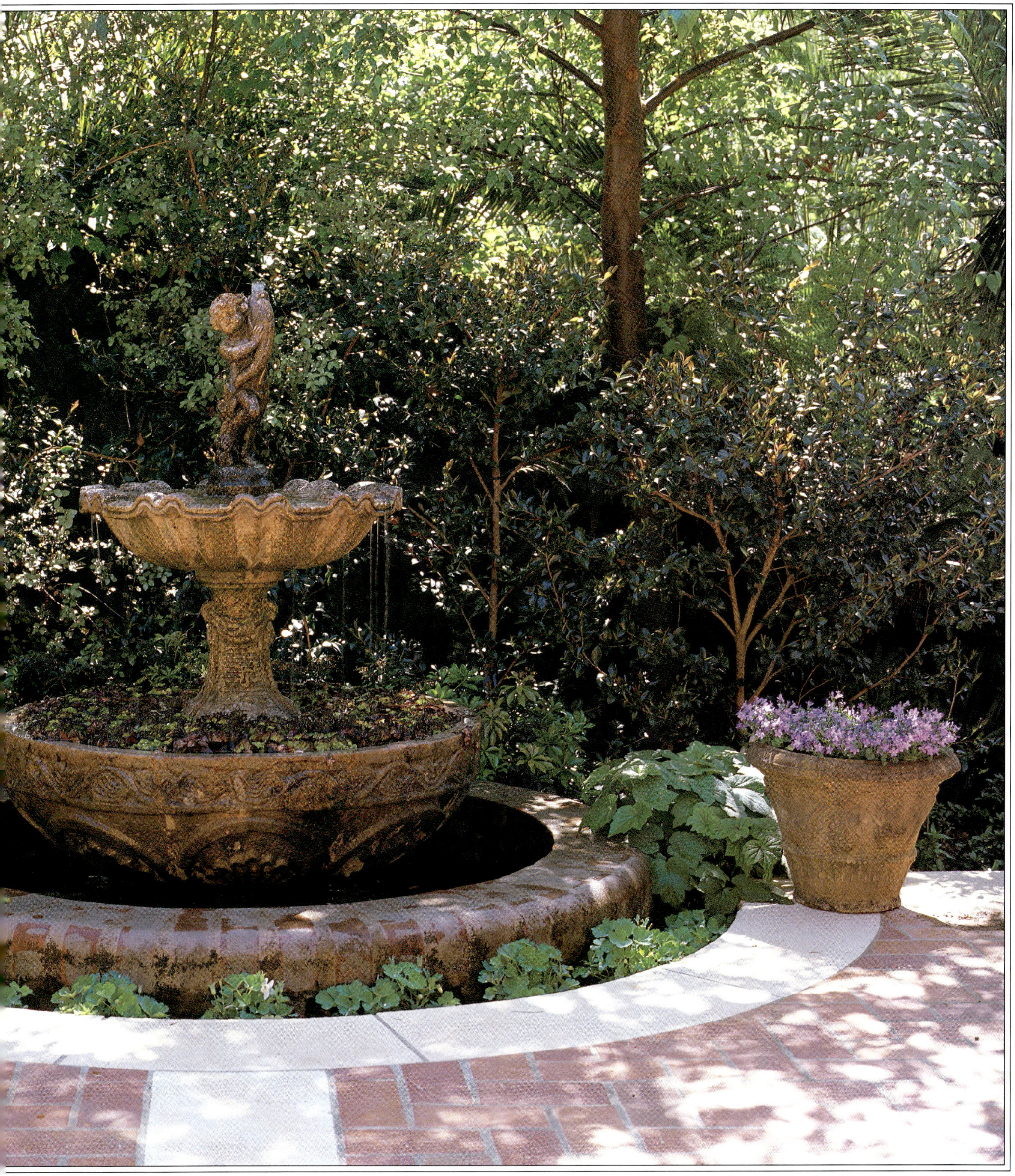

a feeling of coolness and tranquillity. Its mood changes from day to day. One moment it may be responding to the movement of the wind, the next sparkling and glistening beneath the rays of the sun.

Moving water has a restful quality and can be incorporated in the garden by creating a man-made stream leading into a pond or a fountain.

A pond or stream should always be placed thoughtfully so that it becomes part of the structure of the garden. Large country gardens allow more scope for design and informal lines can be used to create large ponds. But in small gardens it is often better to use water in a formal manner or as a sculptural feature like a fountain or water bowl.

The water in a pool should always look clear and sparkling. This can only be achieved by using a recycling system run by a pump or a combination of oxygenating plants, fish and water snails.

Formal use of water

Formal pools are usually made of concrete and are generally in geometric shapes. The edges should be detailed and the pool still and reflective with the occasional breaking of its surface with a clump of irises or waterlilies. Fountains can be used but try to avoid great rushes of water which spoil the effect.

The pool may be level with the ground around it or slightly raised. Raised pools give you the opportunity to sit on the edge and are also safer for children.

Informal pools

The construction of informal pools is a simple procedure if you use black plastic or a rubber pool lining. Butyl rubber lining is made especially for this purpose and is stronger and longer-lasting than black plastic. Making an informal pool is as easy as digging a hollow in the ground, lining it and covering the sides of the lining with rocks or pebbles.

If you wish to keep fish then one section of the pond must be at least 45 cm deep. Fish also require overhanging rocks and vegetation where they can hide from predatory birds.

Streams

Streams should be used to carry water from one level to another in a natural fashion. Streams are only practical in a large garden where the ground contours can be followed in a logical way.

When constructing a stream a fall of at least one in four is usually required to keep the water flowing steadily. The stream should be wide and deep at the mid-point of a curve and shallow along the inside arc, as silt builds up in the curves. Carefully placed rocks in the bends of the stream will cause water to curve around them and rocks which project further into the water will cause ripples, thus creating visual interest.

Waterfalls

A waterfall may be a slight trickle over a group of rocks or a gushing flow — perhaps overflowing from a water basin or flowing into a pond. Often the most successful waterfalls are those between the level changes of small formal pools as these waterfalls provide a strong vertical connection. The most important point to keep in mind when considering the creation of a waterfall is that it is in proportion with the pool and the surrounding garden. A pump will be required to recycle the water. The greater the overflow the larger the pump that will be required. The flow of water from a gentle waterfall can be returned easily by using a submersible pump.

Swimming pools

The most important point when considering a

swimming pool is that it suits the style of the house and garden. In other words the pool and landscape should be designed as one. An informal native garden will blend perfectly with an informally shaped pool while a stylised garden will blend with a formal pool. Often the more simple the shape the more successfully it fits into the garden. The majority of councils require fencing to be placed around the swimming pool and this should be done with subtlety.

If possible it is best to plan the position of your swimming pool when making the initial plan for your garden. The site for a swimming pool should be open and sunny, preferably away from deciduous trees. There should also be space near the pool for storage of the maintenance gear.

This well-designed swimming pool blends perfectly with the rest of the garden.

GARDEN BOUNDARIES

Garden boundaries form the backdrop of a garden. They have a dual purpose. They are used to eliminate anything unsightly or to highlight interesting aspects of the garden.

FENCES

For centuries fences have been used to divide areas of land. Few of us can imagine urban living without fences. They give security and enhance the appearance of our homes while ensuring privacy. A fence can totally conceal a garden or offer tantalising glimpses of it. A fence can also be used as a temporary enclosure while waiting for hedges to grow.

Fences should be appropriate for the style of the house and garden. Think of them as garden fittings which may also be used to show off plants growing in front of or climbing over them to best advantage.

Wooden fences provide privacy and make a good backdrop for the majority of plants. Picket fences look wonderful around older timber cottages. There is a range of picket designs. Picket fences provide shelter for plants by cutting down windflow while allowing light in. Daisies or geraniums growing next to pickets enhance an old-fashioned tone. A clematis can be left to scramble lightly through the pickets as a finishing touch.

Cast-iron fences are perfectly suited to Victorian terrace houses and once painted are permanent structures.

Lattice can be bought in sections and is ideal for use as a fence when painted and covered with climbers. When added to the top of an existing paling fence, lattice will improve privacy.

Wooden and cast-iron fences may be painted the same colour as the house or an appropriate matching colour. A painted fence will also dictate to some extent the colour of plants used next to it. Wire mesh fences are rather ugly unless quickly covered with climbing plants and shrubs. I would try to avoid mesh fences unless you are prepared to endure their ugliness for a couple of years until covered with plant material.

Where traffic noise is a problem the fence should be high and thick and brick or stone are ideal materials. Such a fence can always be softened with climbing plants or correctly placed shrubs.

Fences within the garden are often used to divide certain areas while challenging one to see what is on the other side. Tall fences around utility areas are useful for screening, especially those made of lattice.

Privacy can be created by attaching a trellis to a wooden fence and draping both of them with climbers.

An exquisite white wisteria frames this delightful gate.

It is often necessary to enclose a vegetable garden to keep out dogs and cats and this is achieved most successfully with fencing made of the same material as the boundary fences. Climbing plants like peas and beans can be grown over a fence or you may wish to reap the benefits of growing fresh fruit by draping the fence with passionfruit or kiwifruit.

Hedges: a living boundary

When hedges are formally clipped they will form dense barriers but remember that time has to be allowed for regular pruning. Don't be impatient when planting a hedge as the most common mistake is to plant the shrubs too close together. This often results in some of the shrubs dying when they compete for food and water as they mature. Be sure to plant at the

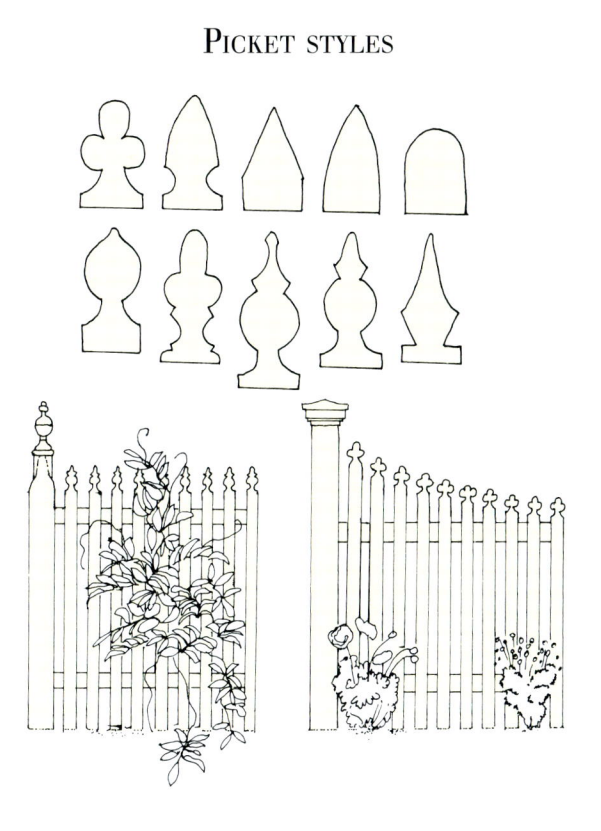

Picket styles

Shrubs for a formal hedge

Name	Height	Comments
Buxus sempervirens	1 m	Very slow growing, but popular as hedging in formal or cottage gardens and as topiary.
Coprosma baueri	2 m	Creates a dense screen when regularly pruned. There is also a variegated variety.
Cotoneaster species	depends on species	Generally grow about 3 m high. Very rampant and hardy growth. Flowers are followed by red or orange berries.
Euonymus japonicus	3 m	Dark green, shiny leaves and reddish fruits in winter. There is also a variegated species.
Photinia robusta	6 m	The new leaves are red. Very fast growing.
Photinia glabra rubens	3 m	Same as above but not as fast growing.
Pittosporum eugenioides 'Variegatum'	6 m	Oval-shaped shrub that can be pruned or left in its natural oval shape.
Pittosporum undulatum	8 m	A good screen where dense growth is required. Does not require pruning.
Taxus baccata (English yew)	2 m	Very slow growing, but long living. Suitable for sun or semi-shade.

A pergola built over a gate and covered with climbing plants makes an interesting and inviting entrance.

recommended distance. Hedges may take a while to grow but they are cheaper than fences.

A well-planted hedge forms the backdrop to the garden and can be trimmed and trained from the beginning. Arches may be formed and the hedge can be clipped to form piers and buttresses.

Informal hedges made from a variety of different trees and shrubs will look very interesting, especially if a selection of flowering shrubs is included. Add several climbing roses or other types of climbers which will ramble through them to create a romantic look.

Gates

A well-designed gate will give a sense of character to an entrance. It invites you to enter someone else's part of the world. The front gate should be in keeping with the house as well as being decorative in its own right.

Gates may be solid for privacy or to keep animals within or without the property. A solid gate creates a feeling of mystery, heightening the anticipation of what is inside. On the other hand a wrought-iron or lattice gate allows you to glimpse the tracery of the garden beyond.

A gate must be functional. It must open and close easily and the piers on either side must be strong enough to support it. It is also important that the gate matches the fence. It does not necessarily have to be built from the same material but it should be in sympathy with it. Various materials blend very well with one another — stone or brick with cast-iron, brick with timber or timber with iron.

Another consideration is the view that will be framed through the gate. A front gate can frame both the house and garden, part of the garden or the path leading to the house.

Planting around the gate may be formal, framed by the sharp outlines of a formally clipped hedge or by an arch draped in a tangle of climbing roses or clematis. The appearance of the gate often suggests the style of the garden within.

Gate piers are as important as the gate itself. They can be creative and ornamental but should be consistent with the style of the house. Brick piers can hold pots or urns spilling over with flowering plants.

Driveway gates should be in harmony with the front gate — preferably made from the same material and in the same style. Wooden driveway gates can look most handsome and the scope for different styles is enormous.

Gateway pergolas

A pergola built over a gate makes an interesting and inviting entrance. Drape it with perfumed climbing plants. Use flower colours which complement the house and the rest of the garden. Choose plants that flower at different times to provide colour for a longer period. Suitable climbers are night-scented jasmine (*Cestrum nocturnum*), *Clematis* species, Carolina yellow jasmine (*Gelsemium sempervirens*), jasmine (*Jasminum* species), honeysuckle (*Lonicera* species), climbing roses (*Rosa* species), star jasmine (*Trachelospermum jasminoides*), or *Wisteria* species.

Right A wire gate forms an elegant entrance to this shaded pathway.

Opposite The old iron gate set in this sandstone fence reveals tantalizing glimpses of the garden beyond.

Garden Boundaries 127

Colour Design

I have always been fascinated by colour. All our attempts in art and architecture to imitate the quality and range of natural colours fall short of the pleasure one can derive from contemplating the tones found in a single flower.

There is no doubt that colour is the most impressive and memorable aspect of the garden. Although a successful garden is based on elements like design, texture and form, it is colour that provides the most enduring impression.

Use of colour

Gardening with colour is an exciting and creative activity. It involves the pleasure of working with living, changing materials. There are, however, many considerations to be addressed before working with colour. For example, the colour of your house is an extremely important factor, especially when you are planting directly next to that colour. Another important consideration is the seasonal colour change that many plants undergo.

Although there are certain principles underlying the choice of a colour scheme for the garden, the ultimate choice is highly personal. Just as the colour range of your clothes reflects your personality, the colours in your garden reflect your character. For some, the attraction is the vibrant effect of a random selection of colours but the idea of having colour themes — using various shades of one colour or specifically matched colours throughout a garden — is becoming popular.

The main point to remember is that colours should always blend with one another. Unfortunately hybridisation has produced flowers with such unnaturally bright colours that they tend to create a jarring visual effect rather than a soft and harmonious one. To avoid disharmony many gardeners are returning to old-fashioned plants which produce soft colours, delightful fragrance and a balance of shapes.

Although trees and shrubs provide the structure for a colour theme, they often have a short flowering period and there is generally a limit to the number you can fit into a garden. But perennials, bulbs and annuals may be planted in abundance, filling the spaces between the trees and shrubs. The skill is in carefully choosing the plants so that they provide continuous, graded colour.

Climbing plants supply vertical colour and are particularly effective when trained along walls and fences, or you can drape them over a pergola or arch to form an impressive entrance.

This drift of bluebells and daffodils is an impressive spring sight.

Colour themes

Colour themes create atmosphere in the garden. White-flowering plants used in contrast with the deep greens of foliage create a tranquil effect, as do white flowers with contrasting grey foliage. Used for the whole theme, especially in a small garden, white and grey give the illusion of space. White reflects the most light of any colour. At night when other colours are subdued, white flowers will shimmer, especially in moonlight, and this can be spellbinding.

Tall flowers like white foxgloves (*Digitalis* species), columbines (*Aquilegia* species) or madonna lilies (*Lilium candidum*) can be planted in sweeping spreads for a bold and arresting effect.

White perennials like Japanese windflower (*Anemone japonica*) can be trusted to reappear faithfully each year. The shasta daisy (*Chrysanthemum maximum*) spreads quickly through the garden and is a delight with its nodding stems of white flowers.

A gold theme may encompass oranges and yellows to provide an enormous scope.

Dark pink and white African daisies add rich colour to this semi–shaded garden bed.

A monochromatic colour theme of sparaxis in shades of maroon looks visually effective in this large garden. The same type of colour theme can also be used in a small garden.

Deciduous trees and shrubs which turn yellow or gold in autumn look very striking. These include *Acer japonicum* 'Aureum', *Acer palmatum* 'Aureum' and *Gingko biloba*. *Fraxinus excelsior* 'Aurea' has young golden-yellow shoots and yellowish branches which are very conspicuous in winter when it loses its leaves.

Sunflowers, with their huge flower heads, can be planted next to African marigolds, which feature varying shades of orange, yellow and lemon.

For a very exotic touch you could try Peruvian lily (*Alstromeria aurantiaca*). Yellow alyssum (*Alyssum saxatile*) is a plant that will lap up sunshine, especially in rock gardens or as a groundcover.

Red looks stunning planted in a bed by itself, when planted to contrast with grey or when combined with white. Red tulips, oriental poppies (*Papaver orientale*) and rose campion (*Lychnis coronaria*) grow well in cool and temperate climates. The single, bright crimson-red flowers of rose campion look outstanding against its silver-grey stems and leaves. Bergamot (*Monarda didyma*), a culinary herb, will thrive in any climate and will reward you with its large whorled heads of bright scarlet flowers in summer. Don't confine it to the herb garden but plant it among other perennials and annuals.

Red bougainvillea gives a brilliant display in hot climates. You can grow it as a climber or prune it to form a shrub. Hibiscus, also a lover of extreme heat, is available in many shades of red and in single or double flowers.

Red native flowering trees may also be included in the theme. The Illawarra flame tree (*Brachychiton acerifolia*) has orange-red flowers which cover the tree in spring before the new leaves appear. The weeping bottlebrush (*Callistemon viminalis*) bows under the weight of its 8-10 cm long spikes of bright red flowers during spring and often again in autumn. Red-flowering gums include *Eucalyptus ficifolia*, *Eucalyptus leucoxylon*, and *Eucalyptus sideroxylon*.

COLOUR COMBINATIONS

Combinations of colour have a harmonious effect, and such combinations can be monochromatic, analogous or complementary as explained below.

MONOCHROMATIC COLOURS

Monochromatic colours are tints and shades of one colour. An example would be blue, various tints of blue and shades of blue-violet. A tint is lighter than the pure colour while a shade is darker. The possibilities offered by this type of colour theme are extensive. When used in small gardens they tend not to be overpowering, and in a large space are visually effective.

ANALOGOUS COLOURS

Gertrude Jekyll was well known for her liking of analogous colour themes. Her perennial borders were based on the concept of the 'tonal garden', the rules of which were very similar to those of an analogous colour scheme. Analogous colours are neighbours on the colour wheel, an example being yellow-orange, orange and red-orange. There is more choice in this type of colour theme because you can also use the various tints and shades of each colour.

COMPLEMENTARY COLOURS

These are colours that are the opposite to each other, for example, red and green and orange and blue. Colours used in this type of theme are vibrant and look wonderful when toned down with silver foliage plants and white flowers.

DRIFTS OF COLOUR

Drifts of one colour have a very natural appearance similar to that of a meadow. Drifts of colour are often used with bulbs, especially bluebells (*Muscari botryoides*), daffodils and jonquils (*Narcissus* species). The most essential aspect of this effect is that the bulbs should not look like they have been planted there. The drift can be created by gently throwing the bulbs where they are going to be planted and then planting them where they fall, or by planting them randomly over the area. The best result is achieved with a large lawn, but if this is impossible, the same look can be achieved with a few bulbs in a limited space underneath a tree, in a corner of the lawn, in a wooded glade or spilling along a country fence.

One of the great advantages of naturalised bulbs is that they can be left undisturbed for many years.

Bulbs suitable for naturalising are *Allium* species, *Alstroemeria aurantiaca*, *Amaryllis belladonna*, *Freesia refracta*, *Fritillaria imperialis*, *Galanthus nivalis*, *Leucojum vernum*, *Lilium candidum*, *Muscari botryoides*, *Narcissus* species, *Scilla campanulata*, *Sparaxis tricolor* and *Watsonia* species.

Annuals also produce delightful colour drifts. Forget-me-nots are hardy little annuals reappearing every year of their own accord to form a beautiful bed of blue. They can be grown in shade and are particularly handy for planting under trees. Pink and white varieties are also available.

Love hearts (*Viscaria* species) form masses of flowers in shades of pink, red, white and blue. The intensity of flower colour is increased and the flowering period is actually prolonged when they are planted in areas of limited shade, making them ideal annuals for under trees.

Blue delphiniums and pink foxgloves are stunning when set against grey foliage.

Pink poppies and deep purple sage combine to wonderful effect.

WHITE FLOWERING PERENNIALS

Plants in this list include varieties from flowers in the colour range from white to cream.

Acanthus mollis – bear's breeches
Achillea ptarmica — yarrow
Anemone blanda — woodland anemone
Anemone japonica — windflower
Anthemis nobilis — camomile
Aster novi-belgii — Michaelmas daisy
Astilbe rivularis — goat's beard
Campanula medium — Canterbury bells
Chrysanthemum frutescans — Marguerite daisy
Chrysanthemum maximum — shasta daisy
Convallaria majalis — lily-of-the-valley
Delphinium species
Lupinus hartwigii — lupins
Papaver orientale — oriental poppy
Penstemon gloxinoides
Polyanthus species
Primula species
Verbena lacinata

BLUE FLOWERING PERENNIALS

Plants in this list include colours from blue and violet to lavender and bluish purple.

Aconitum napellus — monkshood
Anemone blanda — woodland anemone
Anemone japonica — windflower
Aquilegia flabellata — columbines, grannies' bonnets
Brachycome multifida
Campanula medium — Canterbury bells
Delphinium species
Statice species
Lupinus hartwigii — lupins
Meconopsis betonicifolia — Himalayan blue poppy
Primula species
Thalictrum dipterocarpum — lavender shower
Thymus species — thyme
Verbena lacinata

PINK FLOWERING PERENNIALS

Alcea rosea — hollyhock
Anemone blanda — woodland anemone
Anemone japonica — windflower
Aster novi-belgii — Michaelmas daisy
Astilbe rivularis — goat's beard
Bellis perennis — English daisy
Bergenia cordifolia — Norwegian snow
Campanula medium — Canterbury bells
Chrysanthemum frutescans —Marguerite daisy
Delphinium species
Dianthus species — cottage pinks
Digitalis purpurea — foxgloves
Erigeron hybridus — babies' tears
Statice species
Lupinus hartwigii — lupin
Papaver orientale — oriental poppy
Penstemon gloxinoides
Phlox species
Saxifraga umbrosa — London pride
Thymus species — thyme

Plants for a White Garden Theme

Name	Type of plant	Comments
Abelia X *grandiflora*	shrub	Evergreen, bell-shaped flowers in summer
Achillea ptarmica	perennial	Summer flowering
Alcea species (hollyhock)	perennial	Cottage garden favourite
Amaryllis belladonna	bulb	Large trumpet-shaped flowers
Anemone japonica	perennial	Flowers in summer and autumn
Astilbe species (goat's beard)	perennial	Tall growing
Camellia species	shrub	White flowering varieties
Campanula medium (Canterbury bells)	perennial	Flowers summer
Choisya ternata (Mexican orange blossom)	shrub	Fragrant flowers in summer
Chrysanthemum maximum	perennial	Large daisy flowers
Chrysanthemum parthenium (feverfew)	perennial	Fern-like leaves and small daisy flowers
Coleonema alba (white diosma)	shrub	Winter/spring flowers
Cornus florida (white dogwood)	tree	Flowers in early spring
Eriostemon species (wax flowers)	shrub	Star-shaped flowers
Lobularia maritima	annual	Low growing
Melaleuca linariifolia (sweet Alice)	small	White flowers in summer tree attract birds
Petunia hybrids	annuals	White flowering varieties
Philadelphus coronarius (mock orange)	shrub	Scented flowers in spring
Phlox hybrids	perennial	Spring and summer flowers
Pieris japonica	shrub	White flowers in late spring
Primula hybrids	annual	White flowers in winter/spring
Prostanthera nivea	shrub	Native plants with mint-scented leaves
Viburnum species	shrubs	Flowers mainly late winter/spring

Flowers for a Blue Garden Theme

Name	Type of plant	Comments
Aconitum napellus (monkshood)	perennial	Autumn flowering
Anemone blanda (woodland anemone)	perennial	Flowers in early spring
Agapanthus orientalis	bulbous	Flowers in summer
Borago officinalis (borage)	annual	Self-seeding herb flowering in summer
Brunfelsia latifolia	shrub	Very fragrant
Campanula medium (Canterbury bells)	perennial	Flowers mid-spring to mid-summer
Ceratostigma willmottianum	shrub	Flowers summer/autumn
Clerodendrum ugandense	shrub	Flowers summer/autumn
Delphinium species	perennial	Tall flowers in summer and annual
Echium fastuosum	shrub	Stunning deep-blue flowers
Felecia amelloides	shrub	Daisy-like flowers
Hebe species	shrub	Summer flowering
Hydrangea macrophylla	shrub	Acid soils will produce blue flowers
Jacaranda mimosifolia	tree	Summer flowering
Muscari botryoides (grape hyacinth)	bulb	Flowers late winter to early spring
Myosotis species (forget-me-not)	annual	Self-seeding annual
Nigella damascena (love-in-a-mist)	annual	Spring flowering
Psoralea pinnata	shrub	Blue and white flowers
Viola species	annual	Long flowering period
Viscaria species	annual	Grow under trees

Bright orange Californian poppies (Eschscholtzia aurantica) will self-seed readily to create a floral meadow.

A COLOURFUL MEADOW

You should consider transforming areas of the garden into summer meadows. These low maintenance garden areas can be made possible by using old-fashioned plants that self-sow to such a degree that they create floral meadows. The soil for this enterprise should be rich and free-draining, but apart from these requirements it is only a matter of sowing the seed in spring. Once an area is established it will self-sow yearly. Suitable plants include Californian poppy (*Eschscholtzia aurantica*) which has grey fern-like foliage and rich orange flowers; corn cockle (*Agrostemma githago* 'Milas') whose large pale lilac flowers appear for 12 weeks from direct sowing and will continue to flower for nearly 2 months; Flanders poppy (*Papaver rhoeas*) which has rich red flowers with a black blotch in the centre; queen Anne's lace (*Daucas carota*) with its wild look and white flowers and toad-flax (*Linaria vulgaris*) with its miniature snapdragon-like flowers.

GARDEN RESTRUCTURING

Often one is lucky enough to move into a new house with a well-established, very attractive garden. But generally there is always something in the garden that one wants to change. Perhaps the tone of it does not suit your taste. It may be too contrived and need to be softened, or the colour scheme may be too bright and jarring.

STRUCTURE

The first step is to examine thoroughly the existing structure of the garden. You will have to wait for all the seasons to pass so you can see what appears and what flower colours there are. Having done this you must be ruthless and decide what you like and don't like.

I don't recommend removing large trees unless they are definitely in the wrong place. Often they are too close to the house or are causing problems with sewerage. Many gardens contain only trees and shrubs with no underplanting of perennials, bulbs or annuals. This looks very static as the only time something happens is when a tree or shrub flowers for a short period. A garden overplanted with trees and shrubs will also create excessive shade. Some shrubs are required in the garden to retain structure but leave room between them for the softening effect of flowering perennials, annuals and bulbs.

If the garden is bare, choose trees and shrubs carefully. Think about flower and leaf colour as well as leaf texture, height and width.

REDESIGNING

When redesigning a garden you should thoroughly assess the garden beds. Consider whether they are in the position you want or whether they can be changed to create a completely new atmosphere in the garden. Garden paths should be running in the right direction. Some may be purely functional, leading directly to utility areas. It is difficult and expensive to change paths made of concrete but you can always add to these or direct new paths into more interesting areas of the garden. If concrete paths do go in the right directions but are overpowering in appearance, they can be softened by using plant material spilling onto the sides.

Often very simple additions like a woodland theme planted in a corner of the garden will change its feel. A copse of *Betula pendula* or *Eucalyptus scoparia*, both of which have interesting bark, can look quite spectacular.

Privacy is often a problem in a new garden.

The huge trumpet-shaped flowers of Datura cornigera *are quite startling when featured in a small garden.*

A bare lawn can be transformed using this simple plan.

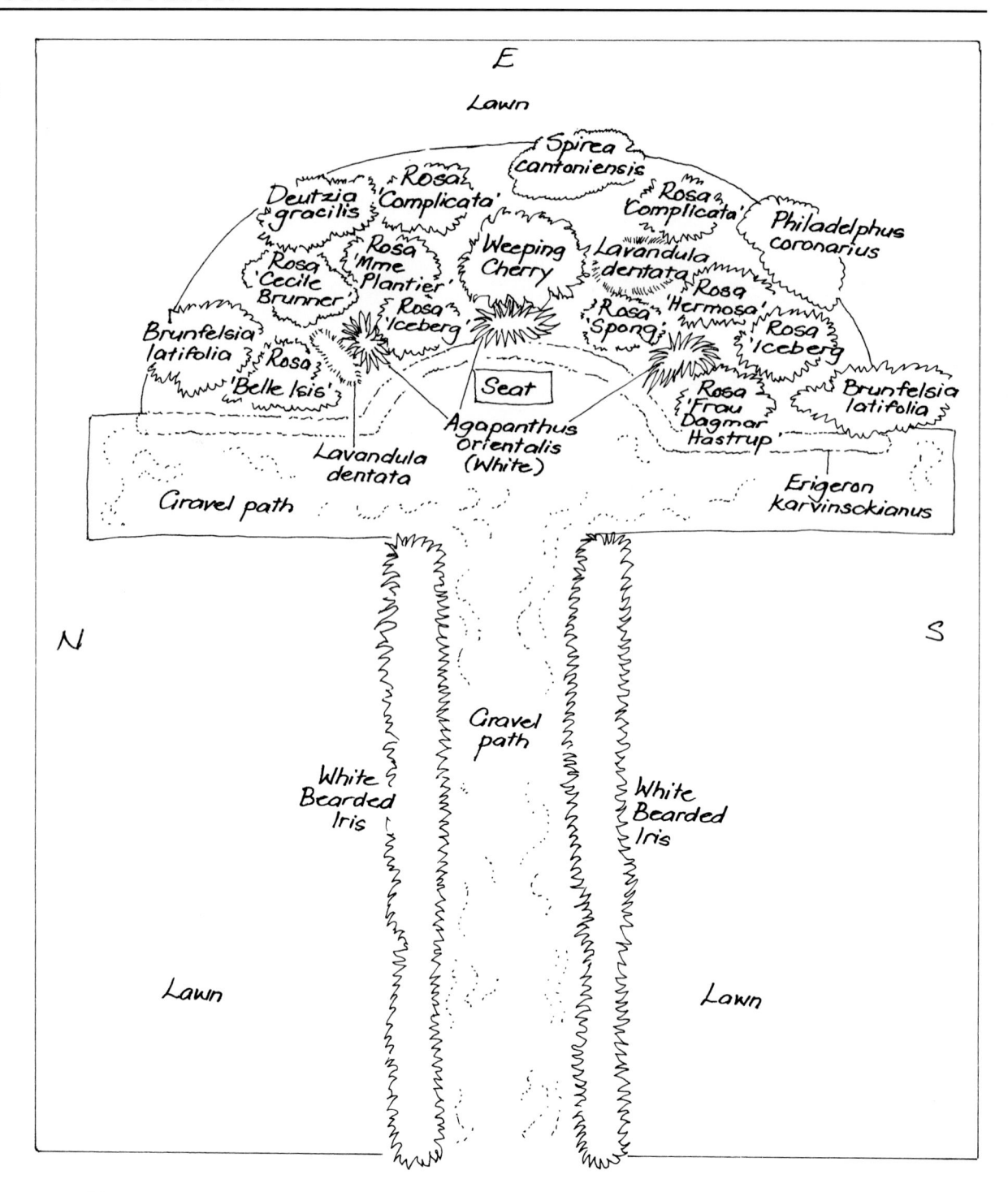

Garden plan (labels, clockwise/around):

- E (top), N (left), S (right)
- Lawn (top, bottom-left, bottom-right)
- Spirea cantoniensis
- Rosa 'Complicata'
- Deutzia gracilis
- Rosa 'Complicata'
- Philadelphus coronarius
- Rosa 'Cecile Brunner'
- Rosa 'Mme Plantier'
- Weeping Cherry
- Lavandula dentata
- Rosa 'Hermosa'
- Brunfelsia latifolia
- Rosa 'Iceberg'
- Rosa 'Spongi'
- Rosa 'Iceberg'
- Rosa 'Belle Isis'
- Seat
- Rosa 'Frau Dagmar Hastrup'
- Brunfelsia latifolia
- Agapanthus Orientalis (White)
- Lavandula dentata
- Gravel path
- Erigeron karvinsokianus
- White Bearded Iris (both sides of gravel path)
- Gravel path

Underplanted with forget-me-nots, grape hyacinth, love-in-a-mist, borage, violets and English daisies.

If the garden is small try to avoid gaining privacy by planting too many large trees as this will create excessive shade. Trellis added to the top of an existing fence and covered with climbers will give privacy but still allow sun to enter. Alternatively, use smaller trees or shrubs — the evergreen alder (*Alnus rhombifolia*), for example, is fast growing and has a pretty habit.

Often a strategically placed arch or trellis

fence can give a garden charm and character. Use trellis to fence off a small area of the garden for a courtyard. This gives the garden an intimate feeling and also invites you to walk around the other side of the trellis to investigate the rest of the garden.

Climbing plants allowed to wander over a fence or trellis can transform the atmosphere of the garden. In small inner-city houses the use of trellis or wire attached to brick walls and covered in evergreen climbing plants will cover an ugly aspect.

Perhaps the structure of the garden can be changed easily by planting a formal box hedge around the perimeter of a garden bed. This will tie the bed together as well as making it a focal point in the garden.

I think that colour is one of the main problems facing the new owner of an existing garden. There are always colours that you cannot live with or which do not fit the colour scheme you have in mind. If you wish to change the colour of the house you may find existing plants next to the house clash dreadfully with the newly chosen colour. Shrubs can always be moved to other areas of the garden, given away or, if necessary, ruthlessly removed.

Soften existing paths by using cascading plants on the side. Place seats at points of interest through the garden. They don't have to be expensive seats. A piece of wood on top of bricks creates a casual-looking, simple seat. Terracotta pots and urns placed thoughtfully beside paths or at the corner of the house create attractive scenes.

Underplanting

Correct placement of flowers under trees and around shrubs is capable of changing the atmosphere of a garden. Choose a mixture of perennials, annuals and bulbs of different heights, leaf textures and colours. A variation in leaf texture is very important as it gives the garden a feeling of softness.

Plant in a way that does not make the garden appear to be too contrived. Make sure you use plants of different heights as the use of one height in a garden bed will look boring.

Use themes throughout the garden. Take note of the colour of each plant and plant for colour harmony. Using only one or two colours through the garden, like pink or blue, can create a very harmonious feeling. Or you may wish to use white or green for a tranquil feeling. Take care that the plants chosen do not all flower simultaneously.

Bright colour schemes can be softened by the use of grey leaved plants or white flowers. They will also be softened by the use of small shrubs with different tones of green leaves.

Gates within a garden invest it with a sense of mystery, tempting you to explore beyond them.

Perennials

Poppies add height and colour to a perennial border.

Perennials have had a rich and varied heritage throughout recorded history. Many garden historians — and I would share their view — regard the nineteenth century English garden as the high point of perennial artistry. It was during this period that the full charm of perennials and the diversity of their possible uses was realised. While the structure of the garden may be centred around trees and shrubs, perennials create the attractiveness, the ambience.

What is a perennial? The simplest definition of a perennial is 'a plant that lives for more than two years'. While many plants fit this category, including trees, shrubs and bulbs, the word commonly refers to perennial flowering plants that are herbaceous. This means that their stems are soft and fleshy, not woody like those of shrubs and trees.

These herbaceous perennials survive the winter because their roots are stronger and more vigorous than those of annuals and biennials. With the onset of cold the tops die down but the roots remain alive in a dormant state sending forth new foliage and flowers each year when the weather warms.

Designing a perennial border

Perennials should not be associated only with cold-climate gardens as most of the plants that were grown in England were imports. There are over 20,000 species of perennials, which come from all over the world and which are suitable for all climates.

There are two types of perennial borders — herbaceous and mixed. Herbaceous borders contain mainly perennial plants with the odd splash of annuals. The major drawback with an herbaceous border is that it can tend to look very bare during winter. A mixed border is one containing shrubs as well as perennials. Shrubs add structure to the border and support the perennials.

Perennial gardens actually require less maintenance than most other types of gardens. It is the consideration given to the initial design of the garden that takes the time.

Perennial borders should be informal and be comprised of plants of varying heights. If planted against the wall of a house perennials should be planted in a configuration which places the low growers at the front and the tallest varieties at the back. To achieve such an informal tapering from the front edge without abrupt changes in height, make the borders at least 1.5 m to 2 m deep. The deeper the bed the more gently the heights of the plants should be tapered.

If the perennial border lines a pathway or can be viewed from both sides, then it must be planned accordingly, with the larger perennials in the middle of the bed and a gradual reduction to lower growing plants on each side.

The design of the perennial border achieves its impact from the combination of plants used. Although there is to be a mixture of plants, don't plant just one of each perennial. At least three or four of the same type need to be planted together to ensure a bold and visually arresting design. A good perennial border will combine colour, form and texture creating a garden picture. You should consider the colour of the foliage as well as flower colour. Annuals should be interplanted to provide wider appeal.

Don't plant perennials in straight rows. A straight row of anything in the garden looks too restrained. Plant them in large drifts and fill the garden bed with different textures and shapes.

Perennial borders can be designed for spring, summer and autumn colour or for continuous display throughout the seasons. A seasonal perennial garden will give a spectacular display,

The combination of plants in this garden is responsible for its arresting visual quality. Tall foxgloves flank the pathway while lower growing perennials spill onto the gravel.

140 Creating your Ideal Garden

Right *A summer-flowering perennial border.*

Below *This summer perennial border is a patchwork of colour. The style is relaxing and pragmatic.*

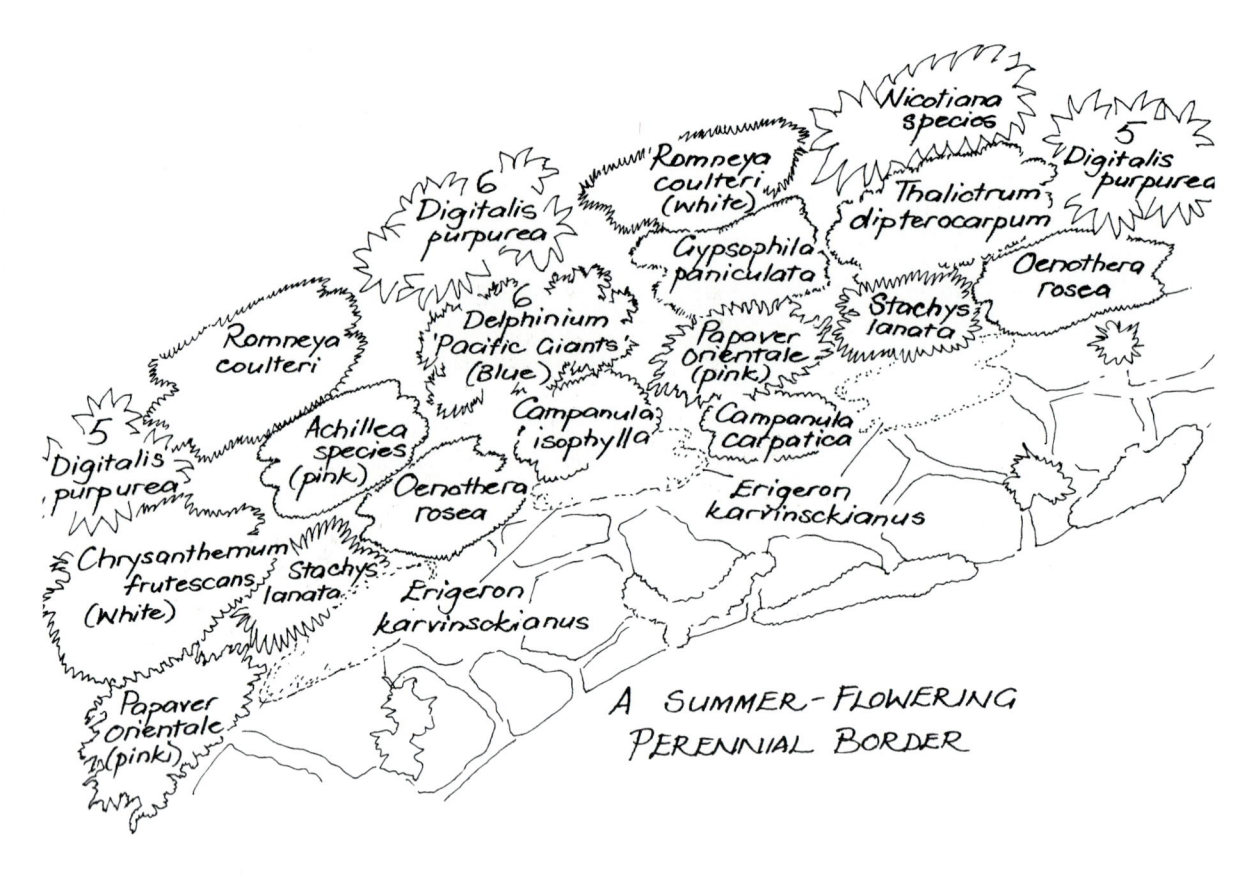

A SUMMER-FLOWERING PERENNIAL BORDER

but should you decide to have one you must be willing to have less flowers during other seasons. For a longer duration of colour, plant for a continuous succession of bloom in which new flowers appear as others fade. Although this may reduce the overall visual effect of garden colour, it will reveal the forms of the plants more clearly. A perennial garden planned for a succession of blooms is always changing, so in this regard it is not one garden but many gardens in one.

Tall growing perennials suitable for the back of the border include: lavender shower (*Thalictrum dipterocarpum*) which has masses of small mauve flowers borne on loose panicles and leaves of similar appearance to maidenhair fern; *Romneya coulteri* which has white poppy-like flowers with crinkled petals surrounding a mass of golden-yellow stamens and Russell lupins which are valued for tall spikes of outstanding flowers. These include a range of pinks, as well as shades of blue and white.

Try yarrow (*Achillea* 'Cerise Queen'), the pinkish-purple flowers of which appear from spring to autumn. In addition there are many varieties of yarrow with colours of white, cream, pink and yellow. The tall stately spires of *Delphinium* 'Pacific Giants' come in shades of pink, blue and white and reach a height of 1.5 m. Cut them back after flowering to encourage another flush in autumn.

The flowers of flowering tobacco (*Nicotiana* species) are very fragrant, especially in the evenings. Flower colour range includes white, lime-green and lilac and the plants reach a height of about 1.5 m.

Medium growing perennials include parrot beak (*Alstromeria pulchella*), whose red-tipped green flowers will remain for several months and peach-leaved campanula (*Campanula persicifolia*), whose bell-like flowers are available in shades of purple, blue and white.

Oriental poppies (*Papaver orientale*) have large flowers in shades of pink, white and red. Left undisturbed, the clumps become most impressive. Baby's breath (*Gypsophila paniculata*) is one of the most elegant perennials and has masses of tiny pink or white flowers.

A spectacular perennial for the front of the border is the pink evening primrose (*Oenothera rosea*). Its large, open-faced, rose-pink flowers open all day and close at night. The flowering is prodigious, lasting all summer.

Lamb's ear (*Stachys lanata*) is full of character with its tiny amethyst flowers, grey woolly spikes and felty leaves. It will harmonise with everything in the garden.

For shady areas of the perennial border you cannot surpass helleborus. It grows in the shade and will start flowering in late winter when other flowers are scarce.

Perennial maintenance

It is a pleasant task to walk into a bed of perennials and forage around in the heady fragrance of flowers to rescue any poor plant which may have been overwhelmed by a stronger growing one. These rescued plants can be transferred to another part of the garden or the dominating plant itself can be removed to a position where it can

---

PERENNIAL DESIGN AT A GLANCE

- Determine at the outset what plants you want.
- Draw a master plan of the perennial garden.
- Consider the height and width of each plant, allowing room for it to spread.
- Plan flower colour and flowering times for colour harmony.
- Consider foliage texture and the structure of the plant. Good structure and texture add strength to the border.
- Place shrubs around the periphery of the bed to give shape to the garden.
- Plant only perennials that will grow in your area.
- Place perennials appropriately with, for example, shade-lovers under trees and sun-lovers in full sun.
- Plant more than one of each type for a massed effect.

---

take over an area without causing harm. If I find one perennial that will thrive in difficult areas of the garden like under trees and in shade I tend to plant that only and let it take over the area. In part of my garden where the ground is dry and partially shaded under larger trees I plant agapanthus and windflowers (*Anemone japonica*). To try and cultivate other types of plants in this area is often disappointing as they simply don't grow or require too much maintenance.

The essential maintenance of perennials usually includes staking the taller growing ones and giving them a supply of food when the new stalks appear. Staking should always be done subtly, using wooden stakes that do not appear above the tops of the perennials or wire stakes placed evenly around the plants.

The soil should be properly prepared before planting by digging in manure or compost and each spring a mulch of the same will not go astray. As the buds start to appear an application of soluble plant food is helpful.

Right *A stunning display of shasta daisies (Chrysanthemum maximum). The use of one type of plant* en masse *can look more spectacular than a range of plants.*

Below *Different heights, textures and forms will help to produce an informal perennial garden.*

Dividing perennials

There are two main reasons for dividing perennials; rejuvenation and propagation.

Division is the most common method of increasing the number of perennials throughout the garden. It is also a point at which perennials can be swapped with other perennial-lovers. Some of my favourite plants have come to me in this way.

The nature of most perennials is to grow larger every year, usually by spreading and making a bigger clump. Often one plant will grow to such a size that it will choke many other desirable plants.

The general rule is to divide spring and summer flowering perennials in late summer or autumn and autumn flowering perennials in early spring. This will allow a whole growing season for re-establishment. The only exception to this rule is in very cold climates where it is best to divide in early spring.

The dividing process is simple. Dig the entire clump out and then pull the root system apart, creating as little damage as possible. Replant the divisions as soon as possible applying a mulch of manure or compost around each plant. Keep the soil moist until the plants have established.

A SELECTION LIST OF PERENNIALS

Acanthus mollis
(oyster plant or bear's breeches)
FLOWER COLOUR Purple and white
FLOWERING TIME Summer
HEIGHT 90 cm
ASPECT Sun or partial shade

Achillea filipendulina
(yarrow)
FLOWER COLOUR Bright yellow
FLOWERING TIME Summer
HEIGHT 75 cm
ASPECT Sun
OTHER SPECIES
A. millefolium — white flowers
A. millefolium 'Rosea' — pink flowers
A. millefolium 'Cerise Queen' — crimson flowers
A. tomentosa — yellow flowers

Aconitum napellus
(monkshood)
FLOWER COLOUR Deep blue
FLOWERING TIME Autumn
HEIGHT 60-80 cm
ASPECT Sun or semi-shade

Aethionema coridifolium
(Lebanon stone cress)
FLOWER COLOUR Rosy-carmine
FLOWERING TIME Spring to mid-summer
HEIGHT 30-45 cm
ASPECT Sun
OTHER VARIETIES
A. coridifolium 'Warley Rose' — rose-pink flowers

Ajuga reptans
(bugle flower)
FLOWER COLOUR Blue
FLOWERING TIME Summer
HEIGHT 20 cm
ASPECT Full or semi-shade
OTHER VARIETIES
A. reptans 'Burgundy Lace' — cream and maroon leave
A. reptans 'Multicolor' — reddish pink, brown and creamy yellow markings on the leaves
OTHER SPECIES
A. pyramidalis — leaves have a metallic purple sheen

Alstroemeria pulchella
(parrot beak)
FLOWER COLOUR Dark-red petals tipped with green
FLOWERING TIME Late spring to summer
HEIGHT 90 cm
ASPECT Sun
OTHER SPECIES
A. aurantiaca — yellow, spotted brown flowers

Alcea rosea
(hollyhock)
FLOWER COLOUR Various colours
FLOWERING TIME Summer
HEIGHT 180 cm
ASPECT Sun

Anemone blanda
(woodland anemone)
FLOWER COLOUR Blue, but pink, violet or white forms are available
FLOWERING TIME Spring
HEIGHT 15 cm
ASPECT Shade

Anemone japonica
(windflower)
FLOWER COLOUR White, dark pink or mauve depending on the variety
FLOWERING TIME Late summer and autumn
HEIGHT 90 cm
ASPECT Partial shade

Anthemis nobilis
(camomile)
FLOWER COLOUR White with a yellow centre
FLOWERING TIME Spring and summmer
HEIGHT 20 cm
ASPECT Sun

Aquilegia vulgaris
(columbines)
FLOWER COLOUR Cream, pink, yellow, white, red or blue depending on the variety
FLOWERING TIME Spring
HEIGHT 75 cm
ASPECT Sun or partial shade
OTHER SPECIES
A. flabellata — white to violet-blue flowers

Arabis albida
FLOWER COLOUR White
FLOWERING TIME Spring
HEIGHT 20 cm
ASPECT Partial shade
OTHER VARIETIES
A. albida 'Flore Plena'— white flowers

Arenaria montana
(sandwort)
FLOWER COLOUR White
FLOWERING TIME Late spring
HEIGHT 15 cm
ASPECT Partial shade

Armeria maritima
(thrift or sea pink)
FLOWER COLOUR Pink
FLOWERING TIME Spring to summer
HEIGHT 12 cm
ASPECT Sun
OTHER SPECIES
A. pseudarmeria 'Giant White' — white flowers
A. pseudarmeria 'Rubra' — rosy-red flowers

Artemisia lactiflora
FLOWER COLOUR Creamy-white
FLOWERING TIME Late summer to autumn
HEIGHT 150 cm
ASPECT Sun or partial shade

Windflower (Anemone japonica) *thrives in partially shaded areas of the garden.*

Marguerite daisy (Chrysanthemum frutescans) flowers continuously from spring to summer.

Aster amellus
(perennial or Italian aster)
FLOWER COLOUR Pale pink and various shades of blue
FLOWERING TIME Summer to autumn
HEIGHT 50 cm
ASPECT Sun

Aster novi-belgii
(Michaelmas daisy)
FLOWER COLOUR Mauve, pink, purple, lilac or white depending on the variety
FLOWERING TIME Mid-summer to autumn
HEIGHT 120 cm
ASPECT Sun

Astilbe hybrids
(goat's beard)
FLOWER COLOUR White, shades of pink or red depending on the variety
FLOWERING TIME Summer
HEIGHT 90 cm
ASPECT Shade

Aubretia deltoides
(rock cress)
FLOWER COLOUR Rose-lilac to purple or blue
FLOWERING TIME Spring
HEIGHT 10 cm
ASPECT Sun

Aurinia saxatilis (syn. *Alyssum saxatile*)
(yellow alyssum)
FLOWER COLOUR Yellow
FLOWERING TIME Spring to early summer
HEIGHT 30 cm
ASPECT Full sun

Bellis perennis
(common or English daisy)
FLOWER COLOUR White tinged with pink and yellow centres
FLOWERING TIME Spring
HEIGHT 10 cm
ASPECT Sun or semi-shade

Bergenia cordifolia
(Norwegian snow)
FLOWER COLOUR Rose-pink
FLOWERING TIME Late winter to early spring
HEIGHT 35 cm
ASPECT Sun or full shade

Brachycome multifida
FLOWER COLOUR Lilac-blue
FLOWERING TIME Spring and summer
HEIGHT 30 cm
ASPECT Sun or dappled shade

Campanula carpatica
(tussock bellflower)
FLOWER COLOUR White, blue, lavender or lilac depending on the variety.
FLOWERING TIME Late spring to summer
HEIGHT 25 cm
ASPECT Sun or partial shade

Campanula isophylla
(Italian bellflower)
FLOWER COLOUR Pale blue
FLOWERING TIME Late spring to summer
HEIGHT 45 cm
ASPECT Sun or partial shade
OTHER VARIETIES
C. isophylla 'Alba' — white flowers

Campanula medium
(Canterbury bells)
FLOWER COLOUR Blue, white, pink or violet depending on the variety
FLOWERING TIME Spring to mid-summer
HEIGHT 90 cm
ASPECT Sun or partial shade

Campanula persicifolia
(peach-leafed campanula)
FLOWER COLOUR Blue or white depending on the variety
FLOWERING TIME Late spring to mid-summer
HEIGHT 90 cm
ASPECT Sun

Campanula portenschlagiana
FLOWER COLOUR Blue
FLOWERING TIME Spring to early summer
HEIGHT 15 cm
ASPECT Partial or dappled shade

Campanula rotundifolia
(English harebell or blue bells of Scotland)
FLOWER COLOUR Violet-blue
FLOWERING TIME Mid-spring to late summer
HEIGHT 50 cm
ASPECT Light shade
OTHER VARIETIES
C. rotundifolia 'Alba' — white flowers.

Centranthus ruber
(red valerian)
FLOWER COLOUR Bright red
FLOWERING TIME Spring to late summer
HEIGHT 75 cm
ASPECT Sun
OTHER VARIETIES
C. ruber 'Albus' — white flowers
C. ruber 'Roseus' — rose-pink flowers

Cerastium tomentosum
(snow in summer)
FLOWER COLOUR White
FLOWERING TIME Spring to summer
HEIGHT 15 cm
ASPECT Sun

Ceratostigma plumbaginoides
(perennial leadwort)
FLOWER COLOUR Blue
FLOWERING TIME Summer to autumn
HEIGHT 30 cm
ASPECT Sun

Chrysanthemum frutescans
(Marguerite daisy)
FLOWER COLOUR White, pink or yellow
FLOWERING TIME Late winter to early summer
HEIGHT 90 cm
ASPECT Sun

Chrysanthemum maximum
(shasta daisy)
FLOWER COLOUR White with yellow centres
FLOWERING TIME Late spring to late summer
HEIGHT 90 cm
ASPECT Sun

Delphinium 'Pacific Giants'
FLOWER COLOUR Pink, white or blue
FLOWERING TIME Late spring to early summer
HEIGHT 1.5 m
ASPECT Sun

Dianthus plumarius
(garden or cottage pink)
FLOWER COLOUR Shades of red, pink, purple-reds, mauves or white depending on the variety
FLOWERING TIME Spring
HEIGHT 30 cm
ASPECT Sun

Dicentra spectabilis
(bleeding heart)
FLOWER COLOUR Deep pink and white
FLOWERING TIME Spring
HEIGHT 1 m
ASPECT Dappled shade

OTHER VARIETIES
D.spectabilis 'Alba' — white flowers

Dictamnus albus
(burning bush)
FLOWER COLOUR White
FLOWERING TIME Spring and summer
HEIGHT 60 cm
ASPECT Sun

Digitalis purpurea
(foxglove)
FLOWER COLOUR Purple, red, maroon, cream or pink.

The dainty flowers of Bellis perennis *appear in early spring.*

Delphiniums reach a height of 1.5 m and are ideal plants for the back of a perennial border.

FLOWERING TIME Summer
HEIGHT 1.5 m
ASPECT Partial shade

Doronicum cordatum
(leopard's bane)
FLOWER COLOUR Yellow
FLOWERING TIME Spring
HEIGHT 25 cm
ASPECT Sun or light shade

Echinaceae purpurea
(purple cone flower)
FLOWER COLOUR Purple-crimson
FLOWERING TIME Mid-summer to autumn
HEIGHT 120 cm
ASPECT Sun

Echinops ritro
(globe thistle)
FLOWER COLOUR Metallic blue-white
FLOWERING TIME Summer
HEIGHT 120 cm
ASPECT Sun

Echium fastuosum
(viper's bugloss)
FLOWER COLOUR Lilac-purple
FLOWERING TIME Mid-spring to mid-summer
HEIGHT 150 cm
ASPECT Sun

Erigeron karvinsckianus
(babies' tears)
FLOWER COLOUR Pink and white
FLOWERING TIME Spring to autumn
HEIGHT 25 cm
ASPECT Sun or semi-shade

Eryngium giganteum
(sea holly)
FLOWER COLOUR Blue
FLOWERING TIME Summer
HEIGHT 2 m
ASPECT Sun

Euphorbia wulfenii
FLOWER COLOUR Green-yellow
FLOWERING TIME Spring

HEIGHT 120 cm
ASPECT Sun

Festuca ovina 'Glauca'
(sheep's fescue)
FLOWER COLOUR Grown for its strap-like blue leaves
FLOWERING TIME N/A
HEIGHT 25 cm
ASPECT Sun

Gazania X *hybrida*
FLOWER COLOUR White, cream, yellow, red or brown
FLOWERING TIME Spring and summer
HEIGHT 25 cm
ASPECT Sun

Geranium sanguineum
FLOWER COLOUR Magenta
FLOWERING TIME Late spring and summer
HEIGHT 45 cm
ASPECT Sun
OTHER VARIETIES
G. sanguineum 'Album' — white flowers
OTHER SPECIES
G. endressii — pale rose-pink flowers
G. himalayense — violet-blue flowers

Geum quellyon
(scarlet avens)
FLOWER COLOUR Scarlet
FLOWERING TIME Late spring to early autumn
HEIGHT 50 CM
ASPECT Sun

Gypsophila paniculata
(baby's breath)
FLOWER COLOUR White
FLOWERING TIME Summer
HEIGHT 90 cm
ASPECT Sun
OTHER VARIETIES
'Bristol Fairy' — double white flowers
'Flamingo' — double pink flowers
'Rosy Veil' — double pink flowers

Hedychium flavum
(ginger lily)
FLOWER COLOUR Yellow with long red filaments

FLOWERING TIME Summer
HEIGHT 1.5 m
ASPECT Sun or partial shade

Helenium autumnale
(sneeze weed)
FLOWER COLOUR Yellow
FLOWERING TIME Summer to early autumn
HEIGHT 150 cm
ASPECT Sun

Helianthemum nummularium
(sun rose)
FLOWER COLOUR Yellow
FLOWERING TIME Mid-spring to mid-summer
HEIGHT 30 cm
ASPECT Sun

Helleborus corsicus
FLOWER COLOUR Yellow-green
FLOWERING TIME Late winter to early spring
HEIGHT 90 cm
ASPECT Shade
OTHER SPECIES
H. niger — white flowers tinged with pink
H. orientalis — shades of purple, pink, crimson, white or cream flowers

Heuchera sanguinea
(coral bells)
FLOWER COLOUR Bright red
FLOWERING TIME Spring to mid-summer
HEIGHT 30 cm
ASPECT Sun

Limonium sinatum
(statice)
FLOWER COLOUR Pink, purple, blue, white or yellow
FLOWERING TIME Summer
HEIGHT 75 cm
ASPECT Sun

Lupinus
(Russell Lupins)
FLOWER COLOUR Yellow, purple, orange, red, white, pink, blue and many bi-colours
FLOWERING TIME Spring and summer
HEIGHT 1.2 m
ASPECT Sun

Lychnis coronaria
(rose campion)
FLOWER COLOUR Bright magenta
FLOWERING TIME Late spring and summer
HEIGHT 60 cm
ASPECT Sun or partial shade
OTHER VARIETIES
'Alba' - white flowers
'Atrosanguinea' — crimson flowers
OTHER SPECIES
L. chalcedonica — bright scarlet flowers
L. chalcedonia 'Rosea' — pink flowers

Meconopsis betonicifolia
(Himalayan blue poppy)
FLOWER COLOUR Blue
FLOWERING TIME Late spring to early summer
HEIGHT 120 cm
ASPECT Semi-shade

Oenothera rosea
(pink evening primrose)
FLOWER COLOUR Pink
FLOWERING TIME Late spring to summer
HEIGHT 50 cm
ASPECT Sun
OTHER SPECIES
O. biennis — yellow flowers

Paeonia lactiflora
(Chinese or common herbaceous peony)
FLOWER COLOUR White, creamy-yellow, shades of pink, red, crimson or rosy-purple depending on the variety
FLOWERING TIME Spring

HEIGHT 1 m
ASPECT Sun or light shade

Papaver orientale
(oriental poppy)
FLOWER COLOUR Red with a black centre but other coloured varieties include pink, white and orange
FLOWERING TIME Late spring to early summer
HEIGHT 90 cm
ASPECT Sun

Penstemon gloxinoides
FLOWER COLOUR Pink, purple, off-white or crimson
FLOWERING TIME Late spring to early summer
HEIGHT 90 cm
ASPECT Sun

Phlox paniculata
(perennial phlox)
FLOWER COLOUR White, mauve, orange, purple, rose-pink, salmon or crimson depending on the variety
FLOWERING TIME Summer
HEIGHT 150 cm
ASPECT Sun

Phlox subulata
(alpine or moss phlox)
FLOWER COLOUR hite, crimson, blue, pink or red depending on the variety
FLOWERING TIME Spring
HEIGHT 15 cm
ASPECT Sun

Physostegia virginiana
(obedient plant)
FLOWER COLOUR Mauve-pink
FLOWERING TIME Summer to autumn
HEIGHT 90 cm
ASPECT Sun
OTHER VARIETIES
'Alba' — white flowers
'Bouquet Rose' — deep pink flowers
'Rosea' — rose-pink flowers
'Speciosa' — pale pink flowers
'Vivid' — rosy red flowers

Platycodon grandiflorus
(balloon flower)
FLOWER COLOUR Blue
FLOWERING TIME Summer

Dianthus *'Pamela pink'* makes a pretty border in a perennial garden.

The large, pink flowers of oriental poppies (Papaver orientale) are a truly arresting sight.

HEIGHT 60 cm
ASPECT Sun or semi-shade
OTHER VARIETIES
'Albus' — white flowers
'Roseus' — rosy-lilac flowers

Polyanthus species
FLOWER COLOUR Large colour range
FLOWERING TIME Spring
HEIGHT 25 cm
ASPECT Light sun or semi-shade

Polygonatum multifolium
(Solomon's seal)
FLOWER COLOUR White
FLOWERING TIME Spring or early summer
HEIGHT 1 m
ASPECT Light shade

Polygonum affine
'Darjeeling Red'
FLOWER COLOUR Deep pink
FLOWERING TIME Summer
HEIGHT 25 cm
ASPECT Sun or partial shade

Primula denticulata
FLOWER COLOUR Lilac, deep purple and rose or deep carmine
FLOWERING TIME Spring
HEIGHT 30 cm
ASPECT Shade

OTHER SPECIES
P. japonica — magenta, white or rose flowers
P. helodoxa — golden yellow flowers

Romneya coulteri
FLOWER COLOUR White
FLOWERING TIME Mid-summer to early autumn
HEIGHT 1.5 m
ASPECT Sun

Rudbeckia laciniata
'Golden Glow'
FLOWER COLOUR Yellow
FLOWERING TIME Summer to autumn
HEIGHT 1.5 m
ASPECT Sun

Salvia farinacea
(mealycup sage)
FLOWER COLOUR Purple
FLOWERING TIME Summer to autumn
HEIGHT 70 cm
ASPECT Sun
OTHER SPECIES
S. leucantha — deep violet flowers
S. patens — deep blue flowers
S. splendens — scarlet flowers
S. aurea — terracotta flowers
S. rutilens — bright red flowers

Sanquisorbia bakusanensis
FLOWER COLOUR Pink
FLOWERING TIME Summer
HEIGHT 90 cm
ASPECT Partial shade

Saponaria officinalis
(soap wort)
FLOWER COLOUR Pink
FLOWERING TIME Summer
HEIGHT 60 cm
ASPECT Sun or partial shade
OTHER VARIETIES
'Alba-plena' — white flowers
'Rosea-plena' — pink flowers

Saxifraga umbrosa
(London pride)
FLOWER COLOUR Pink
FLOWERING TIME Spring and early summer
HEIGHT 45 cm
ASPECT Dappled sun or semi-shade

Silene vulgaris
(sea campion)
FLOWER COLOUR Light pink
FLOWERING TIME Spring and summer
HEIGHT 60 cm
ASPECT Sun or partial shade

Solidago canadensis
(golden rod)
FLOWER COLOUR Yellow
FLOWERING TIME Autumn
HEIGHT 1.5 m
ASPECT Sun

Stachys lanata
(Lamb's ears)
FLOWER COLOUR Rosy purple
FLOWERING TIME Summer and autumn
HEIGHT 20 cm
ASPECT Sun or dappled shade

Stokesia laevis 'Alba'
(Stoke's aster)
FLOWER COLOUR White
FLOWERING TIME Summer to early autumn
HEIGHT 60 cm
ASPECT Sun
OTHER VARIETIES
'Lilacina' — lilac-blue flowers
'Rosea' — rose pink flowers

The lilac blue flowers of Stokesia laevis *'Lilacina' are present from late summer to early autumn.*

Thalictrum dipterocarpum
(lavender shower)
FLOWER COLOUR Mauve
FLOWERING TIME Summer to early autumn
HEIGHT 180 cm
ASPECT Sun or semi-shade
OTHER SPECIES
T. aquilegifolium — rosy-purple flowers

Thymus serpyllum
(wild or creeping thyme)
FLOWER COLOUR Deep lilac
FLOWERING TIME Late spring and summer
HEIGHT 5 cm
ASPECT Sun
OTHER VARIETIES
'Alba' — white flowers
'Coccineus' — crimson flowers
'Magic Carpet' — lilac-pink flowers
OTHER SPECIES
T. citriodora — rosy-mauve flowers
T. pseudolanuginosus — lilac-pink flowers

Tulbaghia violacea
FLOWER COLOUR Lavender-pink
FLOWERING TIME Spring to autumn
HEIGHT 60 cm
ASPECT Sun

Verbena lacinata
FLOWER COLOUR Salmon, rose, lavender or white depending on the variety
FLOWERING TIME Spring and summer
HEIGHT 50 cm
ASPECT Semi-shade
OTHER SPECIES
V. peruviana — crimson flowers

Viola odorata
(sweet violet)
FLOWER COLOUR Reddish-purple, violet-purple, dark violet, rose-pink, deep violet, blue or white depending on the variety
FLOWERING TIME Spring
HEIGHT 10 cm
ASPECT Shade
OTHER SPECIES
V. hederacea — violet-blue and white flowers

Old-fashioned Roses

Above Old-fashioned roses are loved for their simplicity, delicacy of colour and exquisite fragrance. This yellow Charles Austin rose has all those qualities.

Opposite An arch covered with the delightful pink blossoms of Rosa multiflora *'Cathayensis' and* Rosa *'New Dawn' makes an enchanting entrance to this garden.*

Old-fashioned roses become an addiction. Once you discover these beautiful plants you will feel you have to collect them all. Old-fashioned roses are characterised by delicacy of colour, generosity of bloom and most of all their captivating fragrance.

The recent and growing interest in old-fashioned roses reflects a desire in many gardeners to recapture the quietness and graciousness of bygone days. Their highly decorative qualities are appreciated in both the house and the garden.

Roses originated in the northern hemisphere, mainly in North America, Asia, the Middle East and Europe and they were first cultivated around 5000 years ago in China.

These 'original' roses were single flowers comprised mainly of five petals and reproduced readily from seed. They were widely used for medicinal purposes and as a food. The rose-hips of some species supplied vitamin C and the young tips have a nutty flavour.

Landscaping with Roses

Although the more modern types of rose are bedding plants, many old-fashioned varieties are like shrubs and can be planted in shrub or perennial borders. The rambling types may be left to scramble around on garden perimeters.

This chapter is intended to introduce you to the various types of roses and some of the more popular types. To really delve into old-fashioned roses, I would have to write a complete book on the subject.

Old-fashioned roses harmonise perfectly with trees and shrubs and can provide structure to an herbaceous border. Standard roses can be used to provide height in a border or may be used purely as specimen plants in a garden bed.

Climbing roses can be grown over arches or used to soften brick walls. A seat placed under an arch or arbour covered with climbing roses provides a perfect setting to read, contemplate or talk with friends.

Roses create an atmosphere of charm when planted in the herb garden, adding height, colour and fragrance. Dry the petals when they fall and add them to a potpourri.

There is nothing more beautiful than a climbing rose which has woven its way up into a tree. As the rose climbs some of its branches will hang, giving a drooping effect to the tree. Choose a tree that doesn't have much character, perhaps an old fruit tree which doesn't produce much fruit or a tree which is past its prime. Plant the rose at least 70 cm from the tree and on the side which receives the most sun. Help it to begin climbing with chicken

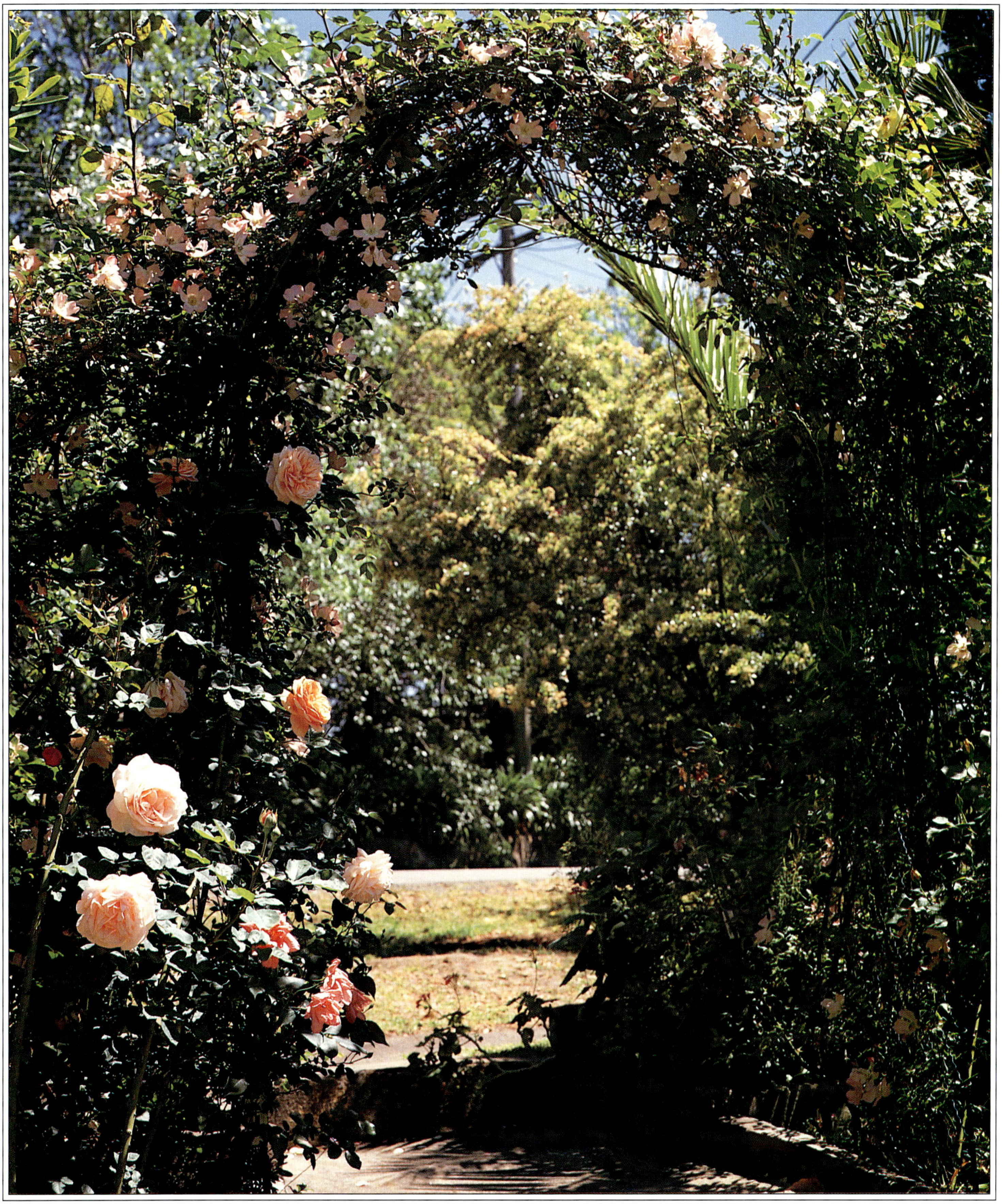

wire placed around the trunk. The wire should remain until the rose is large enough to scramble its way through the branches.

CARE AND MAINTENANCE

Old-fashioned roses are not trouble-free but they certainly do not require as much care as hybrid roses. They are still susceptible to black spot but because of their vigorous growth they tend to throw off the disease easily and do not require the constant spraying required by more modern roses.

Old climbers and rambling roses have such strength and powers of survival that they are often the last plants remaining in the gardens of long-deserted houses. But this does not mean you plant them and forget as they respond magnificently to regular feeding. Mulch them in spring with cow manure or compost as this will reduce the effect of drastic changes in soil temperature and will help to retain soil moisture. I also apply a handful of complete rose food around the base of the plant in spring and again in early summer.

Aphids and black spot are the main problems for roses. I find aphids can be removed easily by spraying a hard stream of water from the hose on them. Alternatively there are many organic garlic preparations on the market which are effective against aphids. A simple solution of soft soap and water also works well.

I do not find black spot a particular problem with old-fashioned roses. I find it often disappears the following season even if I do nothing. But if it is persistent try using a fungicide spray.

The majority of old-fashioned roses do not need pruning as the bushes will remain healthy and floriferous without human intervention. The only pruning generally required is the removal of dead wood or branches that are growing across a path.

Above A seat placed under a rose covered arch makes a fragrant resting spot.

Right A romantic place to sit: a yellow banksia rose forms an interesting canopy over the circular seat.

A SELECTION LIST OF OLD-FASHIONED ROSES

GALLICA ROSES

Many of the Gallicas are thicketing roses and do not grow much more than a metre high. Gallicas have had a considerable influence on the evolution of modern roses. They usually have many upright canes and the flowers have a sweet perfume. Many of the Gallicas were brought back from the East by the Crusaders of the twelfth and thirteenth centuries. Their petals were used at that time for making perfume and for their medicinal properties. It has been estimated that there were 2000 or more varieties once in cultivation but there are not that many left now.

Forms and hybrids of *R. Gallica*

'Agathe Incarnata' Pre-1815
Height: 1 m. Masses of flowers which open to palest pink.

'Belle Isis' c.1845
Height 1.2 m. The strongly perfumed pink flowers are a very soft shade of pink.

'Cardinal de Richelieu' 1840
Height 1.5 m. Rich purple flowers and dark green foliage make this a magnificent rose.

'Charles de mills'
Height: 1.2 m. A vigorous rose with dark green leaves and perfumed flowers in a mixture of purple and deep red.

'Complicata'
Height: 2 m. The single flowers are bright pink with gold stamens.

'Constance Spry' 1961
Height: 2 m. The pure light pink flowers have golden stamens and an intoxicating fragrance of myrrh.

'Duc de Guiche' 1835
Height: 1.2 m. The highly scented crimson flowers appear in abundance during summer.

'Duchesse de Montebello' 1829
Height: 1.2 m. The small but very fragrant double, soft-pink flowers are produced on upright stems.

'Hippolyte'
Height: 1.2 m. The beautifully formed magenta-purple flowers have soft highlights in the centre.

'La Belle Sultane'
Height: 1.5 m. An extremely vigorous rose having dark, rich red velvety flowers.

'Pompon Panachee'
Height: 90 cm. The milky white flowers are splashed and striped with rich rose-pink.

'Rosa mundi' 16th century
Height: 1 m. One of the first striped roses, with a mixture of light crimson and white.

'Sissinghurst Castle'
Height: 90 cm The fragrant flowers are a deep velvety red with golden anthers.

'Tuscany Superb' 1848
Height: 1.2 m. An attractive rose having large, dark green leaves and strongly perfumed dark red flowers.

CENTIFOLIA ROSES

Also known as Old Cabbage Roses, Centifolias are the loveliest of all the roses and are valued for their double, very fragrant flowers. Centifolia roses were hybridised, particularly by the Dutch in the fifteenth and sixteenth centuries. They were said to have introduced over 200 varieties.

Forms and hybrids of Centifolia roses include:

'Bullata' 1815
Height: 1.5 m. The clear-pink, fragrant flowers appear in such abundance that they bow the bush.

'Fantin Latour'
Height: 1.5 m. The soft-pink flowers literally cover the bush.

'La Noblesse' 1856
Height: 1.5 m. The soft, silvery-pink flowers appear in late summer.

'Old Cabbage Rose' Prior to 1597
Height: 1.3 m. A rich-pink rose of classic globular form.

'Petite de Hollande'
Height: 1 m. minature soft-pink blooms cover the bush.

'Reine des Centfeuilles' 1824
Height: 1.5 m. An extremely free flowering rose, bearing masses of double, scented, clear-pink flowers.

'Spong' 1805
Height: 1.2 m. A pretty rose which is covered in masses of small, rose-pink scented flowers in summer.

'The Bishop'
Height: 1.2 m. A stunning rose with full, fragrant flowers which are a mixture of magenta, cerise and purple.

'Tour de Malakoff' 1856
Height: 2 m. A unique rose covered in magnificent flowers which upon

The spectacular rich red flowers of 'La Belle Sultane' contrast perfectly with the golden stamens.

A scented pathway: roses, scented geraniums and herbs form a fragrant border.

opening are cerise fading to lilac-grey.

Moss Roses

Moss roses are the ultimate valentine roses. They are a sport which occurred from the Centifolia roses. moss roses are so-called because of a soft covering on the buds and often on the upper stems. They became quite a novelty when first discovered, and in the eighteenth century there were at least 30-40 varieties listed in nurserymen's catalogues. The flowers are usually very globular and open flat, giving a generous fragrance.

Forms and hybrids of *R. X centifolia muscosa* include:

'A longs Pedoncules' 1854
Height: 1.5 m. A vigorous, sprawling shrub with light, grey-green leaves and beautiful, soft lilac-pink flowers.

'Baron de Wassenaer' 1854
Height: 2 m. The double, fragrant flowers are a rich, bright-red and are borne in clusters on strong stems.

'Comptesse de Murinais' 1843
Height: 1.8 m. The soft-pink flowers change to creamy-white when they are fully open. The moss is a clear rich green which, if touched, exudes a powerful balsam-like odour.

'Golden Moss'
Height: 1.5 m. The beautiful blooms open from mossed buds and are a deep golden-yellow.

'Henri Martin' 1863
Height: 1.2 m. A graceful plant which carries fragrant, medium-sized dark crimson flowers.

'Lane's Moss' 1854
A stunning rose with extremely dark-green moss and double, cupped, very fragrant crimson flowers.

'Little Gem' 1880
Height: 90 cm The clusters of flowers are bright crimson and the stems which are covered in moss carry rich-green leaves.

'Mousseux du Japon'
Height: 1.2 m. This is the most heavily mossed of all the roses. The semi-double, soft lilac-pink, fragrant flowers occur in recurrent flushes during the summer.

'Old Pink Moss'
Height: 1.2 m. A pretty plant with fresh-green moss and clear-pink flowers.

'White Moss' 1817
Height: 1.2 m. A truly wonderful rose covered in large, fully double, white, fragrant flowers in summer. The stems and buds are covered in moss.

Damask Roses

The origin of these roses seems to be lost in time. The autumn-flowering Damasks were valued for their repeat flowering period. 'Quatre Saisons', for example, was capable of producing two crops in a season, and this was particularly valuable as its petals were used for perfume and medicine.

'Botzaris' 1856
Height: 1 m. A fragrant rose that has plump buds which open to very double, flat, creamy-white blooms with a button eye.

'Celsiana' Pre-1750
Height: 1.2 m. An extremely pretty rose which produces clusters of highly scented, clear-pink flowers, fading to white in the sun.

'Gloire de Guilan'
Height: 1.5 m. A graceful rose producing masses of large, fully quartered blooms in a beautiful shade of pink.

'Ispahan'
Height: 1.2 m. A long-flowering rose with semi-double, light pink fragrant flowers.

'Marie Louise'
1813 Height: 1 m. A spreading rose having clusters of rich rose-pink flowers.

'Quatre Saisons', also known as **'Autumn Damask'**
Height: 1.2 m. An extremely ancient and very beautiful rose with clear, silky pink, very fragrant flowers. It flowers prolifically in spring and then repeat flowers in autumn, often having occasional blooms in between.

Alba roses

To my mind these are the most stunning in appearance of all the groups of roses. Some trace the ancient origins of this plant to medieval Europe. All the Albas are delicately coloured in shades of milky white, and creamy or pale pink. They have a beautiful, sweet fragrance and are very hardy and vigorous with an outstanding ability to cope with shade.

Forms and hybrids of *R. X alba*

'Celeste', sometimes known as **'Celestial'**
Height: 1.8 m. A very ancient rose whose date and parentage are unknown but which probably originated in the late eighteenth century. Celeste is a magnificent rose and has beautiful, semi-double, soft-pink flowers which combine well with the soft grey-green foliage.

'Chloris', **'Rose du matin'** Very ancient
Height: 1.5 m. An extremely pretty

rose which has very dark-green leaves and very small thorns. The deep-pink buds open to form a double rose of soft satiny-pink. 'Chloris' is shade-tolerant and tolerant of poor soils.

'Jacobite Rose'
Height: 1.5 m. Covered in spring in creamy-white double blooms.

'Maidens Great Blush' 15th century or earlier
Height: 1.5 m. The very fragrant double, blush-pink blooms appear in great quantities on arching branches which bow down under the weight of the flowers. 'Maidens Great Blush' is tolerant of shade.

'Maxima' or **'Jacobite Rose'** 15th century or earlier
Height: 1.8 m. The branches in spring are laden with creamy-white, very double flowers in an upright cluster of 6 to 8 blooms.

'Mme Plantier' Pre-1848
Height: 1.5 m. A very hardy rose which is covered in creamy-white fragrant flowers.

'White Rose of York'
Height: 1.5 m. The fragrant semi-double pure-white flowers have a centre of golden stamens.

China roses

Chinese paintings depicted hybridised roses as early as the tenth century. When travel became more consistent in the eighteenth century plants including roses were frequently brought back to Europe. The majority of China roses are not very tall and look great when planted in herbaceous borders or herb gardens. They are very free-flowering with a sweet fragrance and some of them will even flower through winter.

Forms and hybrids of *R. chinensis*

'Archduke Charles' 1850
Height: 1 m. The lovely flowers are pale rose-pink edged with crimson and the colour deepens as the flower ages.

'Comtesse du Cayla' 1902
Height: 90 cm. A very free-flowering rose which has highly scented, single, orange flowers with red highlights.

'Hermosa' 1840
Height: 90 cm. A small rose which can be planted in groups in an herbaceous border. The flowers are a delicate mid-pink and are set off by the numerous grey-green leaves. Shade tolerant.

'Louis XIV' 1859
Height: 60 cm. The well-scented, deep-crimson, semi-double flowers of 'Louis XIV' highlight the golden stamens.

'Old Blush' or **'Parsons Pink'** Pre-1750
Height: 1.8 m. This highly scented rose is one of the worthiest of all the old Chinas. It was often planted beside cottage doors and trained to grow up each side. It is free-flowering and will produce clusters of silvery-pink flowers throughout the year.

'Viridiflora' (the Chinese green rose) 1833
Height: 90 cm. An exquisite rose with clusters of tiny, jade-green buds. These buds eventually open to deep-green flowers that gradually burnish with crimson.

Bourbon roses

Bourbon roses developed from a natural cross between China and Damask roses on the Isle de Bourbon, now known as Reunion, around 1817. Bourbon roses were very popular during the mid-nineteenth century when French rose breeders bred them to have characteristics like repeat flowering, almost evergreen foliage, a strong fragrance and very double, fragrant blooms.

Forms and hybrids of *Rosa X borboniana*

'Boule de Neige' 1867
Height: 1.2 m. A stunning rose with large flowers which open to pure white and have a strong fragrance. It has an upright habit, dark-green, glossy foliage and very few thorns.

'Bourbon Queen'
Height: 1.8m. Magnificent semi-double rose-pink flowers with a strong scent.

'Gypsy Boy' 1909
Height: 1.8 m. An extremely beautiful, tall rose which can be trained as a small climber. The double flowers are a very deep crimson bordering on black with yellow anthers. It is shade tolerant.

'Honorine de Brabant' 1874
Height: 1.8 m. A spectacular striped rose which is in shades of lilac with purple markings on a large, cupped flower. The foliage is lush and vigorous and there are few thorns.

'Mme Isaac Péreire' 1881
Height: 2 m. A bold rose with enormous deep-pink blooms carried on a strong bush. The flowers are borne in recurrent flushes even into autumn and have a rich perfume.

'Mme Pierre Oger' 1878
Height: 1.2 m. A beautiful delicate rose and a great favourite for cottage gardens. The tall, arching branches bear cupped, silvery-pink double flowers with the form of small waterlilies. It flowers almost

The rich–pink flowers of 'Monsieur Tillier' have a coppery, silken glow.

The pretty pink flowers of Rosa multiflora *cover this hedgerow in spring.*

continuously throughout summer.

'Souvenir de la Malmaison' 1843
Height: 1.8 m. One of the most beautiful of all the Bourbons. When given plenty of space it makes a beautiful scrambling rose. The flowers are a creamy-blush with powder-pink shadings. It will bear a number of flushes of blooms, and the autumn flush is perfect.

TEA ROSES

Tea roses will flower from spring to spring with scarcely a break. They were very popular roses during the latter half of the nineteenth century. many species have died but the best have survived. They are characterised by their constant flowering, massive blooms and elegant buds. They are probably the only type of old-fashioned rose which needs pruning, but this should be done only lightly. The name Tea rose was derived from the scent which is reminiscent of fresh green tea leaves before fermentation.

'Adam' 1833
Height: 2 m. One of the first Tea roses which is loved for its creamy-apricot petals with tints of pink deep in the centre.

'Anna Oliver' 1872
Height: 90 cm. A fragrant rose which is a mixture of light pink and deep rose. The high-centred blooms are on a vigorous branching bush which has mid-green foliage.

'Catherine mermet' 1868
Height: 90 cm. One of the most popular florists' roses of the nineteenth and twentieth centuries. The pink flowers have a creamy-white base and are held on long stems.

'Devoniensis' (the magnolia rose) 1838
Height: 3.5 m. A spectacular Tea rose covered in large, creamy-white flowers which are slightly blushed with pink in the centre. It has a rich fragrance and is very free-flowering.

'General Gallieni' 1899
Height: 1.2 m. An extremely beautiful rose with buff-coloured flowers heavily overlaid with red and pink with hints of yellow in the base.

'Lady Hillingdon' 1910
Height: 90 cm. This outstanding rose has long pointed buds and large, open, apricot-yellow flowers which have a lovely perfume.

'Lady Hillingdon' climbing form 1917
Height: 4.5 m. A beautiful climber with the same coloured flowers as above. The apricot flowers look stunning against the plum-coloured stems and leaves.

'Monsieur Tillier' 1891
Height: 1.5 m. The rich-pink flowers have a coppery, silken glow with a strong fragrance.

'Safrano' 1839
Height: 1.5 m. The abundance of deep-apricot flowers change to pale buff and are on the plant virtually throughout the year.

RUGOSA OR ROSEHIP ROSES

Rugosa roses are vigorous, thorny shrubs which freely produce long canes. They have been cultivated from the Ramanas roses of Japan. Rugosa roses form dense bushes and make magnificent hedges. They have large fragrant flowers and foliage that colours in autumn. The large hips can be the size of small apples. They are very hardy, cold-tolerant and will also withstand salt winds.

R. rugosa alba
Height: 2 m. One of the best forms of Rugosa with large, white, highly scented flowers. The foliage is deep green and the flowers will appear until winter.

Forms and hybrids of *R. rugosa*

'Belle Poitevine' 1894
Height: 1.8 m. The large flowers are a deep, rich pink while the heavily veined foliage is dark green. 'Belle Poitevine' is shade tolerant and will flower repeatedly.

'Blanc Double de Courbert' 1892
Height: 1.5 m. A very popular plant in earlier days. The huge, semi-double flowers are a pure white and exude a superb perfume. The bush is dense and shrubby with rich, dark-green foliage.

'Frau Dagmar Hastrup' 1914
Height: 90 cm. A stunning rose which has beautiful, clear, silver-pink flowers with pronounced stamens. It flowers from spring into autumn.

'Lady Curzon' 1901
Height: 90 cm. A tall growing shrub with arching branches and dark-green foliage. The large, single, pale rose-pink flowers are very fragrant. Shade tolerant.

'Mrs Anthony Waterer' 1898
Height: 1.2 m. The rich, deep-crimson, semi-double flowers are produced on a vigorous bush which has dark-green foliage. The prolific flowers have a delicate perfume.

'Phoebe's Frilled Pink' 1891
Height: 1.5 m. Dainty, very fragrant pale pink flowers which look similar to a frilled carnation cover this bush. This is one of the prettiest of all the Rugosas.

'Rose à parfum de L'Hay'
Height: 1.2 m. The large globular buds open flat to rich-red, fragrant

flowers which turn a deeper colour in hot sun. It is considered to be one of the most fragrant of all the Rugosas.

'Sarah van Fleet' 1926
Height: 1.8 m. Bears masses of large, semi-double flowers of clear pink which have creamy stamens. Very fragrant and flowers repeatedly.

'Schneezwerg' 1912
Height: 1.5 m. The fragrant, pure-white, semi-double flowers have golden stamens. Flowers endlessly from spring to late autumn.

Hybrid musk Roses

Hybrid musk roses are hardy and will flower in diverse situations. They are recurrent flowering and have been bred from the extremely fragrant wild musk rose of Shakespeare.

'Autumn Delight' 1933
Height: 1 m. Covered in large, almost single, creamy-buff flowers which fade to creamy white. Very fragrant.

'Ballerina' 1937
Height: 1.5 m. A vigorous shrub which is covered in masses of single apple-blossom-like pink flowers which have a tiny white eye.

'Buff Beauty' 1939
Height: 1.5 m. The double gold blooms repeat flower from spring until the end of autumn.

'Cornelia' 1925
Height: 1.2 m. The masses of coral-pink buds open to reveal delicate pink petals. Almost never out of flower.

'Eva'
Height: 2 m. The large single flowers are flame-coloured and appear in spectacular clusters.

'Frances E Lester'
Height: 2.5 m. An extremely vigorous rose whose pale-pink and white flowers are born in clusters of 25-30 blooms.

'Penelope' 1924
Height: 1.5 m. The fragrant semi-double creamy-pink blooms flower recurrently.

'Prosperity' 1919
Height: 1.5 m. A lovely shrub rose with creamy-white flowers and dark-green foliage.

Rambling roses

There are no plants more enchanting than rambling roses. They typify the style of an old-fashioned garden. In the Victorian and Edwardian eras they were grown in abundance over trellises, archways and around doorways, windows and verandahs. The majority of the rambler roses were bred from *R. sempervirens*, *R. multiflora* and *R. wichuriana*. They all have the amazing ability to throw up many branches from the base of the plant, an ability which allows them to completely clothe the side of a wall. Most of the rambling roses are almost evergreen and they are usually well covered with foliage.

'Aglaia' (yellow rambler) 1896
The delicate flowers are a pale primrose colour and appear on almost thornless growth. The foliage is light green and has coppery tints.

'Appleblossom'
Bears huge trusses of apple–blossom-like, pale-pink, single blooms with a white eye and golden stamens.

The rambling rose 'Dorothy Perkins' forms a beautiful arbour. During spring it is covered in delightful pink flowers.

'Aviator Bleriot'
An old Edwardian rambling rose. The yellow buds open to cream, very fragrant double flowers. The glossy foliage is a dark green.

'Chaplin's Pink Climber' 1929
A very beautiful rose which is smothered in clusters of semi-double, soft-pink flowers. It looks spectacular when planted over an arch or pergola.

'Dorothy Perkins' 1902
A lovely rambling rose with cascades of clear-pink, double, small blooms.

'Felicité et Perpetué'
A popular rose in colonial times in Australia. In summer it is smothered in plump, pink buds which open to clusters of creamy-white, very fragrant flowers. The foliage is a deep glossy green.

'Tausendschon' 1906
This delicate rose is almost thornless. The fragrant, pretty flowers appear in just about every shade of pink. It will flower in spring and again in autumn.

Climbing roses

Climbing roses are generally sports of Bourbons, Teas and Hybrid Teas. They are very vigorous but will not usually attain the height or spread of rambling roses.

'Albertine' 1921
One of the most beautiful of all the old climbers, it is covered in an abundance of large, soft-pink, richly perfumed flowers.

'Blackboy' 1919
The fragrant blooms are large and a deep, velvety crimson. It is a very vigorous rose that has the advantage of being mildew-proof. It flowers profusely in spring and is followed by another flush later in the season and again in autumn.

'Cecile Brunner' 1894
This is the climbing form of the lovely little bush rose. The small pink blooms are very fragrant and the plant will carry literally hundreds of flowers annually.

'Courier'
An Alister Clark rose that is covered in large, saucer-shaped fragrant flowers of a glowing salmon colour.

'Cupid' 1915
The petals of the pale, peach–coloured flowers are slightly frilled. This sweetly-scented rose is difficult to obtain but worthwhile if you can find one.

'Iceberg'
A stunning rose which is forever in flower. The dark-green foliage is covered in clusters of double white flowers with a touch of ivory.

'Lady Hillingdon' 1917
A climbing form of one of the popular Tea roses. This very vigorous plant has large, very fragrant golden flowers. The dark-green foliage is a rich bronze when new. It seems to bloom continuously from very early spring.

'Mme Abel Chatenay' 1917
Another climbing form of a famous Hybrid Tea. It is very free-flowering and will flower for long periods. The fragrant flowers are a mixture of rose and light pink in colour.

'Mme Gregoire Staechelin' 1927
Not a very old rose but an extremely beautiful one. It will flower continuously from early to mid-season. The large semi-double flowers are a clear pink with a deeper pink reverse. The fragrance has been likened to the smell of sweet peas.

'Paul's Lemon Pillar' 1915
A stunning rose which carries pale-lemon flowers with a satin-like texture. The flowers, which are produced over a long period, are very fragrant.

'Souvenir de la Malmaison' 1843
The huge, creamy-blush, full flowers appear endlessly from spring to autumn.

'Swan Lake'
A beautiful rose having elegant buds which open to fully double, white flowers with a pink blush in the centre.

OLD-FASHIONED ROSES 159

The enchanting, small, pink flowers of 'Cecile Brunner' appear in abundance over this arch from spring to summer.

CLIMBERS

A garden is essentially a place of beauty, harmony and tranquillity. It should be a retreat from the demands of an often hectic lifestyle. The modern gardener is continually seeking ways of creating an atmosphere of enchantment and climbing plants, because of their softness and varied colours, are important contributors to the creation of such an atmosphere.

LANDSCAPING WITH CLIMBERS

Climbers are used to soften hard architectural lines and conceal the uglier aspects of buildings and walls. They have the advantage of occupying little ground space while spreading their beautiful foliage and delicate flowers over large areas. Unique visual effects and informal lines contribute to their aesthetic appeal.

In their natural habitat climbers form an integral part of the ecology as they grow through trees and shrubs. Despite this many people suffer from the misconception that any climber weaving its way through a tree or shrub will eventually strangle it. While this may be true of wisteria or a large old ivy, softer climbers like clematis or climbing roses imbue a garden with magical charm as they wind through the lower branches of trees. One should plant climbers that flower at different times from the host shrub or tree. This will help provide a long period of colour which may encompass a number of seasons.

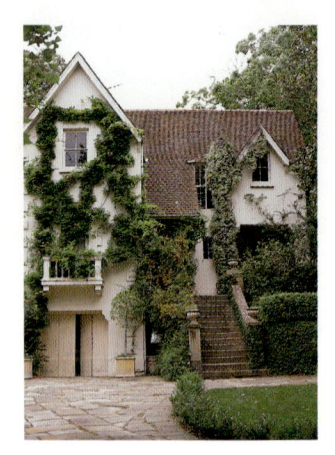

Evergreen climbers are ideal for situations where screening is necessary, while deciduous climbers are excellent for providing shade in summer and allowing the sun through during winter.

In small gardens you can grow climbers over fences as they take less space than a hedge of shrubs. Even an unsightly fence made from steel or mesh will be completely transformed in a couple of years. Plant the climbers close together according to their vigour of growth and train them fanwise from the outset so that the laterals grow horizontally. This will prevent the bottom of the fence becoming bare. A selection of climbers can be used on a fence as long as the colours are co-ordinated and match the colour of your house.

Arches, pergolas and arbours have always been associated with climbers as they provide an excellent vehicle for their cultivation. Different climbers planted each side of the arch may be used to prolong the flowering period. Make sure the colours are complementary if this approach is taken.

Wisteria, Chinese star jasmine (Trachelospermum jasminoides) *and ivy grow profusely on the walls of this house to create a captivating look.*

Arches, pergolas and arbours can be enhanced considerably when adorned with climbing plants which have clusters of flowers or long, drooping flowers. Chilean bell flower (*Lapageria rosea*) produces large, rose-red, waxy, bell-shaped flowers which hang in pendant clusters. The combination of these flowers and the leathery, dark green leaves creates a stunning effect. One variety, 'Alba', has white flowers. The abundant bright orange flowers of orange trumpet creeper (*Pyrostegia venusta*) appear during mid-winter when flowers are scarce. The dense, terminal panicles contain 30-50 flowers. While suitable only for warm climates, orange trumpet creeper will thrive in full sun or partial shade.

There are few more beautiful sights than the pendulous racemes of wisteria when it is in full bloom. The rosy-mauve flowers of *Wisteria floribunda* 'Longissima' appear on slender racemes which are often 100 cm or more long. The sweetly scented flowers open during September and October. The variety 'Alba' has white flowers on shorter racemes while 'Rosea' has pale lilac-pink flowers. Wisteria should be given a sunny, sheltered position.

For very rapid, rampant growth you can't beat dolichos, cobaea or solandra. While *Dolichos lignosus* is an aggressive plant when grown in richer soils, it can be perfect for areas requiring quick cover. The plant is almost covered in pea-shaped, rosy purple flowers during spring. Most situations will suit dolichos, but the flowers are more abundant in full sun. 'Alba' is the white variety.

The growth rate of the cup and saucer vine (*Cobaea scandens*) is truly remarkable. Violet-purple flowers appear freely in spring and early summer among its dense green foliage. Cup and saucer vine's main requirements are a warm climate, sun and protection from strong winds.

Gold cup vine (*Solandra maxima*) is a fast-growing favourite for frost-free climates. Originating in Mexico, this evergreen plant will cover a carport or shed in a summer as it climbs with the aid of its long, stiff stems. The large, shiny green leaves have a pale underside. Large, slightly perfumed, yellow, trumpet-shaped flowers which are 15-20 cm long appear during summer and extend into early winter.

In gardens where ground space is precious climbers may be used to blend the house with the garden by using the walls as a connecting

The ivory–white, fragrant flowers of Chinese star jasmine (Trachelospermum jasminoides) flank this entrance way.

background. Courtyard walls can be draped with sweet-smelling plants, enabling the perfume to pervade both house and garden. Useful for this purpose are pink jasmine (*Jasminum polyanthum*) with its tinted rose-pink and white spring flowers and Chilean jasmine (*Mandevilla laxa*) which is loved for its milky-white summer flowers and quick growth. Give snail flower (*Phaseolus carracalla*) some support and stand back — your wall will be clothed rapidly in unusual light purple and yellow flowers. The flowers have, as the common name suggests, a snail-like appearance. The perfume is heavy and sweet. Carolina jasmine (*Gelsemium sempervirens*), another vigorous climber, gives an extremely decorative display of strongly perfumed, golden-yellow flowers and small, dark green foliage.

For instant perfume and a long flowering period you won't surpass sweet pea (*Lathyrus odoratus*). It grows easily from seed in a sunny position if given an alkaline and well-drained soil.

You should plant self-supporting vines when you wish to cover high walls. Creeping fig (*Ficus pumila*) grows slowly at first but once established becomes quite vigorous. This interesting plant has two kinds of leaves: the small adhering type which are dark green and crinkled and larger dark green ones which grow on arborescent branches. The early spring growth of both types is light brown to green.

Boston Ivy (*Parthenocissus tricuspidata*) is useful for very large walls. The large, glossy green leaves turn to scarlet, yellow and purple in autumn. Silver vein creeper (*Parthenocissus henryana*) has red spring leaves ageing to reddish green with silver veins on the upper surface and purple beneath. During autumn the leaves colour to bright red. Its foliage colour is best when planted in dappled shade.

A trellis covered with a climbing plant makes an ideal screen. It may be used to shield one part of the garden from another, to conceal an ugly view, to provide a windbreak for the vegetable patch or simply to break the monotony of the garden. A screen surrounding a vegetable patch could be covered with climbing fruit like passionfruit, grapes or kiwi fruit. Alternatively climbing beans, peas, chokos or cucumbers may be used.

SELECTING CLIMBERS

It is important when selecting a climber to ensure that its growth habit is equal to its task. The habit should not be too slow or too vigorous and should suit its support. Climbers with hanging flowers, like wisteria, should be displayed over an arch or pergola where the long flower racemes may hang and be fully appreciated. Climbers used on a wall should have

Opposite Old-fashioned enchantment; clematis and wisteria winding over an arch and through a picket fence.

SHADE-TOLERANT CLIMBERS

NAME	TYPE OF SHADE
Beaumontia grandiflora	filtered
Cissus species	full
Clematis aristata	part or dappled
Clematis montana	dappled
Clerodendrum species	filtered
Ficus pumila	full
Fuchsia procumbens	light
Gelsemium sempervirens	part
Hardenbergia comptoniana	dappled
Hedera species	full or part
Hibbertia scandens	part
Hoya scandens	dappled
Kennedia species	part
Lonicera 'Tellmanniana'	full or part
Parthenocissus species	part
Pyrostegia venusta	part
Solanum species	part
Sollya heterophylla	dappled
Stephanotis floribunda	light

Climbers

This extremely old wisteria winds through an aged camphor laurel tree. Surprisingly, the tree does not seem to be affected by this huge plant.

the capacity to cling without support. Climbing plants have various aids which help them to climb. Understanding these aids will enable you to choose the right climber for the right support.

Sucker discs — Some climbers have discs which develop from their long stems for support. The discs find their way into small cracks and joints of masonry or rough timber and hold on with great tenacity. Ivy and Virginia creeper are good examples of climbers which employ sucker discs.

Scramblers — The climbing rose is perhaps the most common example of this type of climber. Scramblers bear hooks or prickles which curve downwards, enabling the plant to attach to another plant or object.

Twiners — The support for this type of climber is given by the stem which coils around itself for support. Wisteria and honeysuckle are good examples.

Tendril climbers — This type of climber spreads by means of thread-like tendrils. Tendrils are usually modified stems, leaves, leaflets or, as in the case of nasturtiums, modified petioles. The entire tendril usually winds itself around the support by developing a spring-like coil.

A SELECTION LIST OF CLIMBERS

Actinidia kolomikta
FLOWER COLOUR White
FLOWERING TIME Late spring and summer
CULTIVATION Grown also for its beautiful leaves which are reddish-green at first, maturing to bright green with the outer half of each leaf white or deep rose-pink. Likes a rich, well-drained soil and a sunny position

Akebia quinata
(five-leaf akebia)
FLOWER COLOUR Lime to slatey-purple
FLOWERING TIME Late winter to early spring
CULTIVATION Prefers full sun but will tolerate some shade

Allamanda cartharica
FLOWER COLOUR Golden; the variety 'Hendersoni' has golden-yellow flowers tinged with brown and purple
FLOWERING TIME Spring and summer
CULTIVATION Needs a warm climate, sunny position and ample summer water
OTHER SPECIES
A. neriifolia — golden-yellow flowers
A. nobilis — bright yellow flowers
A. violacea — reddish-violet flowers

Antigonon leptopus
(Coral vine)
FLOWER COLOUR Bright rose-pink; the variety 'Album' has white flowers
FLOWERING TIME Summer and early autumn
CULTIVATION A sunny position protected from cold winds and a light free-draining soil

Aristolochia elegans
(Dutchman's pipe)
FLOWER COLOUR Purple and white with a yellow-green throat
FLOWERING TIME Summer and autumn
CULTIVATION Requires a hot or temperate climate and a sunny aspect

Bauhinia corymbosa
FLOWER COLOUR Pale rose
FLOWERING TIME Summer
CULTIVATION Suitable for sun or dappled shade in a frost-free area. Keep the soil moist during spring and summer

Beaumontia grandiflora
(trumpet vine)
FLOWER COLOUR White
FLOWERING TIME Spring and early summer
CULTIVATION A fast growing climber that will thrive in a frost-free area in full sun or dappled shade. Likes a great deal of water during spring and summer

Bougainvillea species
FLOWER COLOUR Large colour range depends on the variety
FLOWERING TIME Spring to autumn
CULTIVATION Likes hot, wet summers and dry, mild winters

Campsis grandiflora
(Chinese trumpet vine)
FLOWER COLOUR Terracotta
FLOWERING TIME Summer
CULTIVATION Can be grown in cold and tropical climates but is deciduous in cold climates. Requires full sun

Cissus discolor (trailing begonia)
FLOWER COLOUR Creamy-green but inconspicuous as it is valued for its foliage
FLOWERING TIME Spring
CULTIVATION Likes a warm, humid climate and dappled sunlight or shade
OTHER SPECIES
C. antarctica — bright green leaves

Clematis species
FLOWER COLOUR Depends on the species or variety
FLOWERING TIME Spring to summer
CULTIVATION Most species and varieties will grow in full sun or partial shade. They prefer cool to cold climates and ample spring and summer water
OTHER SPECIES
C. aristata — creamy-white flowers
C. jackmanii — lavender-blue flowers
C. orientalis — orange-yellow flowers
C. montana 'Alba' — white flowers
C. montana 'Rubens' — pink flowers

Clerodendrum splendens
FLOWER COLOUR Brick-red
FLOWERING TIME Late spring to autumn
CULTIVATION Likes a warm climate and partial shade but it will tolerate full sun. Needs protection from strong winds

Clytostoma calliestegoides
(prev. *Bignonia lindleyi*)
(trumpet vine)
FLOWER COLOUR Lavender
FLOWERING TIME Late spring to early summer
CULTIVATION Prefers full sun but will tolerate partial shade. Mulch in spring with manure or compost

This white clematis adds a romantic touch to this gate.

Cobaea scandens
(cup and saucer vine)
FLOWER COLOUR Purplish-green turning violet-purple
FLOWERING TIME Spring
CULTIVATION A sunny aspect with protection from cold wind is ideal. Makes vigorous growth

Congea tomentosa
(shower orchid)
FLOWER COLOUR Pale pink to bright rosy-lilac
FLOWERING TIME Late autumn to early spring
CULTIVATION Requires a warm, frost-free climate and a free-draining soil

Dolichos lignosus
FLOWER COLOUR Rosy-purple
FLOWERING TIME Spring
CULTIVATION A vigorous climber that will thrive in virtually any situation. Prefers temperate and hot climates

Dipladenia sanderi 'Rosea'
FLOWER COLOUR Pink
FLOWERING TIME Throughout the year
CULTIVATION Suitable for full sun or semi-shade. Tip pruning will prevent the growth from becoming scarce

Ficus pumila
(creeping fig)
FLOWER COLOUR Grown for its attractive, dense foliage
FLOWERING TIME N/A
CULTIVATION Suitable for full sun or dense shade. Grows slowly at first but later becomes very vigorous

Fuchsia procumbens
(climbing or trailing fuchsia)
FLOWER COLOUR Red
FLOWERING TIME Late spring through summer
CULTIVATION An excellent plant for seaside gardens as it requires a coarse, well-drained soil. Will grow in full sun or light shade

Gelsemium sempervirens
(Carolina jasmine)
FLOWER COLOUR Golden
FLOWERING TIME Late winter to spring
CULTIVATION Suitable for sunny or partially shaded positions. Tolerant of wind and light frosts

Gloriosa superba
(Glory or climbing lily)
FLOWER COLOUR Lemon-yellow with an orange-scarlet stripe
FLOWERING TIME Summer and autumn
CULTIVATION A warm, sunny position and a temperate to tropical climate

Hardenbergia comptoniana
(native wisteria)
FLOWER COLOUR Deep violet-blue
FLOWERING TIME Spring
CULTIVATION Requires dappled sunlight and a rich, well-drained soil
OTHER SPECIES
H. violacea — deep purple flowers
H. violacea 'Alba' — white flowers
H. violacea 'Rosea' — rosy-lilac flowers

Hedera helix
(English ivy)
FLOWER COLOUR Cream but usually grown for its foliage
FLOWERING TIME Spring to summer
CULTIVATION Thrives in cold climates and is tolerant of poor soil and shade
OTHER SPECIES
H. canariensis 'Variegata' — green leaves edged with cream

Hibbertia scandens
FLOWER COLOUR Yellow
FLOWERING TIME Spring and irregularly during summer and autumn
CULTIVATION A well-drained, sandy soil is the main requirement. Suitable for full sun or partial shade

Hoya carnosa
(wax plant)
FLOWER COLOUR Pinkish-white with a red centre
FLOWERING TIME Summer
CULTIVATION Suitable for warm and tropical climates. Do not cut the flowers as the same flower spurs continue to flower for several years. Prefers partial shade

Hydrangea petiolaris
(climbing hydrangea)
FLOWER COLOUR White
FLOWERING TIME Spring to summer
CULTIVATION Can be grown in sun or partial shade. Prefers a rich, moist soil and should be kept continually mulched

Jasminum polyanthum
(pink jasmine)
FLOWER COLOUR Rose-pink flushed buds that open to white
FLOWERING TIME Spring
CULTIVATION A hardy genus that requires a sunny position and a moderately fertile soil
OTHER SPECIES
J. gracillimum — white flowers
J. nitidum — white flowers
J. officinale 'Grandiflorum' — flowers are white on the inside but reddish outside
J. sambac — white flowers

Kennedia coccinea
(coral vine)
FLOWER COLOUR Scarlet
FLOWERING TIME Late winter and early spring
CULTIVATION A partially shaded position and a well-drained

soil are essential for these Australian native climbers
OTHER SPECIES
K. nigricans — purple-black flowers with a greenish-yellow inner surface
K. prostrata — bright scarlet flowers
K. rubicunda — dusky crimson flowers

Lapageria rosea
(Chilean bell flower)
FLOWER COLOUR Rose-red
FLOWERING TIME Summer
CULTIVATION Prefers a temperate climate and a shady position. The soil should be acidic and ample summer water must be given
OTHER SPECIES
L. rosea 'Albiflora' — white flowers

Lathyrus odoratus
(sweet pea)
FLOWER COLOUR Wide colour range
FLOWERING TIME Spring to summer
CULTIVATION Full sun and protection from wind is required. Sow from seed and water sparingly until the seeds germinate
OTHER SPECIES
L. latifolius — a perennial species

Lonicera 'Tellmanniana'
(honeysuckle)
FLOWER COLOUR Deep yellow-orange. The tips and inside the trumpet are red
FLOWERING TIME Late spring and early summer
CULTIVATION Suitable for full or partial shade
OTHER SPECIES
L. heckrottii 'Gold Flame' — deep rose-coloured flowers which have cream lips

Macfadyena unguis-cati
(cat's paw creeper)
FLOWER COLOUR Yellow
FLOWERING TIME Late spring and early summer
CULTIVATION A hardy climber that can be grown in full sun and in exposed positions in all but the coldest climates

Mandevilla laxa
(Chilean jasmine)
FLOWER COLOUR White
FLOWERING TIME Summer to early autumn
CULTIVATION A trouble-free climber which will grow in full sun or partial shade. Likes ample summer water

Pandorea jasminoides 'Rosea'
FLOWER COLOUR 'Rosea' Pink with maroon throat
'Alba' - milky white
FLOWERING TIME Spring and summer
CULTIVATION An open sunny position and a well-drained soil
OTHER SPECIES
P. jasminoides — white flowers
P. oxleyi — creamy-white flowers
P. pandorana — white flowers with purple markings in the throat

Parthenocissus quinquefolia
(Boston ivy)
FLOWER COLOUR Grown for its large leaves which are purple when they open in spring, change to green throughout summer and become a brilliant red in autumn before falling
FLOWERING TIME N/A
CULTIVATION Can be grown in cold or warm climates. Tolerant of most soils and partial shade but require full sun for good leaf colour
OTHER SPECIES
P. tricuspidata — rich green leaves turn to scarlet, yellow and purple in autumn
P. tricuspidata 'Lowii' — has smaller leaves and more refined growth

Passiflora caerulea
(blue crown passion flower)
FLOWER COLOUR Pinkish-white, blue and purple
FLOWERING TIME Summer and autumn
CULTIVATION Require a frost-free climate and a warm sunny position. The soil should be rich and free-draining
OTHER SPECIES
P. coccinea — vermilion late winter and spring flowers
P. manicata — scarlet flowers with a pale blue centre

Petrea volubilis (purple wreath)
FLOWER COLOUR Violet
FLOWERING TIME Summer
CULTIVATION A warm sheltered position and soil enriched with organic matter

Phaedranthus buccinatorius
(Mexican blood-trumpet vine)
FLOWER COLOUR Orange-crimson with yellow throat
FLOWERING TIME Late spring and early summer
CULTIVATION A warm, sunny aspect with shelter from cold winds and ample summer water

Phaseolus carracalla
(snail flower)
FLOWER COLOUR Light purple and yellow
FLOWERING TIME Summer and autumn
CULTIVATION A warm sunny aspect will produce vigorous growth. Grown in colder climates it becomes partially deciduous

Podranea ricasoliana
(pink trumpet vine)
FLOWER COLOUR Mauve-pink
FLOWERING TIME Summer and autumn
CULTIVATION Suitable for cool and tropical climates in sun or partial shade

Pyrostegia venusta
(orange trumpet creeper)
FLOWER COLOUR Bright orange
FLOWERING TIME Winter to spring
CULTIVATION Suitable for hot and temperate climates. It will grow in shade or sun but flowers better when in full sun

Quisqualis indica
(Rangoon creeper)
FLOWER COLOUR Cream at first

168　CREATING YOUR IDEAL GARDEN

changing to yellow and pink or red
FLOWERING TIME Summer to autumn
CULTIVATION Requires a frost-free area and the warmest part of the garden in full sun

Solandra maxima
(chalice vine or gold cup)
FLOWER COLOUR The bud is yellowish-cream, opening to deep golden-yellow with a dull purple stripe from the throat to each lobe
CULTIVATION A vigorous climber that requires a warm sunny position and soil that is frequently enriched with organic matter

Solanum jasminoides
(potato vine)
FLOWER COLOUR White
FLOWERING TIME Summer and autumn
CULTIVATION Requires a warm sunny position
OTHER SPECIES
S. seaforthianum — blue to violet flowers
S. wendlandii — pale blue flowers

Sollya heterophylla
(Australian blue-bell creeper)
FLOWER COLOUR Pale lavender to deep blue
FLOWERING TIME Spring to mid-summer
CULTIVATION A position in full sun and well-drained soil in a frost free district will produce healthy growth

Stephanotis floribunda
(Madagascar jasmine)
FLOWER COLOUR White
FLOWERING TIME Late spring to early autumn
CULTIVATION Prefers a warm climate and a position in full sun

Stigmaphyllon ciliatum
(Brazilian golden vine)
FLOWER COLOUR Yellow
FLOWERING TIME Summer to autumn
CULTIVATION Requires a hot tropical climate and a sunny position

Tecomaria capensis
(cape honeysuckle)
FLOWER COLOUR Orange-red to scarlet
FLOWERING TIME Summer and autumn
CULTIVATION Requires a frost-free district and a position in full sun

Thunbergia alata
(black-eyed Susan)
FLOWER COLOUR Orange with a black centre
FLOWERING TIME Most of the year
CULTIVATION Hardy plants which will thrive in full sun or partial shade. Tolerant of most garden soils
OTHER SPECIES
T. grandiflora — pale blue flowers
T. gregorii — bright orange flowers
T. laurifolia — pale blue flowers with a yellowish throat

Trachelospermum jasminoides
(Chinese star jasmine)
FLOWER COLOUR Ivory
FLOWERING TIME Late spring to early summer
CULTIVATION A tall climber which is tolerant of most garden soils. Can be grown in full sun or partial shade

Vitis vinifera
(ornamental grape)
FLOWER COLOUR Grown for its vivid crimson autumn leaves
FLOWERING TIME N/A
CULTIVATION Suitable for cold climates only. Grow in full sun and a well-drained soil
OTHER SPECIES
V. amurensis — crimson, orange-scarlet and ruby-red leaves in autumn
V. coignetiae — deep crimson, scarlet and orange leaves in autumn

Wisteria floribunda
(Japanese wisteria)
FLOWER COLOUR 'Alba' — white flowers 'Longissima' — rosy-mauve flowers 'Rosea' — pale lilac-pink flowers 'Violacea Plena' — violet-blue flowers
FLOWERING TIME Spring
CULTIVATION An open, sunny aspect is required with protection from strong winds. Grow in cold to temperate climates
OTHER SPECIES
W. sinensis — lavender blue flowers
W. sinensis 'Alba' — white flowers

FRAGRANT CLIMBERS

Allamanda species
Antigonon leptopus
Bauhinia corymbosa
Calonyction aculeatum
Cestrum nocturnum
Clematis aristata
Dipladenia splendens
Gelsemium sempervirens
Hoya carnosa
Jasminum species
Lathyrus odoratus
Lonicera species
Mandevilla laxa
Phaseolus carracalla
Quisqualis indica
Rosa species
Solandra maxima
Stephanotis floribunda
Trachelospermum jasminoides
Wisteria species

Above *Mauve wisteria scrambling over a pergola imbues this garden with a romantic tone.*

Opposite *A mixture of climbers can transform an otherwise bare paling fence.*

Groundcovers

Groundcovers are a gardener's delight. They enhance the landscape by visually linking unrelated trees and shrubs. On a practical level they are most efficient in hugging and binding the soil on embankments and they are generally easy to maintain. When grown at the base of taller growing trees and shrubs they act as a permanent mulch retaining soil moisture and discouraging the growth of weeds

Landscaping with groundcovers

The name 'groundcovers' is a generic one for a wide range of plant types, including herbs, trailing vines, low growing perennials and shrubs. Annuals will provide quick cover while you are waiting for the slower-growing types to spread.

Most gardens include at least one area situated under trees or eaves in which it is difficult to get anything to grow. Groundcovers are often perfectly suited to such positions and are quite capable of transforming bare earth into a mass of greenery or colour.

It is an unfortunate fact that dry shaded areas have always presented particular difficulties. I have found that ajuga, lamium or ivy will grow successfully in these areas.

Ajuga reptans will grow in sun, dappled or full shade. The bronze-green foliage is highlighted in spring by spires of rich blue-purple flowers. *Ajuga reptans* 'Alba' has glossy leaves which are outstanding when the spikes of white flowers appear. There is also a variegated variety with cream, yellow and green leaves and blue flowers.

Lamium galeobdolon is a rapidly spreading plant which creeps by long arching stolons to form a dense cover. The leaves are evergreen and attractive throughout the year. Beautiful whorled spikes of soft yellow flowers appear in early summer. There is a variegated form with silver and green leaves and the variety 'Silver Beacon' has pure filigree silver leaves. Purple lamium has masses of spires with deep lavender bell-shaped flowers.

Canary Islands ivy (*Hedera canariensis*) will give quick cover, but if it is grown under trees you should ensure that it does not climb them. It will thrive in hot to cool climates. There is also a variegated form. English ivy (*Hedera helix*) will grow well in cold climates, poor soil and shade. There are many varieties including 'Pittsburgh' which has small, dark green, attractively veined leaves. The leaves of 'Aureo-variegata' are irregularly marked and generally tinged with pale yellow, while some

Forget–me–nots form a carpet of blue in spring.

The small daisy–like flowers of babies' tears (Erigeron karvinsckianus), *appear next to the seat in spring and summer.*

are almost wholly yellow. 'Conglomerata' has small dense, dark-green leaves with a ruffled margin and 'Tricolor' features smallish leaves the base colour of which is grey-green overlaid with a creamy-white margin and a reddish edge in autumn and winter.

Helxine soleirolii will fill up shady nooks, and form a bright green carpet of minute, flat, round leaves. The effect is exquisite and the nicest way I have seen them used is as a lawn alternative in a small and infrequently walked-upon area.

Other shade loving groundcovers include *Clivia miniata*, a spreading bulbous plant with long, glossy, deep green strap-like leaves and stems of bright scarlet flowers with a yellow throat in late winter; London pride (*Crassula multicava*) which loves dry shaded areas below trees and produces thick rounded leaves and finely branched tapering spikes of small, starry, pink flowers and *Plectranthus australis* whose dark green leaves have a purplish underside and spikes of light pink lacy flowers in autumn.

Periwinkle (*Vinca major*) is a charming fast-growing old-fashioned groundcover which thrives in both shade and sun. It has shiny leaves and delightful blue flowers throughout most of the spring and summer. The variegated form has deep green leaves handsomely marbled with cream and there is a variety of *Vinca minor* noted for its abundant white flowers.

Fragrant violets have been hybridised for centuries and the leaves and flowers have been used for medicinal purposes, in wine and in fresh salads. According to Greek legend it was customary at Greek burials to cover the dead person with violets to symbolise both beauty and the transitory nature of life. In literature, violets are often associated with modesty and simplicity. In Hamlet Laertes says of his sister Ophelia at her funeral:

*Lay her i' the earth:
And from her fair and unpolluted flesh
May violets spring!*

Violets will thrive in shady areas under deciduous trees. They spread to form a close carpet. *Viola odorata* is the original violet from which many varieties have been formed. It has dark purple flowers and there is also a white form. Worthwhile varieties include 'Culculata' which is vigorous and has extremely fragrant, rich, red-violet flowers; 'Yvonne', whose blue flowers have a pale pink sheen; 'Red Lion' with its magenta flowers which slowly fade to light purple; 'Rosina', loved for its rich pink flowers often used in ladies' posies at the beginning of the century and 'King of the Doubles' which has huge (by violet standards) deep lavender-blue flowers striped with white.

Thyme forms a close-carpeting cover which is ideal for sunny areas between paving stones, on pathways, in the herb garden or underfoot beside a garden seat. Most thymes blossom during summer and the tiny flowers are extremely fragrant. The choice of thymes is enormous and includes the white flowered *Thymus albus* which has been grown since the sixteenth century; *Thymus coccineus*, loved for its deep rosy red flowers; *Thymus* 'Annie Hall' which is a sprawling white-flowered form; *Thymus nitidus* has a mounding habit and soft lavender flowers; grey woolly thyme (*Thymus laniginosa*) whose carpet of grey leaves becomes covered with lavender flowers; golden thyme (*Thymus serpyllum* 'Aureum') which is a golden variety with mauve flowers. *Thymus* 'Magic Carpet' is a vigorous variety having rich pink flowers and parsley thyme (*Thymus integer*) forms a dense mossy carpet the leaves of which (as the common name suggests) smell of parsley.

For very hot sunny areas try woolly yarrow (*Achillea tomentosa*). Its delicate fern-like leaves form a dense mat and are topped with tiny yellow flowers.

Thrift or sea pink (*Armeria maritima*) is an old-fashioned favourite which forms a hummock of mid-grey to green leaves and pink flowers borne on 20 cm tall stems from late spring to mid-summer. This extremely hardy plant will resist drought and sea-spray. Plant it in clumps in front of perennial borders.

Sandwort (*Arenaria montana*) is an enchanting, robust mat-forming plant which is covered in glistening white flowers in spring. Another white flowering groundcover is snow in summer (*Cerastium tomentosum*). Because of its silver-grey leaves it looks wonderful when planted on the border of a white or grey garden or when used to drape over a sunny wall.

My favourite groundcover is babies' tears (*Erigeron karvinsckianus*). These were also favourites of Edna Walling and no tasteful garden should be without them. During spring and summer they are covered in very small daisy-like flowers. They will tumble onto the sides of pathways and because of their self-seeding habit new plants are continually appearing. Babies' tears thrive in full sun and dappled shade but will also grow in full shade, where growth is slower but flowers still appear.

Campanula porsharskyana is a vigorous carpeting perennial which bears a succession of powder blue, bell-like flowers. It will cascade down walls and thrive in the semi-shade.

CHOOSING GROUNDCOVERS

The most important point to consider when choosing a groundcover is that it must be suitable for that particular site. Place shade-lovers under trees and plant the hardier types

GROUNDCOVERS 173

in hot, exposed situations. You must be aware of the groundcover's growth habit, mature size and maintenance requirements. Many groundcovers are rampant and will quickly fill an area as well as taking over anything else in sight. This is fine for areas in which it is difficult to get anything else to grow but the purpose of planting a groundcover will be defeated if time has to be spent removing it from around other plants.

Groundcovers that grow in clumps are generally slower growing than those whose roots run along the ground. Choose leaf colours and texture that will blend with the surrounding plants.

PLANTING

Groundcovers will often survive for years if the soil is properly prepared initially. Before planting, dig in copious amounts of manure or compost. This improves the soil, while feeding the plants. Blood and bone or a soluble complete plant food should be applied in early spring. This will keep the plants healthy and growing at a steady rate.

Mulching around the plants when they are being planted will keep the soil moist and encourage them to grow quickly. To this end use leaf mould, mushroom compost or old grass clippings.

Bugle weed (Ajuga reptans) will often grow where other plants find it difficult. The spires of pretty blue flowers appear in spring.

A SELECTION LIST OF GROUNDCOVERS

Shade-loving Groundcovers

Ajuga reptans (bugle weed)
TYPE OF SHADE Full, semi or dappled
DESCRIPTION The dark green leaves have a metallic purple sheen. Blue flowers are produced on an erect spike during spring and summer.
OTHER VARIETIES
'Burgundy Lace' has cream and maroon leaves.
'Multicolor' has reddish-pink, brown and creamy markings on the green leaves.

Bergenia cordifolia
TYPE OF SHADE Full or semi
DESCRIPTION Large, heart-shaped green leaves make an attractive foliage mass. Stems of rose-pink flowers appear in winter.

Campanula isophylla (Italian bellflower)
TYPE OF SHADE Partial shade in hot climates
DESCRIPTION Violet-blue flowers from late spring until summer.
OTHER SPECIES
C. persicifolia has flowers in shades of blue and white.
C. portenschlagiana has light blue flowers.
C. rotundifolia has violet-blue flowers from spring until summer.

Chlorophytum comosum (spider plant)
TYPE OF SHADE Full or dappled
DESCRIPTION The arching strap-like leaves are striped with yellow or white. New plants are produced on the ends of long shoots.

Convolvulus mauritanicus (glory vine)
TYPE OF SHADE Dappled
DESCRIPTION Shiny green leaves and violet-blue flowers.

Fragaria indica (wild strawberry)
TYPE OF SHADE Semi
DESCRIPTION Strawberry-like leaves and fruit.

Hedera species (ivy)
TYPE OF SHADE Full, semi or dappled
DESCRIPTION Attractive green or variegated leaves. Suitable for areas where nothing else will grow.

Hypericum calycinum
TYPE OF SHADE Full, semi or dappled
DESCRIPTION Green leaves and bright yellow flowers.

Lamium maculatum (dead nettle)
TYPE OF SHADE Full or semi
DESCRIPTION A very hardy groundcover that will thrive in any soil type. Variegated green and silver leaves.

Liriope spicata (lily turf)
TYPE OF SHADE Full or semi
DESCRIPTION Tufts of strap-like leaves and mauve flowers in summer.

Ophiopogon japonicus (mondo grass)
TYPE OF SHADE Full or semi
DESCRIPTION Strap-like dark green and slightly shiny leaves. The white to pale violet flowers appear in summer.

Plectranthus australis
TYPE OF SHADE Full or dappled
DESCRIPTION Dark green leaves with a purplish underside. Light pink or lavender flowers in autumn.

OTHER SPECIES
P. ciliatus has dark green purple-backed leaves and pale mauve flowers.

Saxifraga umbrosa (London pride)
TYPE OF SHADE Semi or light
DESCRIPTION Grown for its rosettes of slightly thick, fleshy mid to dark green leaves. Flower stems are 30-45 cm high and produce loose panicles of small, pink, starry flowers in spring and early summer.

Tradescantia fluminensis (wandering jew)
TYPE OF SHADE Semi
DESCRIPTION Pretty green leaves and flowers.

Vinca major (periwinkle)
TYPE OF SHADE Semi or dappled
DESCRIPTION The glossy almost oval leaves are topped with large mauve-blue flowers.

Viola hederacea (native violet)
TYPE OF SHADE Semi or dappled
DESCRIPTION Kidney-shaped bright green foliage and white to very pale mauve flowers with contrasting violet centres.

Sun-loving Groundcovers

Achillea tomentosa (woolly yarrow)
DESCRIPTION The delicate fern-like leaves form a dense mat. The flowers are a golden yellow.

Armeria maritima (thrift or sea pink)
DESCRIPTION Long green leaves and crowded heads of flowers 3 cm wide on 30 cm stems in white, pink and rosy-red.

Arabis albida (rock cress)
DESCRIPTION A pretty plant having pink or violet flowers in spring.

Arenaria montana (sandwort)
DESCRIPTION An enchanting plant with grey-green foliage and glistening white flowers in spring.

Aurinia saxatilis (basket of gold)
DESCRIPTION Grey-green leaves and bright yellow flowers in spring.

Campanula isophylla (Italian bellflower)
DESCRIPTION A trailing groundcover having pale violet-blue flowers from late spring until summer. The variety 'Alba' has white flowers. In hot climates it requires partial shade.

Campanula persicifolia
DESCRIPTION Flower colour ranges from pale blue to violet-blue and white. In hot climates it requires partial shade.

Campanula portenschlagiana
DESCRIPTION Has green kidney-shaped leaves. Light blue, bell-shaped flowers cover the plant during spring and early summer.

Campanula rotundifolia (bluebells of Scotland)
DESCRIPTION A hardy groundcover which is covered in violet-blue flowers from spring until summer.

Cerastium tomentosum (snow in summer)
DESCRIPTION A low creeping plant that has dense silvery foliage. Daisy-like flowers appear in summer.

Erigeron karvinsckianus (babies' tears)
DESCRIPTION Covered in tiny daisy-like flowers in spring and summer.

Helichrysum species (everlasting daisies)
DESCRIPTION The flowers have a papery texture and are coloured yellow, straw or white. The foliage is silvery.

Phlox subulata (alpine phlox)
DESCRIPTION A fast growing groundcover having an abundance of flowers during spring. The colour range includes blue, pale blue, deep-rose, pink, red and white.

Stachys byzantina (lamb's ears)
DESCRIPTION Has silvery white woolly leaves and rosy-purple flowers.

LAWN ALTERNATIVES

Achillea tomentosa 'Aurea' (woolly yarrow)
Spreads rapidly to give a dense fern-like cover. The foliage is aromatic and yellow flowers appear in summer.

Anthemis nobilis (lawn chamomile)
A perennial groundcover which reaches a height of 10 cm. Prefers a well-drained soil in full sun.

Ajuga reptans (bugle weed)
The dark green leaves have a purple metallic sheen. Can be grown in sun or shade.

Coronvilla varia (crown vetch)
A hardy lawn alternative which will thrive in sun or partial shade. It readily self-sows and has pretty white, pink and lavender clover-like flowers.

Dichondra species (kidney weed)
Forms a dense groundcover remaining green throughout summer. It has kidney-shaped leaves and tiny, white star-shaped flowers. Grow in full sun or partial shade.

Lippia species
One of the hardiest lawn alternatives having bright green leaves and tiny white flowers. Plant in full sun and a well-drained soil. Do not overfertilise.

Mentha pulegium (pennyroyal)
Suitable for shady areas. The leaves have a peppermint taste and fragrance. Plant the divisions 15 cm apart.

Trifolium fragiferum (strawberry clover)
Grows well in all climates, damp conditions and filtered sunlight. Soft pink flowers in summer.

Trifolium repens (white clover)
A pretty groundcover having dark green leaves and white flowers throughout summer. Grows best in full sun but it will tolerate some shade.

Zoysia species
Zoysia grasses reach a height of 15-20 cm and need never be mown. They form a dense felt-like mat and are resistant to heavy traffic. Grow from runners or turf. Very tolerant of salt spray.

A mixture of helleborus and bluebells thrives in dappled shade and looks magical in spring.

Bulbs

Bulbs have an everchanging, enchanting quality. I always find it fascinating that those unimpressive, dull brown bulbs that I take home from the nursery contain the promise of a beautiful flower. A bulb contains the embryo of the entire plant. Roots, stems, leaves and flowers are stored in this form until conditions become favourable for growth. Bulbs have always been associated with spring but it is actually possible to have them flowering throughout the year.

Types of bulbs

We tend to think of any plant that stores its life cycle in an underground fleshy organ as a bulb. But included among these plants are corms, tubers and rhizomes, which have been included in this chapter for simplicity's sake. While the various bulbous plants have their distinct differences, their common factor is their ability to store enough food to sustain them over a period of adverse weather conditions until their above ground growth begins again.

Landscaping with bulbs

Because most bulbs grow in dappled shade they are useful for planting under deciduous trees and in areas of the garden where perhaps other plants may not grow. Left to naturalise, they will form carpets of colour. Bulbs like harlequin flowers (*Sparaxis tricolor*) actually look better if they are left undisturbed, as they resent interference unless very crowded.

Bulbs should always be planted naturally, as if they have been scattered by Mother Nature's free hand. This can be done in lawns or under trees to give a woodland effect.

Clumps or drifts of bulbs should be planted close together so that the random effect is not lost. Use a select few favourite types of bulbs and create flowing patterns of colour. Using one colour and variety in a group will heighten the impact. Daffodils are able to compete with low grass but any foliage must be allowed to die down before being mown. It is during this process that food is stored for the following year's growth.

Bulbs used in garden beds should be in mixed plantings so that their dying leaves are not too obvious. Plant them in perennial borders and plan it so the perennials start flowering as the bulbs are finishing.

Plant fragrant bulbs like lily-of-the-valley, hyacinth and narcissus outside windows, doors and close to garden seats so their perfume can be fully appreciated.

Bulb-filled containers make points of interest when placed through the garden.

BULB CARE

Bulbous plants are among the easiest plants to grow because they are hardy and relatively pest-free. Observing a few precautions will keep them healthy.

The main requirement for healthy bulbs is good drainage. This can be achieved by digging copious amounts of organic matter into the soil before planting.

Bulbs should be fed frequently after the flowers have finished. Bulbs start to store food for the following year at this time and fertilising is important during this period. Either a soluble plant food can be applied or mulch around the plant with manure or compost.

PLANTING DEPTH

A general rule is to plant bulbs at a depth equal to about twice that of the bulb or corm.

CONTAINER-GROWN BULBS

Bulb-filled containers look splendid when placed on patios or verandahs. They also make points of interest when placed throughout the garden. One of the main advantages of growing bulbs in pots is the possibility of bringing them indoors to be enjoyed at the peak of their flowering period. When the bulbs have died down, plant flowering annuals over the top. Most bulbs can be grown in containers but many will thrive loving the crowded root system, and can remain in the same pot for years. Included among these are agapanthus, clivea, freesia, hippeastrum, ixia, muscari, sparaxis and tritonia.

Daffodils and jonquils left to naturalise look spectacular in this woodland setting.

BULB PLANTING DEPTHS

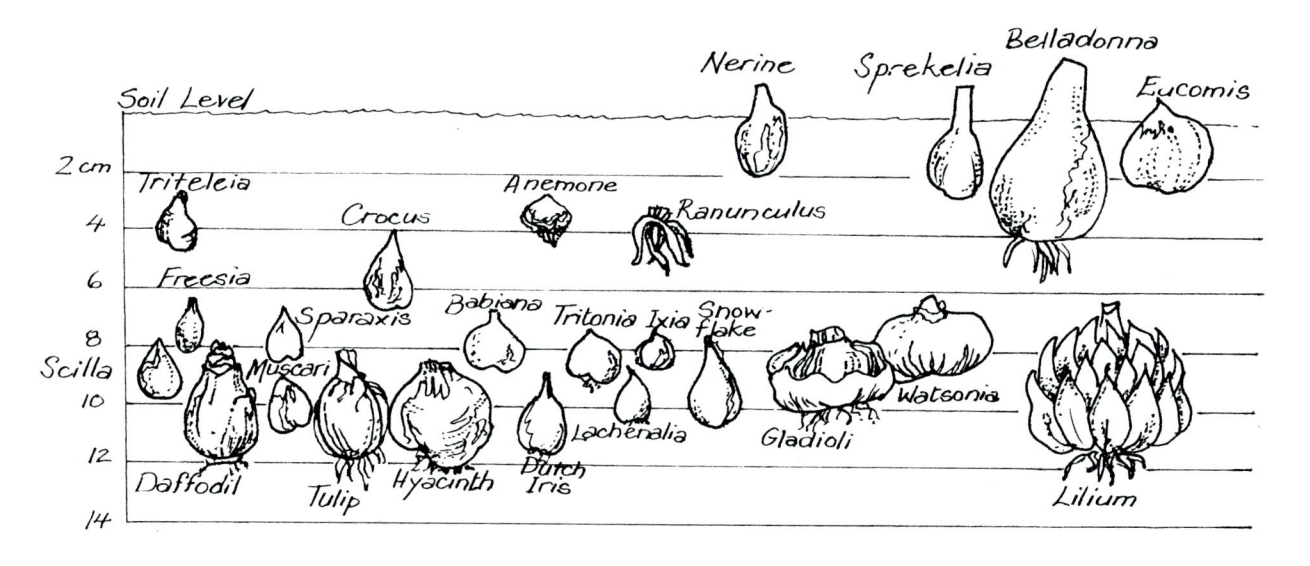

Plant tulips en masse and in one colour only for a stunning effect.

Why bulbs do not flower

True bulbs have already produced the embryo flower within the bulb by planting time. The treatment given to them during the previous season will often determine their performance.

- **Overcrowding** Most bulbs can be left in the ground for years, but sometimes the clumps become so congested they can't produce bulbs of flowering size.
- **Excessive dryness** Lack of water during the flowering season and while the leaves are still green.
- **Too shady** Most bulbs will withstand some shade, but if the bulb is not shade-tolerant it will not be able to make enough food to store for the following year.
- **Foliage removed** The foliage of bulbs should be prematurely allowed to die down naturally.
- **Temperature** Tulips and to a lesser extent daffodils and hyacinths require a cold winter to flower.

A SELECTION LIST OF BULBS

Agapanthus orientalis
(lily-of-the-Nile)
FLOWER COLOUR Blue, white
FLOWERING TIME Summer
CULTIVATION Hardy plants that will thrive in sun or shade
OTHER SPECIES
A. pumila — white and blue flowers

Acidanthera bicolor
FLOWER COLOUR White with purple centres
FLOWERING TIME Summer to autumn
CULTIVATION Open aspect with light shade in hot climates

Allium stipulatum
FLOWER COLOUR Range includes purple, white, pink and yellow
FLOWERING TIME Late spring to early summer
CULTIVATION Resents full shade

Alstroemeria aurantiaca
(Peruvian lily)
FLOWER COLOUR Yellow or orange veined with red
FLOWERING TIME Spring to summer
CULTIVATION Can be left undisturbed for many years. Grow in sum or semi-shade
OTHER SPECIES
A. ligtu — yellow, orange, white, pink scarlet or salmon flowers
A. pulchella — red and green flowers with red-brown spots

Amaryllis belladonna
(belladonna lilies or naked ladies)
FLOWER COLOUR Pink or white, depending on the variety
FLOWERING TIME Summer
CULTIVATION Do not disturb the bulbs unless it is absolutely necessary as they resent root disturbance. Grow in full sun or dappled shade

Bulbinella floribunda
FLOWER COLOUR Bright yellow
FLOWERING TIME Spring
CULTIVATION An acid soil, full sun and a cool or temperate climate are the main requirements

Camassia cusickii
FLOWER COLOUR Pale to deep blue
FLOWERING TIME Summer
CULTIVATION Prefers a heavy, moist soil. Can be left undisturbed for years

Clivia miniata (kaffir lily)
FLOWER COLOUR Scarlet
FLOWERING TIME Late winter to early spring
CULTIVATION A useful plant which will thrive in semi to full shade. Do not overwater

Colchicum autumnale
(autumn crocus)
FLOWER COLOUR Depends on the variety but includes rosy-purple, white, mauve and rose-lilac
FLOWERING TIME Autumn
CULTIVATION Likes a mulch during winter. Grow in full sun or dappled shade

Convallaria majalis
(lily-of-the-valley)
FLOWER COLOUR White
FLOWERING TIME Late winter to early spring
CULTIVATION A well-drained soil and a position in full or semi-shade

Crinum species
FLOWER COLOUR White and shades of pink depending on the species
FLOWERING TIME Summer
CULTIVATION Hardy bulbs in temperate to cold climates. Require full sun and ample summer water

Crocus vernus
FLOWER COLOUR White but there are other colours depending on the variety
FLOWERING TIME Early spring
CULTIVATION Grow in full sun to partial shade and leave the bulbs undisturbed
OTHER SPECIES
C. chrysanthus — golden yellow flowers
C. flavus — yellow flowers but varieties are available in other colours
C. tommasinianus — lilac to pale lavender
C. sativus — lilac to reddish purple and white flowers
C. speciosus — lilac-blue flowers with deeper veins

Cyrtanthus o'brienii (ifafa lily)
FLOWER COLOUR Bright scarlet
FLOWERING TIME Late winter to early spring
CULTIVATION Feed frequently with manure or compost. Will grow in full sun or dappled shade
OTHER SPECIES
Cyrtanthus mackenii — fragrant flowers in tones of white, creamy yellow and pink

Dierama pulcherrimum
(fairy bell)
FLOWER COLOUR Pink
FLOWERING TIME Late spring to early summer
CULTIVATION Adequate moisture is required at all times. Suited to full sun or partial shade

Freesia refracta 'Alba'
FLOWER COLOUR White
FLOWERING TIME Spring
CULTIVATION Avoid overwatering when the foliage has died down. Will grow in full sun or partial shade
OTHER SPECIES
There are many modern hybrids in a variety of colours

The pretty blue flowers of grape hyacinth (Muscari botryoides) appear in late winter. They grow equally well in full sun or partial shade.

Fritillaria imperialis (crown imperial)
FLOWER COLOUR Yellow to rich-red
FLOWERING TIME Spring
CULTIVATION Suitable for cold climates only in a partly shaded position

Galanthus nivalis (true or common snowdrop)
FLOWER COLOUR White with green markings
FLOWERING TIME Late winter to early spring
CULTIVATION Requires a cold climate and a semi-shaded position

Galtonia candicans (cape or summer hyacinth)
FLOWER COLOUR White with green markings
FLOWERING TIME Summer
CULTIVATION Requires plenty of summer water. Will grow in sun or dappled shade. Naturalises freely

Gladiolus species
FLOWER COLOUR Wide range of colours depending on the variety
FLOWERING TIME Summer to autumn
CULTIVATION Prefer a sunny position and a slightly alkaline soil

Haemanthus katherinae (blood lily)
FLOWER COLOUR Salmon-red
FLOWERING TIME Summer
CULTIVATION Suitable for mild climates in a sunny or lightly shaded position

Iris species
FLOWER COLOUR Most colours
FLOWERING TIME Late spring to early summer
CULTIVATION Irises thrive in an open, sunny, sheltered position

Ixia viridiflora (green ixia)
FLOWER COLOUR Metallic blue-green with a dark purple patch at the base of the petals
FLOWERING TIME Spring
CULTIVATION Hardy plants that will thrive in any soil as long as it is well-drained. Will adapt to sun or partial shade

Kniphofia uvaria (red-hot poker)
FLOWER COLOUR Scarlet
FLOWERING TIME Summer
CULTIVATION Good drainage and full sun are the main requirements
OTHER SPECIES
K. uvaria 'Ernest Mitchell' — lemon flowers

Lachenalia aloides (cape cowslip)
FLOWER COLOUR Yellow with a green base and a tip edged in red
FLOWERING TIME Late winter to early spring
CULTIVATION Requires a rich, well-drained soil but will grow in either full sun or semi-shade

Leucojum vernun (spring snowflake)
FLOWER COLOUR White flowers with a green spot on the tips of the petals
FLOWERING TIME Late winter to early spring
CULTIVATION Will grow in any position, sunny or shaded as long as the soil is well-drained

Lilium species
FLOWER COLOUR There are many different species and varieties of liliums in a wide range of colours
FLOWERING TIME Spring to summer
CULTIVATION Liliums prefer a cool to temperate climates. They prefer partial shade especially during the hotter part of the day

Lycoris radiata (red spider lily)
FLOWER COLOUR Red
FLOWERING TIME Autumn
CULTIVATION Spider lily requires a soil rich in organic matter, full sun or lightly dappled shade

Muscari botryoides (grape hyacinth)
FLOWER COLOUR Blue
FLOWERING TIME Late winter to early spring
CULTIVATION Hardy plants that will grow in any garden soil in full sun or partial shade
OTHER SPECIES
M. comosum 'Monstrosum' — the tassel-like flowers are violet-blue

Narcissus species (daffodil, jonquil)
FLOWER COLOUR Colour range is from creamy-whites to yellows and deep rich oranges including pinks and reds
FLOWERING TIME Spring
CULTIVATION Grow in a rich, well-drained soil in full sun or partial shade. A position under deciduous trees is ideal

Nerine bowdenii (spider lily)
FLOWER COLOUR Pink
FLOWERING TIME Autumn

CULTIVATION Full sun and a well-drained soil are the main requirements
OTHER SPECIES
Nerine flexuosa 'Alba' — white flowers *Nerine sarniensis* — crimson flowers

Scilla campanulata (bluebells)
FLOWER COLOUR Blue
FLOWERING TIME Spring
CULTIVATION Prefer a cool, rich soil that is slightly acid. Grow in dappled to half shade
OTHER SPECIES
Scilla peruviana — violet-blue to white flowers

Sparaxis iricolor (harlequin flower)
FLOWER COLOUR Multi-coloured flowers in shades of red, yellow, purple and white
FLOWERING TIME Late spring to early summer
CULTIVATION Can be left undisturbed in the ground for years. Will grow in full sun or semi-shade

Sprekelia formosissima (Jacobean lily)
FLOWER COLOUR Crimson
FLOWERING TIME Late spring to summer
CULTIVATION Likes a warm, sunny situation

Tigridia pavonia (tiger flower)
FLOWER COLOUR Red, spotted with yellow. There are many varieties in a range of colours
FLOWERING TIME Summer
CULTIVATION A warm, sunny position sheltered from strong winds

Tulbaghia violacea (wild garlic)
FLOWER COLOUR Rosy-lilac
FLOWERING TIME Late spring to early autumn
CULTIVATION A sunny or lightly shaded position and a rich soil is required
OTHER SPECIES
Tulbaghia fragrans — lilac-pink flowers
Tulipa species tulips)
FLOWER COLOUR Large range of flower colours depending on the variety
FLOWERING TIME Spring
CULTIVATION A cool climate, sunny or only partly shaded position and a well-drained soil are essential for success with tulips. Feed with a complete plant food when the flowers, stems first appear

Vallota speciosa (Scarborough lily)
FLOWER COLOUR Scarlet-red
FLOWERING TIME Spring
CULTIVATION Prefer a sunny aspect and a well-drained soil

Watsonia species
FLOWER COLOUR Depends on the variety but usually soft pastel colours
FLOWERING TIME Spring
CULTIVATION A hardy plant that is not particular about soil type but prefers a sunny position

Zantedeschia aethiopica (arum or calla lily)
FLOWER COLOUR White
FLOWERING TIME Spring to summer
CULTIVATION A moist soil in a sunny position
OTHER SPECIES
Z. elliotiana — yellow flowers *Z. rebmannii* — wine-red flowers

Zephyranthes atamasco (Atamasco lily)
FLOWER COLOUR White with pink stripes
FLOWERING TIME Spring
CULTIVATION Can be left undisturbed for years. Will grow in sun or semi-shade
OTHER SPECIES
Z. candida — white flowers
Z. citrina — lemon-yellow flowers
Z. grandiflora — rose-pink flowers

The sweetly-scented pink flowers of belladonna lilies (Amaryllis belladonna)

ANNUALS

Nasturtiums flow out of this old wheelbarrow which is being used as an interesting garden accessory.

*Opposite
African daisies (Dimorphotheca species) are hardy spring flowering annuals. Allow them to cascade down banks or along the sides of paths.*

Versatile, colourful and prolific are adjectives that I associate with annuals. Annuals can be interplanted with perennials or spread in drifts throughout the garden. They are perfect in new garden beds when used to cover bare earth and prevent weed growth. Annuals provide quick colour, which can be bold or subtle depending on your garden theme.

LANDSCAPING WITH ANNUALS

Versatile annuals may be used in a variety of ways. They are beautiful when planted *en masse* under trees to create a woodland effect. They are often used as a trim around a garden bed while slower growing hedges or border plants mature. They provide atmosphere and interest planted in terracotta pots and placed in unexpected areas throughout the garden. And, to my mind, they are incomparable when picked and brought indoors for decoration.

Always choose colours that suit the existing colour scheme and ensure that the colours of the annuals don't clash with each other. For example, black pansies associate exquisitely with blue lobelia, blue pansies, or white flowers. Like other pansies, black pansies flower throughout spring and summer. In cool climates they perform year round. They will also grow in semi-shade.

Blue is the first colour to come mind when one thinks of forget-me-nots (*Myosotis sylvatica*). But these pretty annuals are also found in pink and white and thrive in dappled and full shade. Do not remove the plants before they have dropped their seed as all colours will freely self-seed throughout the garden. Their soft growth does not prevent bulbs appearing among them.

Pink catchfly (*Silene pendula*) deserves to be as popular as the forget-me-not because of its ability to grow in sun or semi-shade. Reaching a height of 25 cm, its small pink flowers look delightful in a cottage garden border.

Lovehearts (*Viscaria* species) are also shade-lovers which look marvellous when planted in large drifts under trees. Shade will deepen the colour and prolong the flowering period. Flower colours include mauve, blue and pastel-pink. They are extremely easy to grow, so simply scatter the seeds where they are to grow and flowers will appear twelve weeks later.

The open-faced flowers of busy Lizzie (*Impatiens wallerana*) certainly live up to their common name. Once introduced into the garden (warm climates only) they self-seed and flower prolifically during most of the year. There have been many different colours intro-

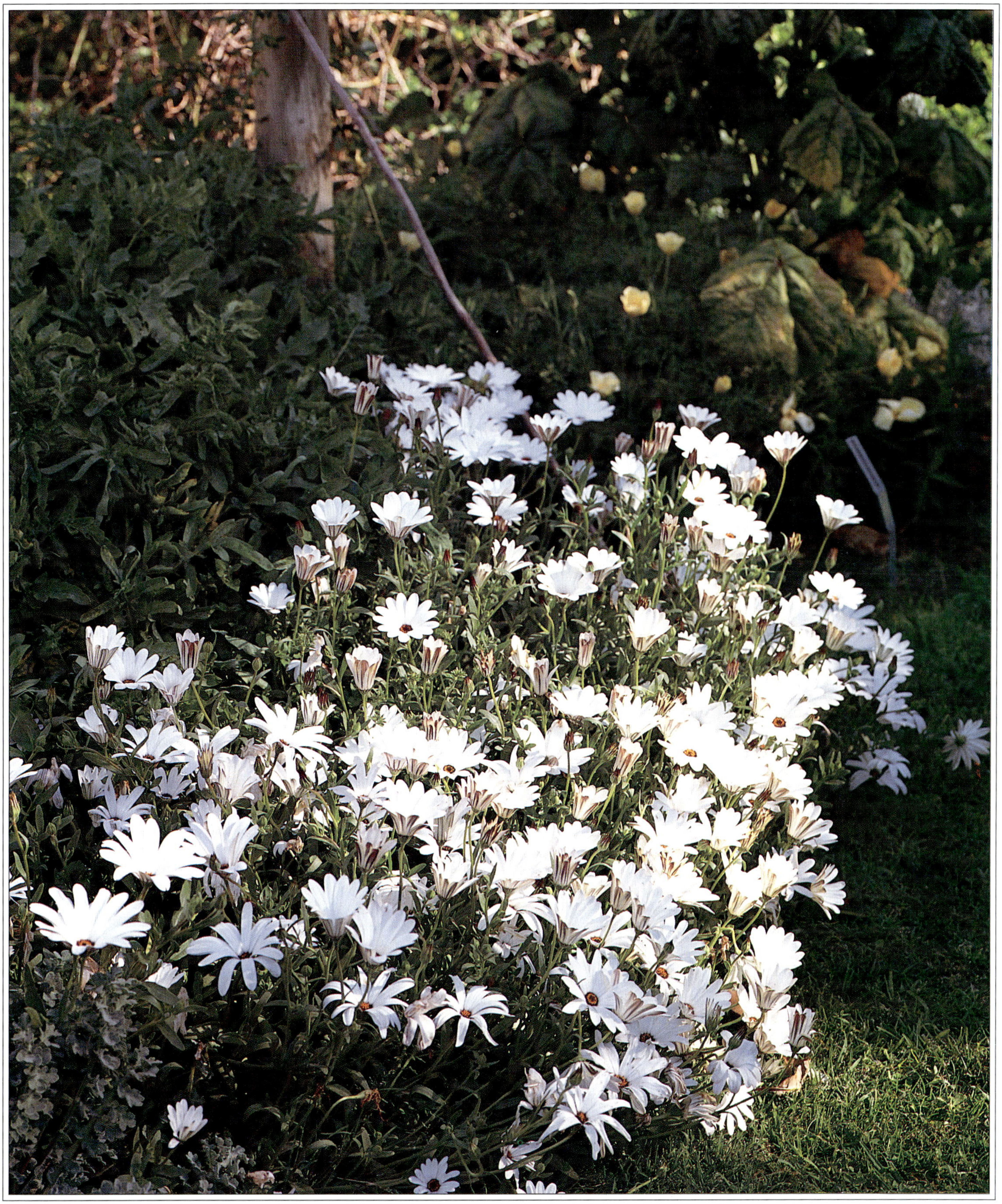

The bright blue flowers of Canterbury bells (Campanula medium) are an interesting sight. Canterbury bells are also available in shades of pink, white, lavender and violet.

duced this season and some of the most attractive are in soft shades of pink and lilac-blue. White is also available and looks spectacular when used in a shade garden among ferns and plants with strap-like leaves.

Honesty (*Lunaria annua*) which is available in white or purple, is an extremely hardy shade loving plant and often thrives where nothing else will grow, reaching a height of about 60 cm. The 'lunar' aspect of its Latin name refers to the silvery-white, moon-like flat seedpods which can be dried and used for indoor decoration. You should always remember to leave some in the garden so that they will reappear the following year.

Wishbone flower (*Torenia fournieri*) has always been a cottage garden favourite. The pretty flower looks like a little deep blue snapdragon with a pale centre. The leaves are bronze-green.

Pincushion flower (*Scabiosa atropurpurea*) has always been a great favourite for bouquets and will thrive and even self-seed in dry soil and a sunny position. The colour range is most attractive with shades of white, blue and purple covering large pincushion-like flowers.

The cleome spider flower is indispensable when attempting to give height to a garden bed. This tall plant grows to 2 m and flowers in whorls of light pink continuously from December to May.

Larkspurs (*Delphinium ajacis*) reach a height of 1 m and will grow in full sun or partial shade. These annual delphiniums have deeply divided leaves and blue, pink, violet or white flowers with a pronounced spur.

Statice (*Limonium sinuata*) is another tall plant that can be picked for indoor decoration and will last for years when dried. Often grown as a perennial, it grows readily from seed and the colour range includes white, yellow, purple, blue and apricot.

Green flowers are rare but when used in the garden they create a cool feeling and tone down brighter colours. Two interesting green-flowering annuals are *Zinnia elegans* 'Envy' which has white and green flowers and grows to 90 cm and bells of Ireland (*Molucella laevis*) which has green bell-shaped flowers. These flowers are produced on long stems and the soft, light green, shell-like leaves provide a compelling feature in annual borders. Both are ideal for cutting and bells of Ireland can be dried easily.

The seed pods of love-in-a-mist (*Nigella damascena*) are highly decorative either in the garden or dried. This freely seeding plant adds a romantic touch to the garden with its feathery mist of pale green, soft, fine foliage. The sky-blue or white flowers appear in spring or early summer in cooler climates.

Plant stocks (*Mathiola incana*) near a window or in a balcony tub so their sweet perfume and subtle colours can be appreciated. The tall flower stalks will last for a several weeks when picked. They are virtually trouble free as long as they are given ample summer water.

Other perfumed annuals include snapdragons (*Antirrhinum majus*) which are favoured for their vivid flowering spikes in cooler weather. They flower twice a year if not removed after the first flush. 'Madame Butterfly F1' has double azalea-like flowers formed with a large and graceful flower spike. Colours include yellow, pink, red and white. The fragrant flowers of wallflowers (*Cherianthus cheiri*) come in rich, deep oranges, purples and burgundy and flower for a long period.

The white African daisy (*Dimorphotheca* species) is ideal when used to cascade down a sunny bank. During spring it is covered in white daisies with a white eye.

The nodding flower heads of poppies are delightful in any garden. Iceland poppies (*Papaver nudicaule*) commence flowering in late winter and will produce masses of flowers for nearly four months. As the name suggests, 'Iceland White' has white flowers but colours include orange, pink and cream. Flanders poppy (*Papaver rhoeas*) is a hardy, self-seeding annual with red flowers and is excellent for naturalising.

CARE OF ANNUALS

The majority of annuals require a rich, well-drained soil. Dig in manure or compost before planting or mulch with the same. When flower buds appear apply a liquid fertiliser and repeat this two weeks later. Always apply liquid fertiliser to a damp soil. If a dry fertiliser is applied make sure it is well-watered around the plant.

SELF-SEEDING ANNUALS

Many annuals have the capacity to shed their seeds throughout the garden and appear the next year in the most unexpected places. Allowing plants to do this gives your garden a sense of intrigue and interest as garden pictures are happening of their own accord.

SELF-SEEDING ANNUALS

Ammi majus	*Nigella damascena*
Eschscholtzia californica	*Papaver* species
Impatiens wallerana	*Primula malacoides*
Lunaria annua	*Silene pendula*
Myosotis sylvatica	*Scabiosa atropurpurea*
Nicotiana species	*Tropaeolum majus*

CHECKLIST FOR GROWING ANNUALS

- Don't plant seedlings too close together. Give plants enough room to reach their full size. You'll receive more flowers.

- Plant sun-loving annuals only in the sun and shade-lovers only in the shade, otherwise the plants will never actually do what they are meant to do.

- Make sure the soil is rich and healthy before planting. Compost or manure can be dug into the soil or used as a mulch.

- Don't plant too early in spring as the soil is colder than the air temperature and the seeds won't germinate.

- Avoid planting in straight rows. Plant in drifts instead for a more informal approach.

A SELECTION LIST OF ANNUALS

Ageratum houstonianum (floss flower)
FLOWER COLOUR White and shades of blue
FLOWERING TIME Warm climates — throughout the year. Cold climates — summer and autumn
CULTIVATION Plant in full sun or lightly dappled shade. Keep moist during summer

Amaranthus caudatus (tassel-flower, love-lies-bleeding)
FLOWER COLOUR Red
FLOWERING TIME Late summer and autumn
CULTIVATION A sunny, dry position with protection from strong winds
OTHER VARIETIES
A. caudatus 'Viridis' — yellowish green flowers
OTHER SPECIES
A. hybridus — red flowers

Ammi majus (Queen Anne's lace)
FLOWER COLOUR White
FLOWERING TIME Spring and summer
CULTIVATION Full sun and shelter from wind

Antirrhinum majus (snapdragon)
FLOWER COLOUR White, cream, pink, red, yellow or orange depending on the variety
FLOWERING TIME Throughout the year
CULTIVATION Place in full sun. Tip prune the plants when they are about 15 cm tall to produce bushier plants and more flowers

Alyssum species (sweet Alice)
FLOWER COLOUR White, lavender or mauve-pink
FLOWERING TIME Spring to summer
CULTIVATION Sow the seed in spring in full sun or partial shade

Calendula officinalis (English or pot marigold)
FLOWER COLOUR Shades of yellow and orange
FLOWERING TIME Late winter and early spring
CULTIVATION Full sun and a well-drained soil are the main requirements

Callistephus chinensis (Chinese aster)
FLOWER COLOUR Shades of pink, white, red, blue and purple
FLOWERING TIME Summer and autumn
CULTIVATION Full sun and protection from strong winds are the main requirements

Campanula medium (Canterbury bells)
FLOWER COLOUR White and shades of blue, lavender, pink and violet
FLOWERING TIME Spring
CULTIVATION Grow in sun or partial shade with protection from drying winds

Celosia cristata (feathery amaranth or cockscomb)
FLOWER COLOUR Red, crimson, yellow or white
FLOWERING TIME Summer and autumn
CULTIVATION Full sun and a well-drained soil

Centaurea cyanus (cornflower or bachelor's buttons)
FLOWER COLOUR Blue, white, pink, maroon or violet-blue
FLOWERING TIME Spring
CULTIVATION Full sun and a rich organic soil

Cheiranthus cheiri (wallflower)
FLOWER COLOUR Orange, yellow, red, brown, crimson or white
FLOWERING TIME Spring
CULTIVATION Grow in full sun and a well-drained soil

Cosmos bipinnatus (cosmos)
FLOWER COLOUR Red, white, or pink with yellow centres
FLOWERING TIME Spring to summer
CULTIVATION Full sun and shelter from strong winds

Delphinium ajacis (larkspur)
FLOWER COLOUR Blue, pink, violet or white
FLOWERING TIME Spring
CULTIVATION Grow in sun or partial shade with protection from winds

Dianthus chinensis (Chinese or Indian pink)
FLOWER COLOUR White, pink, red or lavender
FLOWERING TIME Late winter and spring
CULTIVATION Full sun and a well-drained soil

Eschscholtzia californica (Californian poppy)
FLOWER COLOUR Yellow, orange, scarlet, pink or white

The white flowers of Californian poppy (Eschscholtzia californica) appear in abundance during spring. Once established in the garden, these pretty plants will self-seed every year.

FLOWERING TIME Spring to late autumn
CULTIVATION Full sun. Re-seeds freely every year

Gomphrena globosa (globe amaranth)
FLOWER COLOUR Magenta-purple, violet pink, or white depending on the cultivar
FLOWERING TIME Mid-summer to late autumn
CULTIVATION Full sun and a well-drained soil

Gypsophila elegans (baby's breath)
FLOWER COLOUR White, pink or carmine
FLOWERING TIME Throughout the year
CULTIVATION Easily grown from seed and flowers 8-10 weeks after sowing. Prefers full sun and needs shelter from winds

Helichrysum bracteatum (straw flower)
FLOWER COLOUR White, yellow, orange, tan, rose-pink or red
FLOWERING TIME Early spring to late summer
CULTIVATION Well-drained soil and a sunny position. Ideal for dry inland areas

Iberis umbellata (common annual candytuft)
FLOWER COLOUR Mauve, lilac, pink, purple, carmine or white
FLOWERING TIME Late spring to early autumn
CULTIVATION Require a warm sunny position
OTHER SPECIES
I. amara — white flowers

Impatiens wallerana (busy Lizzie)
FLOWER COLOUR Crimson, red, orange, pink lavender or white
FLOWERING TIME Late spring to late autumn
CULTIVATION A hardy plant that will thrive in poor conditions, sun or semi-shade. Readily self-seeds
OTHER SPECIES
I. balsamina — red, pink, blue or white flowers

Kochia trichophylla (burning bush)
FLOWER COLOUR Flowers inconspicuous. Burning bush is grown for its soft green summer foliage, which changes to reddish-brown in autumn
FLOWERING TIME N/A
CULTIVATION An open sunny position with shelter from strong winds

Lathyrus odoratus (sweet pea)
FLOWER COLOUR All colours except yellow
FLOWERING TIME Late winter and early spring
CULTIVATION A sunny position and a well-drained soil are essential

Linaria maroccana (toadflax)
FLOWER COLOUR Violet-purple, blue, pink, white or yellow
FLOWERING TIME Summer
CULTIVATION Full sun and a neutral soil are the main requirements

Lobelia erinus (edging lobelia)
FLOWER COLOUR Blue to violet colour range and white
FLOWERING TIME Late winter, spring and summer
CULTIVATION Full sun and a well-drained soil will produce an abundance of flowers

Lobularia maritima (sweet alyssum)
FLOWER COLOUR White, lilac, pink or violet
FLOWERING TIME Late winter and spring
CULTIVATION Thrive in any soil in full sun or dappled shade

Lunaria annua (honesty)
FLOWER COLOUR Violet-purple or white
FLOWERING TIME Summer and early autumn
CULTIVATION Suitable for a sunny or shaded situation. Readily self-seeds

Lupinus hartwegii
FLOWER COLOUR Blue, white or pink
FLOWERING TIME Late winter, spring and early summer
CULTIVATION Add lime to the soil before planting. Require a sheltered position in full sun
OTHER SPECIES
L. luteus — yellow flowers *L. mutabilis* — blue, white or pink flowers

Malcomia maritima (Virginia stock)
FLOWER COLOUR Mauve or pink
FLOWERING TIME Spring and summer
CULTIVATION Grow in full sun or partial shade. Flowers appear only six weeks from sowing

Mathiola incana (stock)
FLOWER COLOUR Most colours
FLOWERING TIME Spring
CULTIVATION Stocks appreciate a neutral or slightly acid soil. Plant in full sun with protection from strong winds
OTHER SPECIES
M. bicornis — dark pink flowers

Molucella laevis (bells of Ireland, shell flower)
FLOWER COLOUR Green and white
FLOWERING TIME Summer
CULTIVATION Full sun and a well-drained soil are shell flower's main requirements. Self- seeds freely

Myosotis sylvatica (forget-me-nots)
FLOWER COLOUR Blue, white or pink
FLOWERING TIME Late winter and early spring
CULTIVATION Can be grown in shade or dappled sunlight. Self-seeds freely

Plant stock (Mathiola incana) near a window or on a patio where its delicate but strong fragrance can be appreciated.

188   CREATING YOUR *IDEAL GARDEN*

An informal profusion: pink and white flowering tobacco and borage thrive in this mixed annual and perennial garden.

Nemesia strumosa
FLOWER COLOUR White, cream, yellow, orange, red, scarlet, crimson, blue or purple
FLOWERING TIME Late winter and early spring
CULTIVATION Plant in a mildly acid or neutral soil. Prefers full sun

Nemophila menziesii (baby blue eyes)
FLOWER COLOUR Blue
FLOWERING TIME Spring
CULTIVATION Full sun or partial shade in hot areas

Nicotiana species (tobacco plant)
FLOWER COLOUR White or pink
FLOWERING TIME Spring and summer
CULTIVATION Full sun or partial shade in hot areas

Nigella damascena (love-in-a-mist)
FLOWER COLOUR Blue, pink or white
FLOWERING TIME Spring
CULTIVATION Grow in full sun or partial shade

Papaver nudicaule (Iceland poppy)
FLOWER COLOUR Red, orange, yellow, pink or white
FLOWERING TIME Winter to early spring
CULTIVATION Full sun and a well-drained soil are essential

Papaver rhoeas (Flanders poppy)
FLOWER COLOUR Red
FLOWERING TIME Spring to summer
CULTIVATION A hardy, self-seeding annual which prefers full sun

Petunia hybrida
FLOWER COLOUR Most colours
FLOWERING TIME Summer and early autumn
CULTIVATION Well-drained soil and a sunny position

Phlox drummondii (annual phlox)
FLOWER COLOUR Wide colour range
FLOWERING TIME Summer and autumn
CULTIVATION Full sun with ample summer water

Primula malacoides
FLOWER COLOUR Mauve, purple, pink, white or carmine
FLOWERING TIME Winter and early spring
CULTIVATION Flower abundantly in sun or semi-shade. The soil should be neutral or slightly acid

Reseda odorata (mignonette)
FLOWER COLOUR Shades of red and yellow
FLOWERING TIME Winter and spring
CULTIVATION A rich, well-drained soil in an open sunny position

Silene pendula (pink catchfly)
FLOWER COLOUR Pink
FLOWERING TIME Spring to summer
CULTIVATION Easily grown in sun or semi-shade. Freely self-seeds

Salpiglossis sinuata (painted tongue)
FLOWER COLOUR Wide colour range
FLOWERING TIME Spring and summer
CULTIVATION Full sun with protection from strong winds

Salvia splendens (scarlet sage)
FLOWER COLOUR Shades of red, purple or white
FLOWERING TIME Summer, autumn and early winter
CULTIVATION A sunny position and a well-drained soil. Cut back severely after flowering to induce flowering the following year

Scabiosa atropurpurea (pincushion flower)
FLOWER COLOUR White, blue, purple and pink
FLOWERING TIME Spring to summer
CULTIVATION Will thrive in a dry soil and a sunny position

Schizanthus X wisetonensis (poor man's orchid or butterfly flower)
FLOWER COLOUR White, shades of pink, lavender, mauve, maroon or purple
FLOWERING TIME Winter and early spring
CULTIVATION Likes a warm climate and a position in dappled shade

Senecio X hybridus (cineraria)
FLOWER COLOUR Wide range
FLOWERING TIME Late winter and early spring
CULTIVATION Cinerarias will thrive in shade and well-drained soil

Tagetes erecta (African marigold)
FLOWER COLOUR Lemon, yellow or deep orange
FLOWERING TIME Spring and summer

When the flowers are picked frequently pansies produce increasing numbers of flowers.

CULTIVATION A sunny position and ample water during dry periods are the main requirements
OTHER SPECIES
T. patula — shades of red, yellow and orange flowers

Torenia fournieri (wishbone flower)
FLOWER COLOUR Deep blue
FLOWERING TIME Summer
CULTIVATION Plant in full sun or partial shade

Tropaeolum majus (nasturtium)
FLOWER COLOUR Orange, scarlet, red, yellow or white
FLOWERING TIME Spring, summer and autumn
CULTIVATION Plant in moderately fertile soil, otherwise lush growth appears at the expense of the flowers. Full sun or shade

Verbena x hybrida (vervain or garden verbena)
FLOWER COLOUR Wide range of colours
FLOWERING TIME Late spring, summer and early autumn
CULTIVATION Grow in full sun or partial shade in moderately fertile soil

Viola tricolor (heartsease)
FLOWER COLOUR Wide variety of colours
FLOWERING TIME Late winter and early spring
CULTIVATION Plant in full sun or dappled soil. Although it is a small plant, it requires a rich soil. Picking the flowers regularly encourages more to appear
OTHER SPECIES
V. X wittrockiana — wide variety of colours

Viscaria species (lovehearts)
FLOWER COLOUR Pink, red, white and blue
FLOWERING TIME Spring and summer
CULTIVATION Grow in full sun or dappled shade

Zinnia elegans (youth and old age)
FLOWER COLOUR Wide colour range
FLOWERING TIME Spring and summer
CULTIVATION A warm position and full sun with protection from wind are the main requirements
OTHER SPECIES
Z. haageana — flower colour includes yellow, orange and shades of red

Bird-attracting Gardens

Birds add the dimension of sound to the garden. As the seasons change so do the birds, with some species coming and going throughout the year. One does not need to be an ornithologist to be aware of the presence of different species throughout the year. Honeyeaters probe into flowers looking for nectar while some insect-eating birds help rid the garden of pests.

To successfully attract birds, food, shelter and water should be provided. Food is supplied easily by planting a selection of nectar-rich trees and shrubs. These nectar-producing plants attract both the honeyeaters and the small insects, and the latter attract birds of the insect eating group.

A birdbath, or more simply a shallow bowl, can provide adequate water. Birdbaths should not be placed too far out in the open as most birds feel safer when there is some protective shrubbery around. Tuck birdbaths into corners or place them among plants in an herbaceous border. Better still, place them near a window of the house from which the birds' activities can be observed. Birdbaths should be raised off the ground on a stem to minimise the attention of cats. Most birds prefer water about 25 mm deep.

Trees and shrubs provide a secure vantage point from which birds are able to survey the garden. Tall trees enable birds to check that there no dangers before feeding. They provide the over-storey but lower-growing shrubs are required for an under-storey. Providing a wide variety of plants will ensure that your garden will attract a wide variety of birds.

Many birds are natural predators and provide an organic form of pest control. Chemical pest control is definitely unsuitable if you desire a bird haven and will become unnecessary as biological control takes over. Chemicals kill the butterflies and insects that are food for birds. In a strictly organic garden birds will control insect plagues, feeding hungrily on caterpillars, grasshoppers, shield bugs and dragonflies.

Most species of eucalyptus are visited by parrots from time to time and hollow branches frequently provide nesting sites. *Eucalyptus leucoxylon* can be grown in small gardens and is covered in a profusion of white to deep pink flowers in spring and summer. Another smaller tree that makes an excellent screen plant because of its rounded habit is *Eucalyptus lehmannii*. The dense clusters of yellow-green flowers appear in spring or summer.

Other native trees include species of callistemon. *Callistemon salignus* is particularly attractive, with its long cream bottlebrush flowers in spring and summer. The red flowers

Honey–eaters flock to the large amounts of nectar found in Callistemon flowers.

of crimson bottlebrush (*Callistemon citrinus*) appear in early summer and again during autumn. The many species of melaleuca, commonly called honey myrtles or paperbarks, are rich with nectar. The species range in size from tall trees to dwarf shrubs and will grow in habitats ranging from dry to damp. Another favourite tree is the lilli-pilli (*Syzygium luehmannii*) which has a wealth of white fluffy flowers in spring followed by red pear-shaped berries. The fruits can be turned into a delightful jam if you are able to pick them before the birds get them.

Surprisingly enough, it is not necessarily the flowers of wattle (*Acacia* species) that attract birds. A nectar-producing gland at the junction of the leaf and stem actually provides them with food. *Acacia pycnantha* — the acknowledged floral emblem of Australia — is most beneficial in a bird-attracting garden as it regenerates readily and will often form thickets. The large flowers appear in spring.

The large, cone-like flowers of the banksia genus are unique. Two popular winter flower-

Tucking birdbaths among shrubbery or tall growing perennials makes birds feel secure.

Opposite The red flowers of Callistemon citrinus *are rich in nectar. Just one or two native trees in the garden will attract birds.*

ing species are *Banksia ericifolia* and *Banksia spinulosa*. All the species are bird-attracting as the nectar is replenished daily and provides a continual supply to honey-eating birds. The hard seeds are a favourite food for the yellow-tailed black parrots.

Calothamnus is a valuable plant, as it has an extremely long flowering period during spring and summer. During the remainder of the year there are always some flowers on the bush. Rough netbush (*Calothamnus asper*) has drooping heads of dark red flowers and *Calothamnus rupestris* has showy deep pink or red flowers.

Grevillea, like calothamnus, flower prolifically and generally have some flowers on the plant throughout the year. For some reason birds are often more attracted to the species with red or pink flowers. *Grevillea aspleniifolia* has deep pink flowers throughout the year as does *Grevillea hookerana* with its red toothbrush-like flowers. The long flowering pink spider flower (*Grevillea sericea*) has white to deep pink flowers.

Bird-feeders hung from trees will encourage the presence of birds.

Bird-attracting plants

Name	Type of plant	Comments
Acacia species (wattle)	trees/shrubs	Different species flower at various times throughout the year.
Anigozanthos species (kangaroo paw)	rockery	Flowers last for a long period.
Banksia species	trees/shrubs	Large flowers attract honeyeaters.
Beaufortia orbifolia (Ravensthorpe bottlebrush)	shrub	Lime-green and red flowers.
Callistemon species	trees/shrubs	Bottlebrush-like flowers in various colours.
Calothamnus quadrifidus (net bush)	shrub	Bright red flower spikes.
Calothamnus rupestris	shrub	Pine-like leaves and red flower spikes.
Correa species	shrubs	Tubular flowers.
Epacris impressa (common heath)	shrub	Tubular flowers of white, pink or red.
Eucalyptus species	trees	Flowers rich in nectar.
Grevillea species	shrubs	Birds especially attracted to red and pink-flowering species.
Hakea species	trees/shrubs	Nectar-filled flowers attract honeyeaters.
Kunzea baxteri (Baxter's kunzea)	tree	Bright red flower spikes have gold tips.
Melaleuca species	trees/shrubs	Bottlebrush-like flowers.
Melia azedarach 'Australasica'	tree	Parrots particularly attracted to the fruit.
Olea paniculata (native olive)	tree	Birds love the bluish-black fruit.
Prostanthera species	shrubs	Aromatic leaves and masses of flowers usually in spring.
Syzygium species (lilly-pillies)	trees	Fruits particularly tasty to humans and birds.
Telopea species	shrub	Large red flowers filled with nectar.

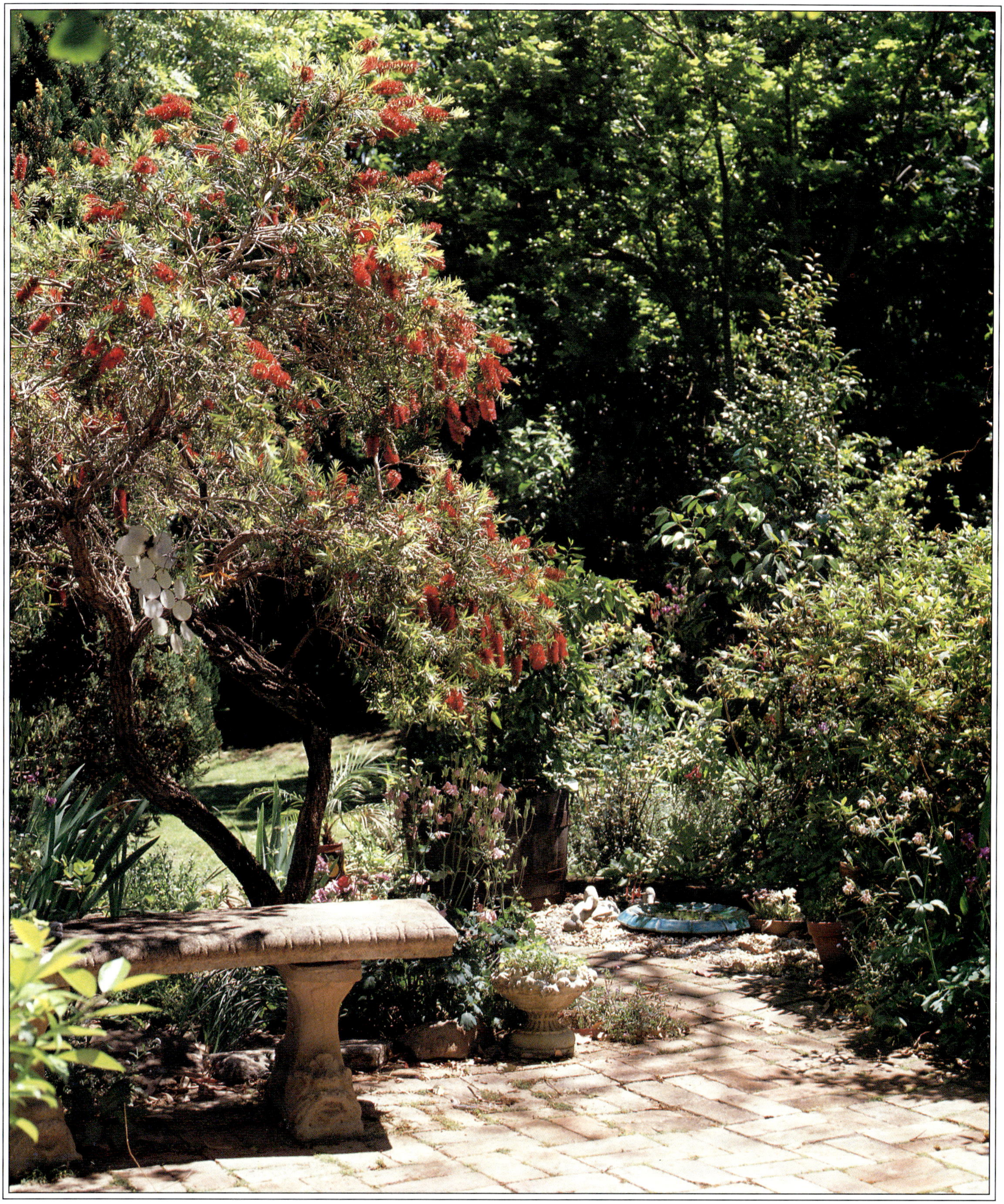

A Butterfly Garden

Gardens are living entities, full of changes centred around plant life and a range of living beings including butterflies. The delight experienced by watching the colour and movement of butterflies cannot be overstated. Spring, which we always associate with blossoms and warm weather, also brings a proliferation of butterflies.

Butterflies can be attracted to any sized gardens by the presence of nectar-producing plants which provide their food. Despite the popular misconception that they chew leaves, butterflies in fact live solely on flower nectar. For this reason no native butterflies are garden pests. The common 'white butterfly' which feeds voraciously on cruciferous plants is an introduced species.

A mixture of native and exotic plants will attract butterflies just as effectively as a fully native garden. The essential criteria for butterfly attracting plants are the production of nectar and the presence of scent. Unfortunately, many modern over-cultivated species have little nectar and virtually no scent and should thus be avoided.

Among the natives the soft-white to cream, daisy-like flowers of flannel flower (*Actinotus helianthii*) and the golden flowers of the everlasting daisy (*Helichrysum bracteatum*) are absolutely irresistible to butterflies. Flowers of both these species are produced from spring until summer.

Other spring/summer *Bird-attracting Gardens* native flowers include the matted pea bush (*Pultenaea pedunculata*), a trailing plant with yellow-orange pea-flowers; showy parrot-pea (*Dillwynia sericea*) with its massed spikes of orange to yellow pea-like flowers; purple coral pea (*Hardenbergia violacea*) which is a popular climbing or trailing plant that becomes covered in rich purple flowers and, of course, several species of the crimson-flowered callistemon or bottlebrush species and cultivars.

The butterfly bush (*Buddleia davidii*) with its lilac-like flower spikes is best known of the exotic butterfly-attracting plants. Not a summer day passes without butterflies hovering over its nectar rich flowers.

Other sought after plants include French or English lavender, yarrow (*Achillea millefolium*), thrift (*Armeria maritima*), wild strawberry (*Fragaria alpina*), pinks (*Dianthus* species), Michaelmas daisies (*Aster novi-belgii*). The flowers of most herbs and cornflowers will also attract butterflies.

Citrus trees provide a rich source of nectar,

Butterflies are attracted to the nectar of flowers.

and some butterflies like the Orchard Swallowtail and the Dingy Swallowtail seek out the trees and lay their eggs on young shoots.

Even a lazy gardener can have a butterfly garden as many butterflies depend on weeds for their existence. Small soft grasses left unmown will quickly attract the common Brown Butterfly and milkweed will attract the Monarch or Wanderer Butterfly. The milkweed itself is a source of larval food. The larvae are generally safe from attack as birds find them distasteful.

A profusion of flowers in a summer perennial border will entice numerous butterflies.

BUTTERFLY-ATTRACTING PLANTS

NAME	TYPE OF PLANT	COMMENTS
Achillea millefolium (yarrow)	perennial	Yellow flowers during summer.
Actinotus helianthii (flannel flower)	annual	Soft white to cream daisy-like flowers.
Armeria maritima (thrift)	perennial	Pink flowers.
Aster novi-belgii (Michaelmas daisy)	perennial	Wide colour range of flowers.
Buddleia davidii (butterfly bush)	shrub	Lilac flowers.
Centaurea cyanus (cornflower)	annual	Blue, pink or white flowers.
Dianthus species (pinks)	perennial	Pink carnation-like flowers.
Dillwynia sericea (showy parrot pea)	shrub	Orange to yellow pea flowers.
Fragaria vesca (wild strawberry)	perennial	Red fruits are edible.
Helichrysum baxteri (everlasting daisy)	annual	White and yellow flowers.
Helichrysum bracteatum (golden everlasting)	annual	Large golden flowers.
Hyssopus officinalis (hyssop)	perennial	Rose coloured to bluish-purple flowers.
Iberis umbellata (candytuft)	perennial	White flowers.
Lavandula species	shrubs	Purple, lilac, white or pink flowers depending on the species.
Lunaria annua (honesty)	annual	Purple or white flowers.
Olearia cillata (fringed daisy bush)	shrub	Pale to bright purple daisies.
Pimelea ferruginea	shrub	Pink flowers.
Primula species (polyanthus)	perennial	Range of flower colours.
Pultenaea pedunculata (matted bush pea)	shrub	Orange/yellow and red flowers.
Syringa species (lilac)	shrub	Mauve, purple or white flowers.
Thymus species	perennial	Pink, white or lilac flowers.
Viola odorata (violets)	perennial	White, pink or purple flowers.

SHRUBS

The choice of shrubs is a key element in creating a garden. As a garden designer, I have found that the placement and qualities of shrubs are sometimes overlooked. This is because shrubs provide the background setting for a garden scene and most people give their attention to the colourful, more spectacular foreground plants. But it should be remembered that it is against the shrubs that everything else is seen.

LANDSCAPING WITH SHRUBS

Shrubs give structure, form and texture to the garden. In my view, groupings of shrubs should be bold and simple. Balance is the essence of good design when using shrubs, and this principle applies to both formal and informal gardens. In a formal garden the balance will be more obvious, but in an informal garden care must be taken that balance is not overlooked.

A correct balance leads to a sense of continuity when different types of plants are used. It is important to taper the shrubs in order of height, with taller ones at the back, medium ones in the middle and low growers at the front.

Place shrubs with light coloured foliage in front of those with dark foliage. The sun shining on the lighter leaves looks particularly intense and striking against a dark backdrop.

Do not base your choice of shrubs completely on flower colour as the different hues of green in the foliage give a sense of contrast in the garden. In addition to green foliage many shrubs have grey, red, purple, yellow or variegated foliage. And one should not overlook seasonal colour changes that come with the bare bark and branches of winter, the bright new growth and flowers of spring, the more muted tones of summer, and the fruits and changing foliage of autumn.

Variety can be achieved by selecting shrubs with different base, branching forms and leaf texture. Small leafed shrubs make the garden seem larger as they create an illusion of space while larger leaves seem to attract your attention and lessen the feeling of distance.

Feature shrubs, the stars of your garden, should be used to maintain sculptural and colour interest throughout the year.

Azaleas and rhododendrons are among the most popular of flowering shrubs. Vireya rhododendrons are hybrids of the tropical varieties and will thrive in warm climates if given light shade. The bell-like flowers are generally held in loose clusters. Pink shades include 'Pink Delight', 'Carillon Bells', 'Flaming Lady' (a very bright pink as the name

The simple white flowers of mock orange blossom (Philadelphus coronarius) *have a subtle fragrance.*

Azaeleas thrive in the dappled shade of this enchanting woodland setting.

suggests) and 'Lady Di' which is the softest of pinks. *Rhododendron lochae* is a northern Australian native featuring bright red flowers.

Many shrubs have aromatic foliage which is interesting throughout the year. 'Where rosemary rules, so does the mistress' is an early saying, and whether this is true or not, rosemary is certainly one of the most aromatic shrubs. Plant it alongside pathways or let the prostrate variety tumble over walls. Rosemary makes an effective garden divider when clipped as a small hedge.

The silver foliage of cotton lavender (*Santolina chamaecyparissus*) has a chamomile-like redolence. The bright, lemon-yellow flowers in summer add to its appeal.

The Australian native mint bushes (*Prostanthera* species), are popular because of their rapid growth, wealth of spring flowers and the mint-like fragrance of their leaves which led to their common name. *Prostanthera caerulea* is covered in an abundance of blue flowers during spring; *Prostanthera incana* is popular because its mauve flowers stay on the shrub for a long period; *Prostanthera lasianthos* will grow in full shade or sun and is a very useful screen plant.

The bark, stem, twigs and buds of deciduous shrubs offer a kaleidoscope of winter textures. The effects may be either delicate and subtle or bold and dramatic. Plant deciduous shrubs among or in front of evergreens. A particularly interesting deciduous shrub with

Rhododendrons and azaleas flank a charming pathway.

SHRUB SHAPES

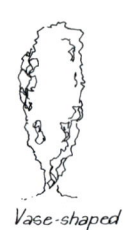

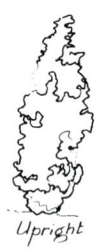

Rounded

Vase-shaped

Upright

Spreading

contorted, corkscrew-like branches (*Corylus avellana* 'Contorta') has the common name Harry Lauder's walking stick after the well-known comedian. Reaching a height of 2-3 m, it is at its best when the long, pendulous catkins appear before the leaves.

Other deciduous shrubs for winter effects include Tartarian dogwood (*Cornus alba*) the twigs of which create interesting patterns; red osier (*Cornus sericea*) with its red branches; *Acer palmatum* 'Dissectum Atropurpureum' which has bronze branches and witch hazel (*Hamamelis mollis*) which carries fragrant golden-yellow and red flowers on its bare branches.

Where large, fast-growing shrubs are needed for screening try *Abelia grandiflora*, *Coprosma repens*, *Feijoa sellowiana*, *Hakea salicifolia*, *Jasminum mesnyii*, *Photinia robusta*, *Pittosporum eugenoides* and most shrubby wattles (*Acacia* species). It is often difficult to find shrubs that are tolerant of the seaside but there are some that will actually thrive there. Included among these are *Cassia bicapsularis* with its golden-yellow flowers; rock rose (*Cistus purpureus*) whose large rose-red, saucer-shaped flowers have a yellow centre with a chocolate blotch at the base of each petal; *Cistus laurifolius*, another rock rose but with white flowers; *Leptospermum laevigatum* which has white flowers in spring; Indian hawthorn (*Raphiolepis umbellata*) which will grow in sun or shade and has white flowers in dense terminal panicles and coastal rosemary (*Westringia fruticosa*) which bears white flowers for most of the year.

For shady areas try Chinese lanterns (*Abutilon* species) but give them no less than half shade if a good flower display is required; Mexican orange blossom (*Choisya ternata*) with its abundant clusters of crisp, white, fragrant flowers; *Fatsia japonica* which is grown for its large, leathery handsome leaves; hydrangeas with their large blue, pink or white flower heads; *Mahonia* species whose yellow flowers provide an interesting variation and *Luculia gratissima* which is loved for its extremely fragrant pink winter flowers.

For a truly arresting visual display, plant *Acalypha hispida*, whose rosy-red flowers resemble foxtails and reach 50 cm in length.

Calliandra tweedii is an adaptable shrub suitable for tropical or temperate climates. Its bright red, pompom like flowers sit above the finely divided dark green foliage.

For beautiful blue flowers you can't surpass the blue butterfly bush (*Clerodendrum ugandense*) which certainly resembles its common name. This hardy shrub will grow in temperate or tropical climates and will adapt to full or half sun.

Euphorbia wulfenii is a handsome, small, soft-wooded shrub with deep bluish-green leaves. Each stem terminates in a large umbel of greenish-yellow bracts. It makes an interesting, low growing feature shrub.

A large bird is the feature of this topiary garden. Neatly clipped hedges surround pathways and rose beds.

Below This dog tucked away in a corner of the garden creates an element of surprise.

The male catkins of the silk tassel bush (*Garrya elliptica*) hang from the outer branches like strings of silk-textured beads and look wonderful against its dark, leathery foliage. Plant the silk tassel bush in cool or temperate climates.

Laburnums are among my favourite shrubs, and one of the loveliest is *Laburnum vossi*, which has long (35 cm), yellow flowers and graceful arching branches. When planted on both sides of a path it forms a lovely arch.

Hedges within the garden

Hedges may be used to separate areas of the garden or be used formally to surround a kitchen or herb garden, a rose garden or maybe a perennial garden brimming with flowers. Hedges used in this manner were part of the cottage garden tradition. Areas of lawn can be divided into shaped beds, and inside an orderly profusion of vegetables and flowers can grow in harmony.

A low growing hedge bordering a path or driveway will look elegant and arresting. Or perhaps a small hedge can be used as a *piece de resistance* at the back of a small pool, fountain or statue. Suitable plants for small hedges include lavender (all species), box, yew, rosemary, *Artemisia lactiflora* and clipped azaleas.

TRAINING A FORMAL HEDGE

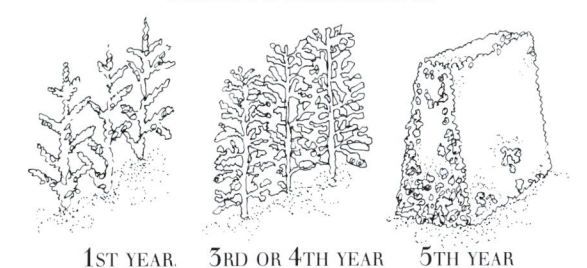

1ST YEAR.   3RD OR 4TH YEAR   5TH YEAR

The variety of shrub shapes in this garden maintains sculptural and colour interest throughout the year.

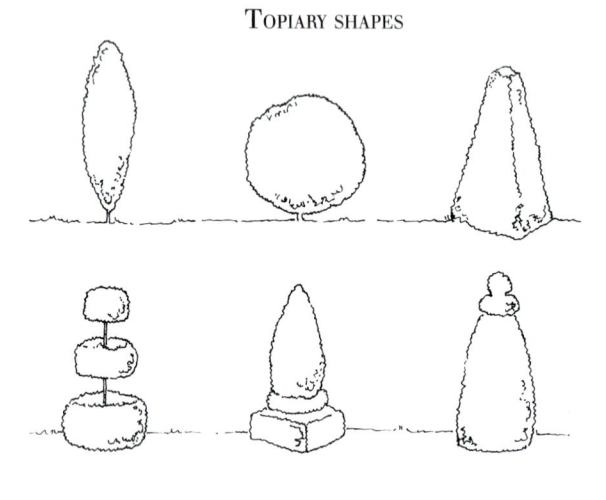

TOPIARY SHAPES

Topiary

Topiary was practised extensively by the ancient Egyptians and Romans and was used as a strong decorative element in the garden. Over the years a variety of plant shaping possibilities have emerged. Topiary designs may be classical, contemporary, simple or elaborate. Topiary may consist of a perfectly shaped hedge with windows or arches cut through it or an animal shape, like a duck or horse.

There is a revival of this form of gardening and the design elements that have been practised over the centuries can be used to our advantage.

Topiary can be used as living sculpture providing a softer alternative to stone statuary. Topiary hedges are often used to frame a garden or one strategically placed topiary plant may be used as a centrepiece. A pair of topiary shapes may also be used to flank a set of steps or a pathway. Topiary adds elegance to a garden by reinforcing the layout of a formal garden, providing a backdrop for a cottage garden or adding an element of surprise. You do not need a classical garden, as topiary is suited to any design. Where possible design the topiary, whether it be a hedge or just one piece, with the initial garden ground plan.

Large terracotta pots containing a topiary shape will enliven even the dullest areas. The two chief plants used for topiary are yew (*Taxus baccata*) and box (*Buxus sempervirens*) but I have seen magnificent topiary shapes formed from grevillea (*Grevillea rosmarinifolia*), holly and bay tree (*Laurus nobilis*).

Topiary hedges

Apart from topiary shapes, hedges have formed a major aspect of topiary. This aspect is ideal for today's smaller gardens where space is limited, because you can control the dimensions. Hedge topiary takes up less space than an informal row of trees and shrubs. Once the desired height of a hedge has been achieved, you can embellish the design by creating piers, windows or arches in the hedge. A window or arch cut through the hedge should highlight a view. An arch may lead to another part of the garden or to a quiet sitting area. Piers can be square, round, or perhaps shaped like an imaginary mythical bird or beast.

Other simple decorations for a hedge might include finials, turrets, scalloping or some other type of sculptural detailing.

Topiary hedges used as a backdrop for a garden seat or a large statue can look stunning.

Knot gardens

Knot gardens evolved from medieval kitchen gardens which contained separate beds for medicinal and cooking herbs to avoid confusion. These gardens originally consisted of four square compartments within a larger square. In each compartment there were different patterns. There were literally hundreds of different designs and third dimensions were added by dotting the corners or centres of each knot with ornamental topiary shapes. The hedges for these knot gardens were traditionally herbs but boxwood (Buxus sempervirens) has remained the most popular because of its slow growth and small, dark green leaves. The garden beds within the knot can be filled with a profusion of flowers and herbs or the knot itself can become the design focus, with the spaces filled with gravel or bare earth. This makes an interesting but low maintenance garden and one that looks just as good when viewed from an upstairs window or at ground level.

Parterre gardens

Parterre gardens derived from knot gardens. The name comes from the French *par terre*, meaning 'on the ground'. These parterre gardens were very large and made in intricate patterns, unlike the predominantly square knot gardens. These amazing gardens were made in interesting and extensive patterns

A mock orange (Philadelphus coronarius) and camellia frame this delightful courtyard. The white flowers of the camellia contrast wonderfully with its dark leaves to form a pretty spring picture.

KNOT GARDEN PATTERNS

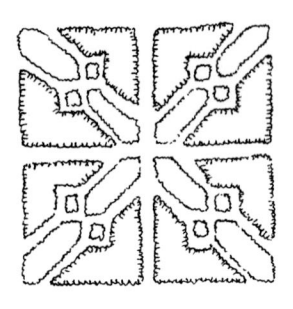

like embroidery. They were formed from clipped boxwood, flowers, grass and stone. Unless you have a great deal of spare time it would be very difficult to maintain one of these gardens but when recreated on a smaller scale they can make an outstanding garden feature.

STANDARD SHRUBS

A standard is characterised by a crown of growth on top of a single, erect stem. The shape is simple and clearly defined with the contrasting straight stem and leafy head. Standard shrubs may be used in pots to flank a doorway or may form an inviting start to a flight of steps. Almost any plant can be used as long as it has a straight stem. Among the most spectacular are citrus trees, camellias, azaleas, box, yew, roses, geraniums, bougainvilleas, grevilleas — especially *Grevillea rosmarinifolia* which responds well to clipping — pittosporum, hibiscus and marguerite daisies.

The head of a standard is usually fashioned into a sphere but may also be shaped into pyramids, cones or mushrooms. Shapely variations are possible with single-stem standards, including multiple discs or balls along the stem instead of the traditional single crown of growth. You may wish to depart from tradition and twist the young stem into corkscrews or knots. Another interesting effect is to use several plants in one pot, or a multi-stemmed plant, and twine or braid the stems into one.

Standard plants are usually expensive but if you have the time it is not difficult to cultivate your own in about two seasons. Purchase a vigorous, straight-growing shrub. It is important that the plant develop a thick, healthy stem. Remove the lower branches from the stem but try to retain the side leaves along the central stem as these help to feed the plant. Staking the main stem will assist the plant to remain straight. As the plant reaches the desired height, allow some side shoots to grow where the head will be. When the plant reaches the desired height pinch out the centre shoot to encourage side growth. When the resulting new growth forms pinch it back just below a leaf node. This will give it a bushier appearance and the process should be repeated until the head is well branched.

PLANTING SHRUBS

An initially well-planted shrub will grow quickly and maintain its health. Water it well before planting and leave it in the container until everything is ready for planting. Dig the hole at least twice the width of the container. Place compost, well-rotted manure or leaf mould into the bottom of the hole. Plant the shrub on top of this. The roots should be spread out slightly if they have started to become pot-bound and any damaged ones should be cut off. Mix any remaining compost or manure with the soil from the hole and place this mixture around the roots, firming it down carefully. When the hole is full, tamp down the soil around the shrub with your foot. It is essential that the shrub be kept well-watered until established.

A SELECTION LIST OF SHRUBS

Abelia x Grandiflora
FLOWER COLOUR Pinkish-white
FLOWERING TIME Summer
HEIGHT 2 m
CULTIVATION Will grow in full shade or sun. Prune by removing the old canes
OTHER SPECIES
A. schummanii — mauve-pink flowers

Abutilon hybridum
(Chinese lantern)
FLOWER COLOUR Wide colour range
FLOWERING TIME Summer and autumn
HEIGHT 2.5 m
CULTIVATION Likes a warm climate and a well-drained soil

Acalypha hispida
FLOWER COLOUR Red
FLOWERING TIME Summer
HEIGHT 2 m
CULTIVATION Suitable for tropical climates. Requires at least half sun

Adenandra uniflora
FLOWER COLOUR White with a rose-pink rib down the centre of each petal
FLOWERING TIME Spring and summer
HEIGHT 1 m
CULTIVATION Requires at least half sun and a warm climate

Azalea species
FLOWER COLOUR Wide colour range
FLOWERING TIME Spring
HEIGHT Depends on the species
CULTIVATION Grow in dappled shade in soil enriched with leaf mould. Keep the roots mulched with cow manure

Boronia denticulata
FLOWER COLOUR Pink
FLOWERING TIME Spring
HEIGHT 1 m
CULTIVATION Prefers a well-drained, gritty soil. Do not use heavy fertilisers. A sprinkling of blood and bone in spring is sufficient
OTHER SPECIES
B. megastigma — yellow flowers

Brunfelsia latifolia
(yesterday, today and tomorrow)
FLOWER COLOUR Open violet-blue, fading to lavender and eventually white
FLOWERING TIME Mid-spring
HEIGHT 3 m
CULTIVATION Grow in partial shade or full sun
OTHER SPECIES
B. paucifolia — same as above but only reaches a height of 1.5 m

Buddleia davidii (butterfly bush)
FLOWER COLOUR Lilac
FLOWERING TIME Summer
HEIGHT 3 m
CULTIVATION A hardy, fast growing shrub that will grow in full sun or partial shade

Buxus sempervirens
(box or boxwood)
FLOWER COLOUR Grown for its dense, dark green leaves
FLOWERING TIME N/A
HEIGHT 1 m
CULTIVATION Likes a moist, well-drained soil and a temperate to cold climate. Grow in shade or sun

Calluna vulgaris
(scotch heather)
FLOWER COLOUR Usually mauve-pink to lilac
FLOWERING TIME Summer
HEIGHT 75 cm
CULTIVATION Prefers a cool climate and a moist, acidic soil

Cantua bicolor
(sacred flower of the Incas)
FLOWER COLOUR Carmine red and buff
FLOWERING TIME Winter and early spring
HEIGHT 1.5 m
CULTIVATION Requires at least half sun in a frost-free position

Ceratostigma willmotteanum
FLOWER COLOUR Royal-blue
FLOWERING TIME Late spring to autumn
HEIGHT 1.5 m
CULTIVATION Grow in full or half sun in well-drained soil. Cut back in late winter to encourage spring flowers

Chaenomeles japonica
(flowering quince)
FLOWER COLOUR Soft pinks, terracotta or rich crimson depending on the variety

A large hawthorn (Crategeus oxycantha) frames the gate leading to this leafy pathway. A splendid variety of shrubs with differing leaf types and colours lines the pathway.

FLOWERING TIME Spring
HEIGHT 2.5 m
CULTIVATION Will grow equally well in cold or hot climates. Prefers full sun but will tolerate some shade

Choisya ternata (Mexican orange blossom)
FLOWER COLOUR White
FLOWERING TIME Spring
HEIGHT 2 m
CULTIVATION A good shrub for shady corners but it also tolerates sun

Chorizema cordatum (Western Australian flame pea)
FLOWER COLOUR Reddish-orange and purple
FLOWERING TIME Late winter and early spring
HEIGHT 1 m
CULTIVATION Will grow in any well-drained soil in full sun or dappled shade

Cistus purpureus (rock rose)
FLOWER COLOUR Rose-red with a yellow centre and a chocolate blotch at the base of each petal
FLOWERING TIME Spring
HEIGHT 1 m
CULTIVATION Rock rose thrives in a dry, sunny position but it will tolerate half sun
OTHER SPECIES
C. laurifolius — white flowers

Convolvulus cneorum
FLOWER COLOUR White
FLOWERING TIME Spring and summer
HEIGHT 1 m
CULTIVATION Requires at least half sun and a well-drained soil

Crategeus oxycantha (hawthorn)
FLOWER COLOUR White but varieties include pink and rose-red
FLOWERING TIME Summer
HEIGHT 5 m
CULTIVATION Grow in cold or temperate climates. Prefers full sun

Daphne odora
FLOWER COLOUR Pink and ruby-red
FLOWERING TIME Late winter
HEIGHT 1 m
CULTIVATION Daphne will thrive in slightly acid, well-drained soil. For best results plant daphne and leave it alone except for the occasional mulch of leaves
OTHER SPECIES
D. odora 'Alba' — creamy-white flowers
D. cneorum — pink flowers
D. mezereum — rosy-purple flowers

Deutzia gracilis
FLOWER COLOUR White
FLOWERING TIME Spring
HEIGHT 2 m
CULTIVATION Requires a well-drained soil and a position in full sun. Remove the old canes from the base every three years or so
OTHER SPECIES
D. rosea — pink flowers

Echium fastuosum (viper's bugloss)
FLOWER COLOUR Purplish-blue
FLOWERING TIME Spring and early summer
HEIGHT 2 m
CULTIVATION Suitable for cool or semi-tropical climates. Plant in full sun. Is resistant to salt winds

Enkianthus campanulatus
FLOWER COLOUR White
FLOWERING TIME Spring
HEIGHT 2 m
CULTIVATION Requires at least half sun and a moist soil
OTHER SPECIES
E. campanulatus — bronze-red flowers

Epacris impressa (native fuchsia)
FLOWER COLOUR Crimson-red tipped with white
FLOWERING TIME Late winter and early spring but tends to be spasmodic
HEIGHT 1.5 m
CULTIVATION Mulch the soil with leaf mould and keep moist. Prefers dappled sunlight

Erica species (heath)
FLOWER COLOUR Ranges from white to deep-red depending on the variety
FLOWERING TIME Late winter to spring
HEIGHT 1.5 m
CULTIVATION Grow in half sun or dappled shade. The acidic soil should be moist but well-drained

Euphorbia wulfenii
FLOWER COLOUR Greenish-yellow
FLOWERING TIME Spring
HEIGHT 1.2 m
CULTIVATION Will thrive in full sun or partial shade in either cold or semi-tropical climates

Euryops pectinatus
FLOWER COLOUR Yellow
FLOWERING TIME Winter and early spring
HEIGHT 1.5 m
CULTIVATION Grow in full sun or partial shade. Picking the flowers and trimming the old flower stems will encourage a bushier habit

Exochorda racemosa (pearl bush)
FLOWER COLOUR White with a greenish centre
FLOWERING TIME Spring
HEIGHT 3 m
CULTIVATION Requires a position with at least half sun and a moist but well-drained soil

Felecia amelloides (kingfisher daisy)
FLOWER COLOUR Blue with a yellow centre
FLOWERING TIME Spring but usually some flowers on the plant throughout the year
HEIGHT 75 cm
CULTIVATION Plant in full sun. It is not fussy about soil type as long as it is well-drained. Cut back lightly after a flush of flowers has finished
OTHER SPECIES
F. angustifolia — soft-lilac flowers

Fuchsia species
FLOWER COLOUR Wide range of colours
FLOWERING TIME Spring and summer
HEIGHT Depends on the variety
CULTIVATION Thrive in shade or half sun. The soil should be sandy and on the alkaline side

Gardenia jasminoides
FLOWER COLOUR White
FLOWERING TIME Late spring and summer
HEIGHT 1.5 m
CULTIVATION Gardenias thrive in a richly composted, well-drained soil in temperate and hot climates. A position with at least two-thirds of the day's sun, preferably with protection from the afternoon sun

Grevillea species
FLOWER COLOUR Range includes orange, red, apricot, yellow, mauve, pink and white
FLOWERING TIME Depends on the species
HEIGHT Depends on the species
CULTIVATION There is a species of grevillea for almost every soil type and climate from tropical to cold. Prune lightly after flowering if it becomes too leggy

Hebe species
FLOWER COLOUR White, lilac, pink or blue
FLOWERING TIME Spring or summer
HEIGHT Depends on the species
CULTIVATION Most species require at least half sun to flower well. The soil should be well-drained. Prune back every couple of years when the plant becomes straggly

Hibiscus species
FLOWER COLOUR Wide colour range
FLOWERING TIME Spring, summer, autumn or winter
HEIGHT Depends on the species or variety
CULTIVATION Prune the deciduous types during winter and the evergreen varieties in spring. Pruning in late summer in tropical climates will encourage winter flowers

Hydrangea macrophylla
FLOWER COLOUR Blue, pink or white
FLOWERING TIME Summer
HEIGHT 1.5 m
CULTIVATION Will thrive in shady areas. Lime or slightly alkaline soils produce red or pink flowers and acid soils produce blue flowers

OTHER SPECIES
H. aspera — blue flowers
H. paniculata — white flowers turn pink
H. quercifolia — creamy-white flowers

Hypericum calycinum (rose of Sharon)
FLOWER COLOUR Yellow
FLOWERING TIME Summer
HEIGHT 45 cm
CULTIVATION A hardy, low growing shrub-like plant that will thrive in any soil type and in sun or shade
OTHER SPECIES
H. chinense — deep yellow flowers

Jasminum mesnyi (yellow jasmine)
FLOWER COLOUR Bright yellow
FLOWERING TIME Winter and spring
HEIGHT 3 m
CULTIVATION A fast growing shrub useful for quick cover. Prune back after spring flowering if necessary

Kalmia latifolia (mountain laurel)
FLOWER COLOUR Soft rose-pink
FLOWERING TIME Late spring
HEIGHT 2 m
CULTIVATION Grow in dappled sunlight for best results. In cold climates it will tolerate full sun but this often results in burnt leaves. The soil should be slightly acid and well-drained. Keep mulched with leaf-mould throughout the year

Kerria japonica (Japanese rose)
FLOWER COLOUR Yellow
FLOWERING TIME Spring
HEIGHT 1.5 m
CULTIVATION Suitable for full sun or light shade. A hardy plant which will grow in cold to semi-tropical climates

Kunzea ambigua (tick bush)
FLOWER COLOUR White
FLOWERING TIME Spring
HEIGHT 3 m
CULTIVATION Requires a free-draining soil and a sunny position
OTHER SPECIES
K. baxteri — scarlet flowers
K. capitata — violet-pink flowers

Laburnum vossi
FLOWER COLOUR Golden-yellow
FLOWERING TIME Late spring
HEIGHT 5 m
CULTIVATION Prefers a cool to cold climate and a position with at least half sun

Lavandula angustifolia (lavender)
FLOWER COLOUR Lilac, blue, white or pink
FLOWERING TIME Spring and summer
HEIGHT 1 m, but depends on the variety
CULTIVATION Lavender prefers cool to temperate climates, a position in full sun and well-

Lavandula angustifolia forms a fragrant lawn border.

drained soil
OTHER SPECIES
L. dentata — lilac or blue flowers
L. stoechas — deep purple

Leonotus leonurus (lion's ear)
FLOWER COLOUR Deep orange
FLOWERING TIME Spring and summer
HEIGHT 2 m
CULTIVATION A great plant for seaside plantings as it is very tolerant of wind and salt spray. Needs at least half sun

Leucothoe fontanesiana (fetter bush)
FLOWER COLOUR Creamy-white
FLOWERING TIME Spring
HEIGHT 2 m
CULTIVATION Grow in dappled or light shade in a slightly acid soil. Mulch around the roots in early spring

Loropetalum chinese (Chinese witch-hazel)
FLOWER COLOUR Creamy-white
FLOWERING TIME Spring
HEIGHT 2 m
CULTIVATION Grow in full sun or light shade in slightly acid, well-drained soil

Luculia gratissima
FLOWER COLOUR Soft-pink
FLOWERING TIME Winter
HEIGHT 2.5 m
CULTIVATION Grow in partial shade with some protection from strong winds. The soil should be well-drained and slightly acid. Even though it prefers cool to cold climates protection from frosts is essential
OTHER SPECIES
L. tsetensis — white flowers

Montanoa pipina ifida (Mexican daisy bush)
FLOWER COLOUR White daisies with yellow centres
FLOWERING TIME Winter
HEIGHT 4 m
CULTIVATION A hardy plant that will grow in full sun and well-drained soil. Cut the bush back by about two-thirds when flowers have finished. This encourages healthy growth and more flowers the following year

Muraya exotica
FLOWER COLOUR White
FLOWERING TIME Spasmodic bursts from spring until autumn
HEIGHT 3 m
CULTIVATION Can be grown in full sun or light shade

Paeonia suffruticosa (tree peony)
FLOWER COLOUR Pink, mauve, purple or white depending on the variety
FLOWERING TIME Spring
HEIGHT 2 m
CULTIVATION At least half sun is required in cold areas but in warmer areas dappled sunlight is sufficient. Keep the soil continually mulched with leaf-mould or manure

Pelargonium species
FLOWER COLOUR Wide range of colours
FLOWERING TIME Mid-spring and summer
HEIGHT Depends on the species
CULTIVATION Suitable for all climates except the very humid. In cold climates they need protection from the winter frosts. They are drought-resistant and prefer the soil drying out a little before watering. Grow in full or half sun

Philadelphus coronarius (mock orange blossom)
FLOWER COLOUR White with golden centres
FLOWERING TIME Late spring
HEIGHT 3 m
CULTIVATION Suitable for sun or semi-shade. If the plant becomes too straggly cut the old canes back in early winter just above where new canes are emerging

Pieris japonica (lily-of-the-valley shrub)
FLOWER COLOUR Creamy-white
FLOWERING TIME Spring
HEIGHT 2 m
CULTIVATION Prefer cold to temperate climates and an acid soil. Requires half sun
OTHER SPECIES
P. forrestii — cream flowers

Prostanthera caerulea (mint bush)
FLOWER COLOUR Blue
FLOWERING TIME Spring
HEIGHT 2.5 m
CULTIVATION Require perfect drainage and near to full sun
OTHER SPECIES
P. incana — lavender-violet flowers
P. lasianthos — white flowers suffused with violet-blue
P. ovalifolia — purple flowers

Protea neriifolia
FLOWER COLOUR Dark pink with black tips
FLOWERING TIME Spring but some flowers on the plant throughout the year
HEIGHT 3 m
CULTIVATION A well-drained slightly acid soil with plenty of compost added. Full sun

Prunus glandulosa 'Rosea-plena' (dwarf flowering plum)
FLOWER COLOUR Pink
FLOWERING TIME Spring
HEIGHT 1.5 m
CULTIVATION Suitable for full or half sun

Romneya coulteri
FLOWER COLOUR White with yellow stamens
FLOWERING TIME Summer
HEIGHT 2 m
CULTIVATION Likes a well-drained light sandy soil and at least half sun. Can be pruned heavily in winter

Rondeletia amoena
FLOWER COLOUR Pink
FLOWERING TIME Spring to early summer
HEIGHT 4 m
CULTIVATION Requires full sun but can withstand some shade. Can be pruned back to just above the lower leaves on the branch as flowers finish

The Mexican daisy bush (Montanoa pipina ifida) *has gorgeous flowers.*

Rosmarinus officinalis (rosemary)
FLOWER COLOUR Pale lavender
FLOWERING TIME Spring
HEIGHT 1.5 m
CULTIVATION Likes a well-drained sandy soil with some lime content. Prefers full sun but will tolerate half shade
OTHER VARIETIES
R. officinalis 'Prostratus' — same as above but with a prostrate habit

Santolina chamaecyparissus (cotton lavender)
FLOWER COLOUR Golden
FLOWERING TIME Late spring and early summer
HEIGHT 70 cm
CULTIVATION A sunny position in a well-drained soil. A cool to temperate climate

Spirea cantoniensis (May bush)
FLOWER COLOUR White
FLOWERING TIME Late winter to early spring
HEIGHT 2.5 m
CULTIVATION Suitable for half or full sun. A hardy shrub that will thrive in most soil types
OTHER SPECIES
S. japonica — rosy-red flowers

Syringa vulgaris (common or English lilac)
FLOWER COLOUR Range includes pink, lilac, claret-red, purple and various tones of mauve and blue
FLOWERING TIME Spring
HEIGHT 2.5 m
CULTIVATION Likes a rich soil with added manure or compost. Lilac thrives in full sun but will tolerate a little shade
OTHER SPECIES
S. persica — lilac flowers

Viburnum macrocephalum (Chinese snowball tree)
FLOWER COLOUR Light green to white
FLOWERING TIME Spring
HEIGHT 4 m
CULTIVATION Suitable for full or half sun in any well-drained soil
OTHER SPECIES
V. opulus — green flowers change to lime then white *V. plicatum* — white flowers

Weigela florida
FLOWER COLOUR Rose-pink but varieties include white and crimson-red
FLOWERING TIME Spring
HEIGHT 3 m
CULTIVATION An open, sunny aspect is preferred but some shade is tolerable

Trees

Trees determine the nature and quality of our environment more than any other plant. Because they live for many decades, they invest the landscape with stability. Trees are an exciting reminder of the changing seasons: the brilliant colours of autumn, the strong silhouettes of winter, the flowers and soft green tones of spring and summer. Trees are barriers against wind, they provide shade and they add structure to the garden. In addition they produce fruits, nuts and berries.

Using trees in the landscape

Trees for ornamental effect should be chosen for their form and foliage as well as their flowers. Many flowering trees do not have the sculptural qualities of those admired for foliage.

Most of the *Acer* species are valued for their leaves as well as their shapely branches and autumn foliage. The soft silver bark of silver birches adds interest to the garden as does the bark of the golden ash (*Fraxinus excelsior* 'Aurea'). Its young, golden-yellow shoots are very conspicuous, as are its yellowish branches after losing leaves in winter.

The most common mistake when planting trees is to overplant. In a small garden this limits the choice of plant material and creates too much shade, making it difficult for other plants to grow. Trees are sometimes planted to provide privacy but in a small garden this can often be achieved more efficiently by other methods. Trellis draped with climbing plants, whether attached to the top of a paling fence or used on its own, will generally provide more privacy than a tree and cast less shade. In small gardens remember to choose trees for their shape and texture as well as their flowers.

Crab apples (*Malus* species) are marvellous trees for small gardens. They seldom grow any higher than 5 m and their umbrella shape gives a pleasant effect when not in flower. *Malus floribunda* is covered in spring with carmine red buds that open into starry, single pale pink flushed flowers which fade to white.

Other trees for small gardens include *Albizzia julibrissin*, a fast growing, small deciduous tree with finely divided fern-like foliage which folds closely together at night. In summer it is covered in a mass of pompom-like, rosy-pink flowers which fade to white at the base. It is suitable for all areas except very hot tropical ones.

The Judas tree (*Cercis silquastrum*) is deciduous and reaches a height of only 7 m.

The stunning colours of a pink variety of angel's trumpet (Datura cornigera) appear through spring and summer.

During spring its branches are clustered with bright rose-pink flowers at about the same time that the interesting two-lobed leaves appear.

Golden rain (*Koelreuteria paniculata*) is another interesting small deciduous tree. This elegant tree has a fairly flat top and decorative frond-like leaves which turn gold in autumn. The panicles of small, fragrant golden flowers appear in late spring and are followed by papery-brown inflated seed pods. This tree reputedly inspired the Chinese Willow pattern. It is suitable for temperate or cold climates.

Flowering cherries and peaches provide a wealth of spring colour. Flowering peaches (*Prunus persica*) will grow in temperate to cold climates. They usually do not grow any higher than about 5 m and standard plants are generally available. Varieties include 'Lilian Burrows' with its soft pink flowers, 'Alba Plena' which is loved for its pure white blooms and 'Magnifica', the flowers of which are a lovely rosy-red.

Colder areas are suitable for growing the

The delightful coloured leaves of this golden elm (Ulmus glabra) *provide interest during spring and autumn.*

beautiful flowering cherries (*Prunus serrulata*) which have truly magnificent pendulous flowers. There are many different varieties including the white 'Mt Fuji' and the rosy-purple 'Kanzan'. Other varieties, of course, produce the many shades of pink for which prunus is well known. The weeping varieties are the most spectacular with their shades of deep pink ('Pendula Rubra'), white ('Pendula') and pink ('Pendula Rosea').

Shade trees should have a medium to fast growth pattern in order to fulfil their purpose. They should be flat-topped and open-headed to provide the necessary shade as well as allowing the movement of breeze through the branches. The lowest branches should be high enough up the trunk to allow standing room beneath. *Acer negundo* 'Aureo-marginatum' is a fast growing tree which provides shade and makes a notable feature in the garden. The large green leaves are margined with gold. It will grow in temperate coastal regions or cold districts and will also stand some inland heat. The variety 'Variegatum' has silver margins.

It will often be more visually arresting to create a woodland effect in a small area rather than featuring one tree. A group of graceful, slender silver birch trees (*Betula pendula*) with their beautiful silver white trunks is a stunning sight. There is also the bonus of the green leaves changing to a golden yellow in autumn. The branches of weeping birch (*Betula pendula* 'Youngii') are so pendulous that they hang almost to ground level.

For creating a native grove *Eucalyptus scoparia* is one of my favourites. The cream and silver trunks are tall and straight, and are particularly beautiful at dusk or in the moonlight.

Many of the *Eucalyptus* species have outstanding flowers. *Eucalyptus sideroxylon* 'Rosea' reaches a height of approximately 12 m, is of rapid growth and has clusters of pendulous rose-pink flowers which contrast beautifully with the grey-green leaves.

Red flowering gum (*Eucalyptus ficifolia*) will grow in cool to semi-tropical climates but definitely thrives best in the sandy soils of

The light pink flowers of a flowering cherry create a romantic tone.

Melbourne and Perth. It is a small tree with heads of large, spectacular deep-scarlet flowers. The wider distribution of the tree has caused the colour to vary from scarlet to white.

Gungurru (*Eucalyptus caesia*), a native of Western Australia, is a well shaped, fast growing small tree reaching a height of 7 m. During late winter and early spring it is covered in large clusters of brilliant rose-pink flowers which contrast strikingly with its silver calyces and powdery-white branches.

The pink-flowering whitewood (*Eucalyptus leucoxylon* 'Rosea') reaches a height of only 10 m. It looks most ornamental during late winter and spring when its pink flowers appear.

The native frangipani (*Hymenosporum flavum*) is unequalled for fragrance. It is a slender evergreen tree with an erect trunk and layered foliage which gives it a picturesque, pagoda shape. The five-petalled cream and yellow flowers appear in branched clusters above the dark, glossy foliage.

During spring *Virgilia capensis* is covered in clusters of softly perfumed mauve-pink, pea-like flowers. It is one of the fastest growing evergreen trees and this makes it ideal for rapid screening. Unfortunately it has a lifespan of only 15-20 years. Pruning it after flowering helps keep it bushy and may prolong its life.

Black locust or false acacia (*Robinia pseudoacacia*) has 20 cm pendulous racemes of fragrant, white pea flowers. Black locust is an elegant tree with attractive foliage and it makes an effective shade tree of gentle appearance.

TREE SHAPES

It is important when selecting trees to be aware of their eventual shape, size and colour. Tree shapes can be broadly categorised into the following: pendulous or weeping; columnar; round-topped; open or columnar. These shapes help determine the appropriate position for the tree. A columnar tree can be used as a screen because the growth is usually dense while a more open tree should be used as background planting because it allows light through, enabling plants to grow beneath.

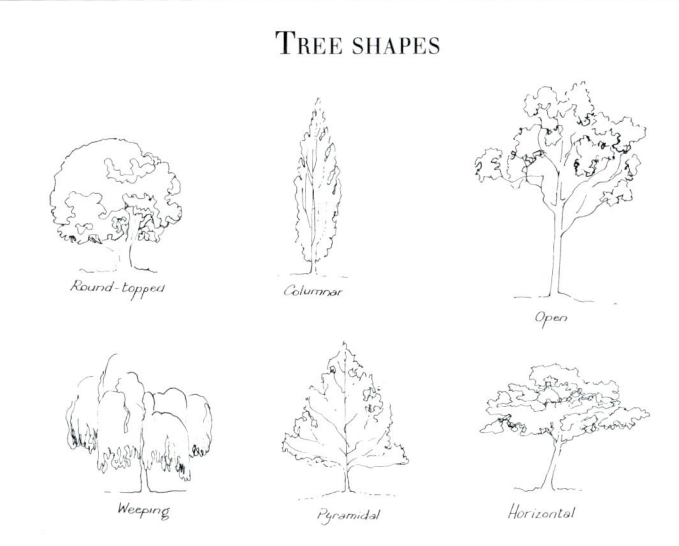

TREE SHAPES

Round-topped   Columnar   Open

Weeping   Pyramidal   Horizontal

A group of silver birches (Betula pendula) *creates a woodland effect. The silver bark is a feature throughout the year.*

This large Japanese maple (Acer palmatum) turns brilliant shades of orange and red during autumn.

Pleaching

Pleaching is the training of deciduous trees on a frame to enable their branches to entwine and form a green wall or canopy. The young trees are started against supporting posts and wires. They are encouraged to grow on one plane only, which assists their branches to interwine. In autumn stop the vertical growth above pairs of chosen buds which are then left to grow horizontally along the wire. When the desired height is reached new growth on the framework merges to form a mass of foliage. During summer clip the foliage to the desired shape.

Pleached trees are marvellous for small gardens where space is limited. An avenue formed by two rows makes an impressive garden walk. For example, an arbour made using lime (*Tilia* species) is deliciously fragrant during summer.

Broad-leaved trees such as beech, hornbeam and lime are usually trained for this effect.

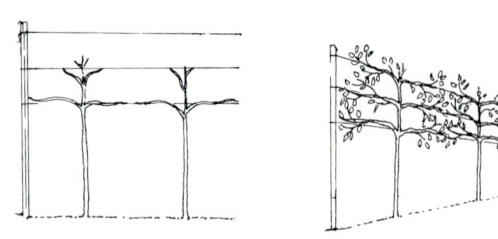

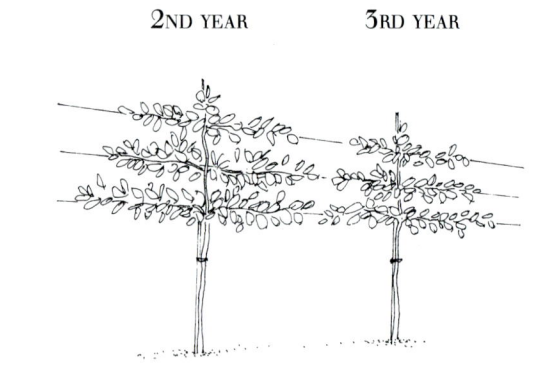

1ST YEAR

2ND YEAR   3RD YEAR

AN AVENUE OF PLEACHED TREES

Espalier

Espalier is most effective when used with fruit trees. It increases the crop and creates interesting forms and shapes in the garden. Pears, nectarines, apples, cherries and plums all lend themselves to this treatment. But, of course, purely ornamental trees can be used. Crab apples, which look most effective when in flower, are especially suited to espalier.

Trees can be espaliered against a wall or can be free-standing with support wires strung between posts. Free-standing espalier can be used to divide the garden or to make an avenue within the garden. The use of espalier means that there is no longer an excuse for not having fruit in a small garden. In cool regions warm micro-climates can be made by espaliering fruit trees against a white wall.

Espalier does take time and continual pruning. It is similar to pleaching trees, where growth away from the lines of the supporting wires is removed annually.

Pruning

Trees can be pruned sympathetically to form interesting shapes, to emphasise their original form or as a maintenance procedure for older trees. It is often undertaken to remove dead, diseased or injured limbs or to remove branches which interfere with other branches or block out light and air.

Large limbs should always be removed in three stages and should be painted with tree paint to prevent fungus and decay entering the wound.

General maintenance

It is most important that careful maintenance is carried out on newly planted trees. This will determine the health of the tree for many years

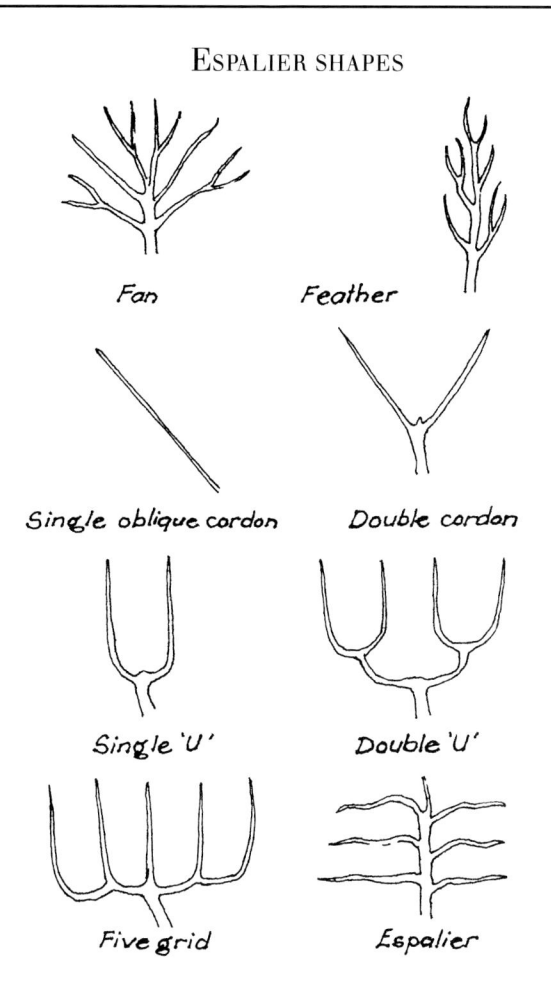

Espalier shapes

Fan

Feather

Single oblique cordon

Double cordon

Single 'U'

Double 'U'

Five grid

Espalier

and encourage prolific growth. All newly planted trees require regular watering to help them become established. Trees planted in windy areas should be staked so their growth will remain upright.

Planting

Dig the hole for the tree twice as wide as its container. Place the tree in the middle of the hole and fill around it with soil. Form the soil into a saucer shape and keep mulched, especially during summer.

Feeding

Mulch young trees with compost or manure. This will keep the soil moist and supply essential plant food. In spring and again in early summer apply a complete soluble fertiliser around the base of the tree. Larger trees can be root fed.

A SELECTION LIST OF TREES

Name	Height	Description
Acacia baileyana (Cootamundra wattle)	10 m	Dense silvery-grey foliage and golden flowers during late winter and early spring.
Acacia decurrens (black wattle)	10 m	Dark bark and fern-like foliage. Yellow flowers.
Acacia elata (cedar wattle)	20 m	Fast growing, long-lived wattle. Cream flowers.
Acer japonicum 'Aureum'	3 m	Smooth, golden-green leaves in the shape of a fan. Deciduous.
Acer japonicum 'Filicifolium'	4 m	Large, deep matt green leaves which turn a rich coppery-red in autumn. Deciduous.
Acer negundo	15 m	The green leaves turn gold in autumn. There are cream and yellow variegated types. Deciduous.
Acer palmatum (Japanese maple)	5 m	A pretty, small tree with a bushy habit. The leaves turn red, gold and purple in autumn. There are many different varieties.
Acer platanoides (Norway maple)	15 m	A tall, upright, fast growing tree. The leaves have five pointed lobes and turn orange-yellow in autumn.
Acer pseudoplatanus (sycamore maple)	15 m	A rapid growing tree whose green leaves turn yellow in autumn. The variety 'Purpureum' has purple on the underside of the leaves.
Acer saccharum (sugar maple)	15 m	The light green, lobed leaves turn yellow, orange and scarlet in autumn.
Agonis flexuosa (willow myrtle)	7 m	Small, umbrella-shaped shade tree with weeping outer branches.
Ailanthus altissima (tree of heaven)	15 m	Attractive-looking tree with dark green leaves and green flowers that later develop coppery tones.
Albizia julibrissin (silk tree)	4 m	A fast-growing small deciduous tree with fern-like foliage and rosy-pink flowers which fade to white.
Alnus glutinosa	15 m	Deciduous tree with pendulous outer branches.
Banksia integrifolia	12 m	A good tree to provide shelter from salt winds. The cylindrical flowers are lime to yellow in colour.
Banksia serrata (old man banksia)	7 m	An interesting tree having ridged, corky-grey and brown bark and large green-grey flowers.
Bauhinia variegata (butterfly tree or orchid tree)	6 m	A small, semi-deciduous tree the leaves of which are divided to about one-third their depth, suggesting a butterfly shape. Flowers are a deep-purple.
Betula pendula (silver birch)	10 m	A delightful tree having pendulous branches and dark green leaves which turn gold in autumn. The bark is silver. The variety 'Dalecarlica' has leaves cut deeply, almost to the midrib; 'Purpurea' has purple leaves; 'Youngii' has very drooping branches which almost reach the ground.
Brachychiton acerifolium (flame tree)	12 m	The leaves drop when the beautiful trusses of scarlet flowers appear. *B. hybrida* has pink flowers.
Callistemon species	depends on species	Delightful small trees with bottle brush-like flowers. *C. citrinus* has creamy-white flowers; *C. viminalis* has bright red flowers; *C. salignus* has cream flowers.
Cassia fistula (golden shower tree)	9 m	A slender tree having racemes of pale yellow flowers in summer.

Cassia nodosa (pink shower tree)	9 m	A beautiful tree the flowers of which open white to pale pink, deepen to rose then fade again.
Castanospermum australe (black bean)	12 m	A broad, dome shaped Australian native with yellow to red flowers in summer.
Catalpa bignonioides (Indian bean)	12 m	A fast growing deciduous tree. The late spring flowers are white with two yellow stripes and purple-brown spots inside.
Cedrela sinensis (Chinese cedar)	3 m	A small deciduous tree which usually produces three or more tall, slender suckers. The new spring leaves unfold to a deep ruby-rose, paling as they grow to become peach, buff and green.
Cercis silquastrum (Judas tree)	7 m	A deciduous tree having two-lobed leaves and clusters of bright rose-pink flowers during spring.
Chionananthus virginicus (fringe tree)	9 m	A small deciduous tree with glossy green leaves and panicles of ivory to white flowers in spring.
Crataegus oxycantha (English hawthorn)	6 m	Tall, erect growth with slender branches. White flowers. The variety 'Paulii' has bright scarlet flowers; 'Plena' has double white flowers; 'Rosea' has double rose-pink flowers.
Datura cornigera (angel's trumpet)	3 m	A small, deciduous tree or large shrub with rough green foliage and large greenish-white, ribbed, trumpet-shaped flowers.
Diospyros kaki (persimmon)	6 m	A beautifully shaped tree having lovely autumn foliage. The large, orange edible fruits remain on the tree after the leaves have fallen.
Eucalyptus citriodora (lemon-scented gum)	20 m	A tall, slender, high-branching tree suitable for planting in groves. The trunk is creamy-buff in summer, silvery-grey in winter and at times displays both colours. Leaves are lemon-scented.
Eucalyptus caesia (gungurru)	7 m	A small tree with drooping, powdery-white branches. These have curling reddish flakes which disclose green strips.
Eucalyptus ficifolia (red flowering gum)	8 m	A small tree having spectacular heads of red or pink flowers that almost cover the foliage.

Below left *Long pendulous racemes of yellow, pea like flowers cover* Laburnum vossi *in spring.*

Below right *Evergreen alders* (Alnus rhombifolia) *planted next to trellis help to provide privacy.*

Eucalyptus scoparia	12 m	Tall trees with creamy-coloured bark. Good trees to use close together to create a woodland effect.
Gingko biloba (maidenhair tree)	15 m	A beautiful deciduous tree having bluish-green fern-like leaves which turn a soft-gold in autumn.
Grevillea robusta (silky oak)	25 m	A tall evergreen tree with attractive fern-like leaves. During spring and summer orange flowers cover the tree.
Jacaranda mimosifolia	18 m	During late spring the tree is covered in lavender-blue flowers which make a delightful carpet when they fall to the ground. The leaves are soft and fern-like.
Laburnum vossi	6 m	A large, deciduous shrub or small tree having long, slender, pendulous racemes of yellow pea-like flowers. The oval leaves are a deep green.
Lagerstroemia indica (crepe myrtle)	6 m	A small tree having smooth bark and shiny leaves which colour before they fall in autumn. The crepe-like textured flowers come in a variety of colours including pale mauve, pink and red.
Lagunaria patersonii	7 m	A hardy, quick-growing small tree, the flowers of which are cream upon opening but darken to rose-pink. Suitable for exposed seaside planting.
Liquidambar styraciflua	25 m	A tall, stately tree suitable for large gardens. The green leaves turn yellow, crimson and purple before they fall in autumn.
Liriodendron tulipifera	20 m	A shapely tree with large yellow-green tulip-like flowers. The leaves turn golden in autumn before they fall.
Magnolia grandiflora	10 m	A large evergreen tree with stiff, glossy leaves, large white flowers and a sweet perfume.
Magnolia campbellii	9 m	The large, cup-shaped flowers are white and pink inside and crimson outside.
Magnolia denudata	6 m	The pure white, sweetly perfumed flowers appear before the leaves.
Magnolia soulangiana (tulip tree)	5 m	The flowers are white inside and purple outside and appear before the leaves.
Malus floribunda (crab apple)	5 m	A shapely tree suitable for small gardens. The flowers are reddish in bud but open to pure white.
Malus spectabilis	5 m	Has vigorous upright growth. The deep rose buds open to blush-pink.
Melaleuca armillaris (bracelet honey myrtle)	4 m	A graceful small tree. Suitable for planting near the coast. White bottlebrush-like flowers.
Melaleuca styphelioides	10 m	An attractive round-headed tree with creamy-white flowers.
Melia azedarach (white cedar)	10 m	A shapely, fast growing tree with lilac flowers. Thrives in dry conditions.
Metrosideros tomentosa (pohutukawa)	10 m	The red bottlebrush-like flowers appear in summer. The green leaves have a woolly underside.
Nyssa sylvatica	12 m	A fast growing deciduous tree having beautiful autumn foliage.
Parrotia persica	7 m	A pretty deciduous tree with attractive foliage and appealing bark. The leaves turn scarlet, orange and golden during autumn.
Paulownia tomentosa (princess tree)	10 m	A showy, quick-growing deciduous tree having clusters of pale lavender flowers.
Pistacia chinensis	9 m	A shapely, small, deciduous tree grown for its attractive green leaves which colour red, yellow and purple in autumn. Makes a good shade tree.

Plumeria rubra (frangipani)	4 m	A small tree grown for its perfumed cream flowers. The stems are thick and soft.
Prunus species	varies	Beautiful flowering peaches, cherries, plums and nectarines. Many suitable for small gardens.
Quercus species (oak)	varies	Deciduous trees suitable for large gardens, cool climates and deep, moist soils.
Tilia europea (Linden or lime)	8 m	A beautiful tree having small creamy flowers.
Ulmus parvifolia (Chinese weeping elm)	9 m	An open-headed tree with pendulous growth and mottled, peeling bark.
Ulmus procera 'Vanhouttei'	16 m	The pale, yellowish-green leaves deepen to a rich golden yellow in autumn.
Virgilia capensis	10 m	An extremely fast growing evergreen tree having heavy clusters of mauve-pink, pea-like flowers in spring.

Below right *The Japanese flowering apricot (Prunus nume) is a welcome relief from the barren look of winter.*

Top left *Trees of different heights make an efficient windbreak for this tranquil garden.*

Below left *An avenue of silver birches line this spectacular driveway.*

The Herb Garden

The cultivation and use of herbs has a long history, going back thousands of years before Christ and recorded in detail from the early years AD when the Romans traded in herbs throughout the world. They have been used by many civilisations for many centuries — in religious ceremonies and for both culinary and medicinal purposes.

The Romans received many of their herbs and spices from their colonies along the Mediterranean, and later from Britain. Although the use of herbs died out in Britain for several centuries, it was revived by the monasteries after the sixth century. The Chinese and Indians both used herbs and spices extensively in their cooking and medicines and still do.

During the early fifteenth and sixteenth centuries it was considered important to grow fragrant flowers and herbs, for it was thought that their perfumes would clear the air of pestilence and it was customary to add fresh-smelling clippings from these plants to the rushes which were strewn over the floors of houses.

A formal herb garden

Traditionally herb gardens were paved and laid out in a formal chessboard pattern or in circular gardens arranged like the spokes of a wheel. The herbs grown in the squares of a chessboard pattern can vary in height without encroaching upon or overshadowing their neighbours. Each plot is generally about 1 m square but of course this depends on the overall size of your garden and how much of it you want to allocate to a herb garden.

Hedges of lavender, rosemary, sage or bay can be grown around the perimeter of the garden to provide protection. A sundial, birdbath or seat can be the centrepiece of a formal herb garden. A seat allows you to appreciate the beautiful aromas, especially during the heat of the day.

Of course, more complicated designs may be used but it is advisable to draw a pattern before implementing any plan. Intricate designs like those based on the Elizabethan knot gardens are interesting. The beds were edged with dwarf boxwood, thyme, violets, and santolina. Plants within the beds were arranged so that the maximum effect was derived from the juxtaposition of each kind of plant with its neighbours. Contrasting leaf patterns added dimension and texture to the overall design.

An informal approach

You don't need a formal herb garden to grow herbs as they have always been part of the

A rare variety of white flowering borage.

A combination of herbs and perennials abound in this enchanting herb garden.

cottage garden scene. It creates an element of surprise to see a border of parsley or a drift of borage in the garden bed. Herbs add charm and fragrance when situated among perennials and shrubs and they attract bees and insects to the garden.

In early cottage gardens herbs were always planted among flowers and vegetables in what were called kitchen gardens. These gardens contained simple flowers like marigolds, violets, roses, irises, and primroses. The flowers and herbs were grown for cosmetics, medicines, flavours and food but not for aesthetic value.

Their very presence makes a garden seem

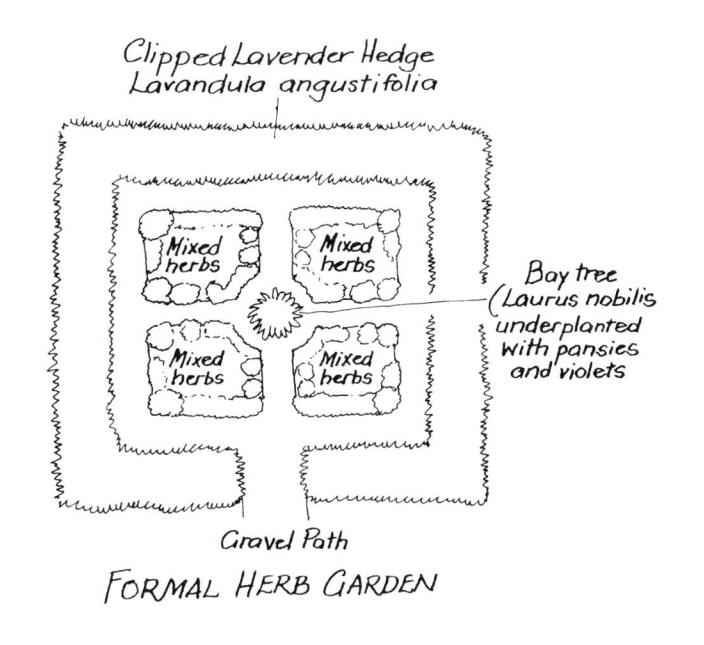

Clipped Lavender Hedge
Lavandula angustifolia

Bay tree (Laurus nobilis) underplanted with pansies and violets

Gravel Path

FORMAL HERB GARDEN

The soft–green lacy leaves of tansy frame a perfumed thyme pathway.

special. Many have a dainty appearance with leaf colours varying from grey to dark green. Foliage texture is also variable, as herbs like chervil have very fine fern-like foliage while sorrel or comfrey have larger, bolder leaves. Their flowers contribute to an overall garden design, with the soft lilac flowers of chives or the long flower stalks of garlic adding a distinct charm.

Many herbs will self-seed annually, often springing up in the most delightful places. Borage, for example, with its star-like, clear-blue flowers will self-seed reliably. The edible leaves have an interesting texture and colour and the flowers can be added to summer salads or frozen in ice-cubes and mixed with summer drinks.

The grey-green leaves of comfrey and marjoram look wonderful among other flowering perennials and among the darker leaves of many groundcovers. Perennial sorrel provides an abundance of leaves for soups, salads and quiches during spring, summer and autumn, while the apple-green leaves have a brightening effect on surrounding plants.

Most of the mints will grow in shady, damp corners in which other plants will often not survive. Lemon balm seems to create a beneficial and tranquil atmosphere and should thus be planted in an area of the garden where you like to sit. Dill, with its feathery foliage, has a softening effect on other plants.

Groups of the same botanical family can form interesting herb borders or simply be placed among other plants in an herbaceous border.

Cultivation of herbs

Herbs are among the easiest plants to grow and have few specific cultivation needs. With little exception, herbs thrive in a free-draining soil and enjoy a sunny location. Taller species should be given protection from the wind.

Herbs in pots

Herbs grown in containers look most attractive, often looking more pleasing than being lost or tucked away in the garden. They are easy to grow and especially enjoy the good drainage that containers allow. Container-grown herbs also give you the versatility to meet their cultivation needs throughout the year as the containers can be shifted around to catch the sun.

Small-space gardeners will like this method as it allows more room in the garden for other essentials. Flat-dwellers can also have a yearly supply of herbs this way. Most herbs can be grown inside as long as they are given a sunny position and fresh air.

One large terracotta pot will hold a variety of herbs, or plants can be cultivated individually in separate pots.

Always use a good free-draining potting

mixture and feed the plants every six weeks with a complete soluble plant food.

HARVESTING AND PRESERVING HERBS

Herbs can be harvested and used as you need them throughout the season. Use scissors or your fingernails to take sprigs from a few inches down the stem, just above a set of leaves. Do not take too much growth at once from young plants as you may weaken them. Select healthy leaves, remembering as you harvest the leaves you are determining the shape of the plant. The more you harvest the fuller and bushier the plant becomes.

Pinching out the flowerbuds of edible perennials will increase leaf production. If allowed to flower early, the leaves will become tough as the seeds are set. But remember that you will want to let one or two plants develop through their full cycle so that they will self-seed through the garden or supply you with seed for the next planting season.

HARVESTING FOR PRESERVATION

The majority of herbs are harvested when the flowers are about to open and the oils are most heavily concentrated. Harvest first thing in the morning before the hot sun brings out the oils.

An exception to this rule is sage, which should be cut when the buds appear. Other exceptions include hyssop, oregano and thyme, which are not harvested until the flowers are full. Parsley, borage, salad burnet and

This fragrant garden features an informal profusion of herbs and flowers.

White gravel covers the paths in this formal herb garden. White 'Iceberg' roses, foxgloves and daisies contribute to its tranquil tone.

winter savory are harvested when the leaves are young.

Shrubby perennials like marjoram, rosemary and lavender should be cut back to half the year's growth at the end of the season.

Seedheads are ready when they turn colour. Cut off the entire head or stem and drop them into paper bags, where they can be left until they open.

Hang-drying

Drying is the oldest method of preserving the leaves, flowers and seeds of herbs. Hang-drying is also very decorative and efficient. Herbs hung in the corner of a kitchen have a charming presence. Hang-drying is as simple as taking a bunch of one kind of herb, tying the ends of the stems together with string and hanging the bunch upside down in a warm place away from direct sunlight. Hang the bunch with space around it to enable the circulation of air and prevent mildew.

It usually takes about two to three weeks for most species of herbs to dry. They should feel crisp and crumble easily.

Store them in airtight bottles out of light so they retain flavour. Dark jars or ceramic bottles are best, but clear bottles can be used as long as they are kept away from sun or bright light. Stored correctly they should keep their taste for at least a year.

Freezing

Basil, fennel, tarragon, chives, dill, parsley and salad burnet can be frozen. Simply make a small bundle of the herb by tying the stems together and blanch it for five seconds in a pot of boiling water. Cool the bundle immediately by plunging it into iced water for a couple of minutes. (Blanching is not necessary for basil, chives and dill.) Gently shake off excess water, place into small bags and freeze.

Sugared borage flowers

Preserved borage flowers look delightful when used for cake decoration. A simple way of preserving borage flowers is to paint them with an egg-white mix and sprinkle them with sugar before drying.

- borage flowers
- 1 egg white
- 1 tbsp water
- caster sugar
- fine paintbrush

Place the egg white and water in a cup and stir with a fork to mix lightly. Paint each side of the flower very thinly with the egg and water mix. Do not use too much. Sprinkle each flower lightly with sugar. Lay the flowers face upwards on a sieve to dry. Put them in an airing cupboard or in the oven on the lowest heat with the door open.

When dry, lift the flowers gently and store

Pressed dirt pathways add informality to this flower and herb garden.

in a tin or jar protected between layers of greaseproof paper.

Herb and flower potpourri

This is a refreshing potpourri which can be placed directly into pretty bowls and left to dry. The subtle fragrances are there when the flowers are fresh and dry.

- 1 cup of lavender flowers
- 1 cup of rosemary leaves and flowers
- 1 cup of mixed flowers from herbs (This can be made up from whatever you have in the garden, such as marjoram, oregano and thyme)
- 2 cups of rose-petals

Mix all ingredients thoroughly and place in an open bowl.

Herb vinegars

An interesting way to use excess herbs in the garden is to make herb vinegars. They add subtle tastes to salads as well as making ideal gifts. Use white wine or apple cider vinegar as the base.

The flavouring procedure is simple. The herbs are steeped in the vinegar in a large glass jar and then decanted into individual bottles. Use approximately 2 cups of leaves for every litre of vinegar. For best results bruise the leaves slightly and pour the vinegar over the top. Leave for a week in a warm place and then test the flavour. If the mix is not strong enough the process can be repeated. Strain and pour into individual bottles adding a sprig of the

Thyme and santolina make a magnificent border to this herb garden pathway.

herb inside each bottle. Cap tightly and store.

If you require flavoured vinegar in a hurry, bring the vinegar and spices to the boil, simmering for about twenty minutes. Pour into fresh bottles and cap, adding a fresh sprig to the bottle. It is now ready to use.

Herbs in ice-cubes

The leaves and flowers of herbs look enchantingly beautiful frozen into ice-cubes for summer drinks.

Herbal teas

Centuries ago herbal teas were called 'tisanes' and were drunk for their flavour and their medicinal value. Herbal teas have a light aromatic flavour that is soothing and cooling in hot weather. The herbs can be used either fresh or dried.

Suitable herbs are basil, borage, camomile, elder flowers, fenugreek, lemon balm, lemon grass, marjoram, mint, rosemary and sage.

A SELECTION LIST OF HERBS

Allium sativum (garlic)
Garlic has long, strap-like leaves and white flowers tinged with purple. It is reputed to keep insects at bay when planted among other herbs.

Allium schoenoprasum (chives)
Chives look attractive when grown as edging plants or planted with perennials and annuals through a garden bed. The grass-like leaves and the delicate purple pompom-like flowers can be eaten.

Anethum graveolens (dill)
Dill is a delicate annual plant which has slender, finely- divided leaves and yellow flowers during summer. Plants can reach 1 m high and 40 cm wide. This quick growing herb is a good companion plant for most plants.

Angelica archangelica (angelica)
A striking, tall perennial herb which has shiny green leaves. Grown at the back of the border or garden bed it has a certain presence. The flowers are greenish-white and appear in compound umbels, from which come a honey-like odour.

Anthemis nobilis (camomile)
A most appealing plant which has soft green, delicate leaves and pretty, daisy-like yellow and white flowers. The flowers can be used in herbal teas. Camomile makes a great groundcover.

Anthriscus cerefolium (chervil)
This delightful annual herb has delicate lace-like green foliage and white flowers during summer. The whole plant has a pleasant fragrance.

Artemisia dracunculus (tarragon)
This woody perennial grows to a height of 90 cm and has an equal spread. Tarragon has a branching habit with narrow, needle-like green leaves. The French consider tarragon the king of all culinary herbs.

Borago officinalis (borage)
Once established, borage will attract bees, as they love the pretty blue spring flowers. The leaves are a grey-green with a hairy appearance. Borage will self-seed every year.

Carum carvi (caraway)
Caraway is one of the most ancient of all herbs and spices and is loved for its feathery foliage and the umbels of creamy-white summer flowers. It is a biennial plant, reaching a height of 60 cm in the second year.

Coriander sativum (coriander)
Coriander is a small annual plant that has been cultivated for thousands of years. This tall herb looks great amongst herbaceous perennials with its delicate leaves and its pinky-white flowers which appear during summer.

Foeniculum vulgare (fennel)
Fennel is a perennial herb which is most commonly grown as an annual. Grown at the back of the garden the fine leaves make a pleasant contrast with broader leafed plants. Small yellow flowers are formed in flat clusters in late summer and early autumn. It reaches a height of 1 m. Both the leaves and seeds have an anise flavour.

Borage self-seeds freely through the garden.

Hyssopus officinalis (hyssop)
An attractive shrubby plant with dark-green leaves and pretty blue flowers which exude a strong aroma, especially from the foliage.

Laurus nobilis (bay)
This small tree has dark green, shiny leaves which impart a wonderful flavour to soups, stews and casseroles. The leaves can be harvested any time of the year or dried for later use. Dry the leaves by hanging a bunch upside down in the kitchen and then store in a jar.

Melissa officinalis (lemon balm)
A charming and fragrant perennial with dark-green leaves that have a distinctive lemon scent, and creamy flowers during summer. It makes a good groundcover as it spreads easily, but dies back during winter. Plant lemon balm near a seat in a meditative part of the garden as it tends to radiate a tranquil effect.

Mentha species (mint)
There are many species of mint which are all rambling perennial plants spreading quickly through the garden. They are best planted in areas where they have considerable space and where they won't dominate the surrounding plants. Peppermint, spearmint, curled mint and apple mint are the most commonly grown varieties. Golden applemint has variegated leaves.

Monarda didyma (bergamot)
A perennial plant with highly scented reddish-coloured leaves and stunning scarlet flowers. Fresh leaves added to a pot of tea impart a wonderful aroma.

Ocimum basilicum (basil)
This splendid herb should be grown for its culinary uses as well as its attractive appearance. It is a low growing plant and can be placed in front of taller perennials.

Origanum majorana (marjoram)
Marjoram is one of the most fragrant and popular of all herbs reaching only 30 cm high and spreading up to 60 cm wide. The small, oval, grey-green leaves are velvety to the touch.

Origanum vulgare (oregano)
Often referred to as wild marjoram but much coarser than marjoram, with larger foliage and a sharper aroma, although the latter varies according to growing conditions. It is a hardy perennial, reaching 50 cm high and having small pink or white flowers.

Petroselinum crispum (parsley)
Parsley makes an ideal border plant, lasting for two years before going to seed. Grow parsley from seed. Soaking the seeds for twelve hours prior to sowing will hasten germination. Sow the seed in a punnet and cover with a piece of wet towelling. Check the seed after one week, leaving the towelling on until germination. When the seedlings are about 7.5 cm high transfer them to the garden bed in a dense row, as parsley will tolerate crowding.

Pimpinella anisum (anise)
This attractive herb has dainty light-green leaves and creamy-white flowers during summer. The seed of the plant is what is commonly known as aniseed, and the distinctive flavour and aroma of the plant comes from the anise oil found inside the seed.

The pretty, mauve–pink flowers of comfrey appear during summer.

Rumex acetosa (garden sorrel)
Rumex scutatus (French sorrel)
Sorrel has delightful apple green leaves similar in appearance to English spinach. Most of the sorrels are vigorous-rooted perennials found growing wild in damp meadows and roadsides in almost every corner of the globe. Some varieties, however, have been cultivated. Sorrel reaches 60 cm in height, but the flower stalks may reach 120 cm. Being a perennial, it will die down in winter but appears in abundance the following spring to provide leaves until autumn.

Ruta graveolens (rue)
Rue is commonly known as the Herb of Grace, named by Shakespeare for its strong aroma and flavour. It is a perennial plant having small grey-green leaves and yellow flowers in summer.

Salvia officinalis (sage)
Sage is a woody perennial plant with oblong, woolly, grey-green leaves. It reaches a height of 90 cm or more. The flowers are purple and appear on tall spikes.

Sanquisorba minor (salad burnet)
Salad burnet is a most attractive, lacy-looking plant but despite its delicate appearance, it is hardy and can survive a frosty winter. Once established in the right position it is easy to grow and will self-seed every spring.

Satureia hortensis (savory)
Savory is an annual plant with a strong aroma that grows wild throughout the Mediterranean area and is widely cultivated as a kitchen herb elsewhere. It has small dark green leaves and either white or mauve flowers.

Symphytum officinale (comfrey)
This perennial herb is valued for its large, hairy, grey-green leaves and its whitish or pale purple flowers. Once established in the garden it will reappear annually, but beware of comfrey's tendency to dominate other plants.

Tanacetum vulgare (tansy)
Tansy is an attractive perennial plant which, if planted outside doors or windows, is reputed to repel flies. It is an easily cultivated plant which has delicate, lacy, soft-green leaves and flat, yellow, daisy-like flowers.

A cook's garden

These plants are indispensable ingredients in the kitchen. Plant them near the kitchen door for easy access.

Basil, bay, chives, chervil, caraway, coriander, cumin, dill, garlic, horseradish, hyssop, lavender, marjoram, oregano, parsley, rosemary, sage, savory.

Herbs as companion plants

Anise	Sprinkle coriander and anise seeds together to assist germination.
Basil	Basil will grow happily in conjunction with most plants except rue.
Borage	Plant with strawberries.
Caraway	The long roots of caraway help to break down heavy soils making it easier for shallow-rooted plants to grow. Do not grow close to fennel.
Camomile	Compatible with most ornamental plants.
Chives	Plant chives underneath roses to keep aphids and black spot away. Planted underneath apple trees they will prevent apple scab.
Garlic	Roses and garlic are mutually compatible, and the smell of the garlic helps to keep aphids away.
Hyssop	Plant hyssop near grapes. It is a good general insect repellent in the garden.
Lemon balm	Lemon balm always radiates a tranquil atmosphere. Plant in a quiet area of the garden where you enjoy sitting.
Nasturtium	Grow near apple trees to prevent woolly aphid.
Parsley	Compatible with roses and tomatoes.
Rue	It is reputed to deter houseflies when grown near windows and doors.
Sage	Grow next to rosemary.
Tansy	Will repel ants and flies and is also a good moth repellent. The leaves rubbed into the fur of pets will repel fleas. Added to the compost heap it will assist fermentation.
Thyme	Beneficial to most plants in the garden.
Yarrow	Increases the aromatic qualities of most herbs.

THE PRODUCTIVE GARDEN

Growing fruit and vegetables is one of life's true delights as great enjoyment can be achieved from watching the crops grow and eventually picking them for the table. And there are many good reasons in these days of environmental and health awareness for making the effort to grow fresh produce.

THE ART OF VEGETABLE CULTIVATION

The noble art of vegetable cultivation is an important and civilising aspect of any society. All you need to produce fresh, chemical-free vegetables is a little ground space or, if that isn't available, some large pots.

Apart from the ordinary, well-known vegetables there are now many interesting cultivars suitable for the home garden. In addition to the staple vegetables you should include crops which are a delight to the palate and not easily obtainable from the greengrocer.

When planning your garden, be bold and include vegetables in garden beds. The inclusion of vegetables in a predominantly decorative planting creates a surprise element. Perhaps you could have a border of carrots, mignonette lettuce or beetroot. The texture and colour of some vegetables' leaves will certainly add interest. For example, two new varieties of silverbeet with impressive leaves are 'Ruby Chard' with its bright red stalks and veins and 'Five Colour Mix' which has stems of red, yellow, orange, cream and white.

It is, of course, usually easier to grow vegetables in plots of their own. Design the vegetable garden to fit in with the style of your house and garden. A Federation style house with a cottage garden could perhaps have a small picket fence around the plot. A native garden, with its natural appeal, might have its vegetable plot surrounded with logs.

Vegetable gardens are well-suited to be used as features in themselves. They may be formally designed with highly structured lines like herb gardens, or informal with pathways meandering through them.

SITING THE VEGETABLE GARDEN

This is one of the most important considerations if a good yield is to be achieved. There are certain essential ground rules if maximum results are to be expected. The most important considerations are undoubtedly sun, wind protection and good drainage.

SUN

Vegetables require as much sun as possible and should be planted out of the shade of high

Carrots thrive in an old wheelbarrow. The use of such unusual containers adds visual interest, particularly to vegetable gardens.

buildings, trees and fences. The only exceptions to this rule are some lettuce and beetroot which prefer a little shade in summer, but this requirement can be fulfilled by planting them on the south side of a large crop like corn or tomatoes.

Wind

Sheltered vegetable gardens have been proved to increase their yield by up to 50 per cent over those subject to windy conditions. A windbreak can be created by using small shrubs. Shade cloth battened to posts is also very effective.

Drainage

Good drainage is essential for vegetables. The easiest method of treating poorly drained areas is to raise the garden beds. There are two effective methods of creating raised beds. The first is to dig a trench around the outside perimeter of the garden and then raise the bed by using the soil from the trenches. To ensure good drainage throughout the entire garden dig trenches in rows from one side of the bed to the other. The trenches, which should be from 30 cm to 40 cm wide and about 20 cm deep, can then be used as paths to facilitate access for maintenance and harvesting. If the bed is still not sufficiently raised, dig in copious amounts of compost, manure or topsoil.

The second method is to build a wall around the outside of the garden, or around individual sections with lower pathways between the sections. Railway sleepers, bricks, concrete blocks or logs can be used. The garden bed can now be built up with a mixture of topsoil, compost or manure to make it level with the top of the wall.

Soil

The secret to success lies in the preparation of the soil. Improve the soil before planting by digging in copious amounts of manure a couple of weeks before planting. I prefer chicken manure or mushroom compost.

Buttercrunch lettuce form a pretty flower garden border. The inclusion of vegetables in a predominantly decorative planting creates an element of surprise.

Space-saving techniques

Where space is limited consider what is known as the 'space/yield ratio'. Spinach, Chinese cabbage, radishes, carrots, beetroot, shallots and lettuce require minimal space but have a high yield.

You should also consider growing crops vertically, as any sunny area against a fence or the side of the house is suitable. You may plant beans, peas, chokos or even cucumbers as long as they are given sufficient support to keep the weight from pulling the vines off the fence.

Another space saving tactic is the growing of climbing pea or bean crops on teepees made from wooden stakes. Plant the seeds at the base of each stake. Crops preferring a little shade like lettuce and beetroot should be planted underneath.

A wandering pumpkin runs riot through this herb and vegetable garden.

Crop rotation

Crop rotation is not practised as commonly today as it once was. Crop rotation used to be the major method of pest and disease control and its main advantage is that the nutrients available in the soil can be used sequentially for crops with different feeding requirements which are planted progressively. For example, leaf crops which require plenty of nitrogen should be followed by root crops which do not. The roots of legumes will reach down into deeper soil layers and absorb essential elements which are then brought to the surface where they become available to other plants. The roots of legumes are also inhabited by nitrogen-fixing bacteria which are capable of taking large amounts of nitrogen out of the air and making them available to the roots of other plants.

Vegetables can be divided into two groups — heavy feeders and light feeders. Heavy feeders, like cabbage, cauliflower, tomatoes, lettuce, endive, spinach, celery, leek, pumpkin and cucumber, should be planted initially in newly built up and fertilised soil. Follow these with crops of lighter-feeding plants like beans, peas, carrots, beetroot, radishes, mustard, cress, turnips or shallots.

Rotate the crops annually so that those from the one family are not planted in the same spot.

Succession planting

Plant vegetables at fortnightly intervals so that one planting will come into harvest as another finishes bearing. This ensures a continuous supply of vegetables rather than an oversupply of one crop.

An additional way to extend the harvest is to plant vegetables with different maturity dates. Certain vegetables are classified as 'early', 'mid-season' or 'late'.

Garden layout

A vegetable garden may be used as a feature. I have seen circular gardens with paths laid out like the spokes of a wheel as in traditional herb gardens and large beds brimming with vegetables and herbs used as a garden's centrepiece.

It is a good idea to keep track of the varieties you plant. If one is a disappointment or does not grow well in your area, switch to another variety the next year. You will eventually build up a preferential list of plants that grow well in relation to the amount of work you are willing to do. Leave an area in the garden for perennial vegetables such as asparagus and horseradish.

The size of your garden is usually dictated by the amount of available land, the time you wish to spend tending it and the number of people for whom it is to provide food.

Nasturtiums in the vegetable garden

The leaves and flowers of nasturtiums make interesting additions to salads and the presence of the plant in the garden is invaluable. Nasturtiums secrete a mustard oil which many insects find attractive and they will thus seek nasturtiums out in preference to any cabbage, broccoli, cauliflower, kohlrabi or turnips growing nearby. The orange flowers of nasturtiums are also reputed to repel aphids. It makes good sense to grow them around the edge of the vegetable garden or interplant them with the rows of crops. Planted next to radish they will improve the taste and planted next to cucumber they will repel cucumber beetles. A spray made from nasturtium leaves will control the spread of woolly aphid on apple trees. Alternatively, let the climbing varieties twine up the trunks of apple trees.

Companion planting with vegetables

Wherever plants are grown in the wild there are always mixtures which, in accordance

CIRCULAR HERB AND VEGETABLE GARDEN

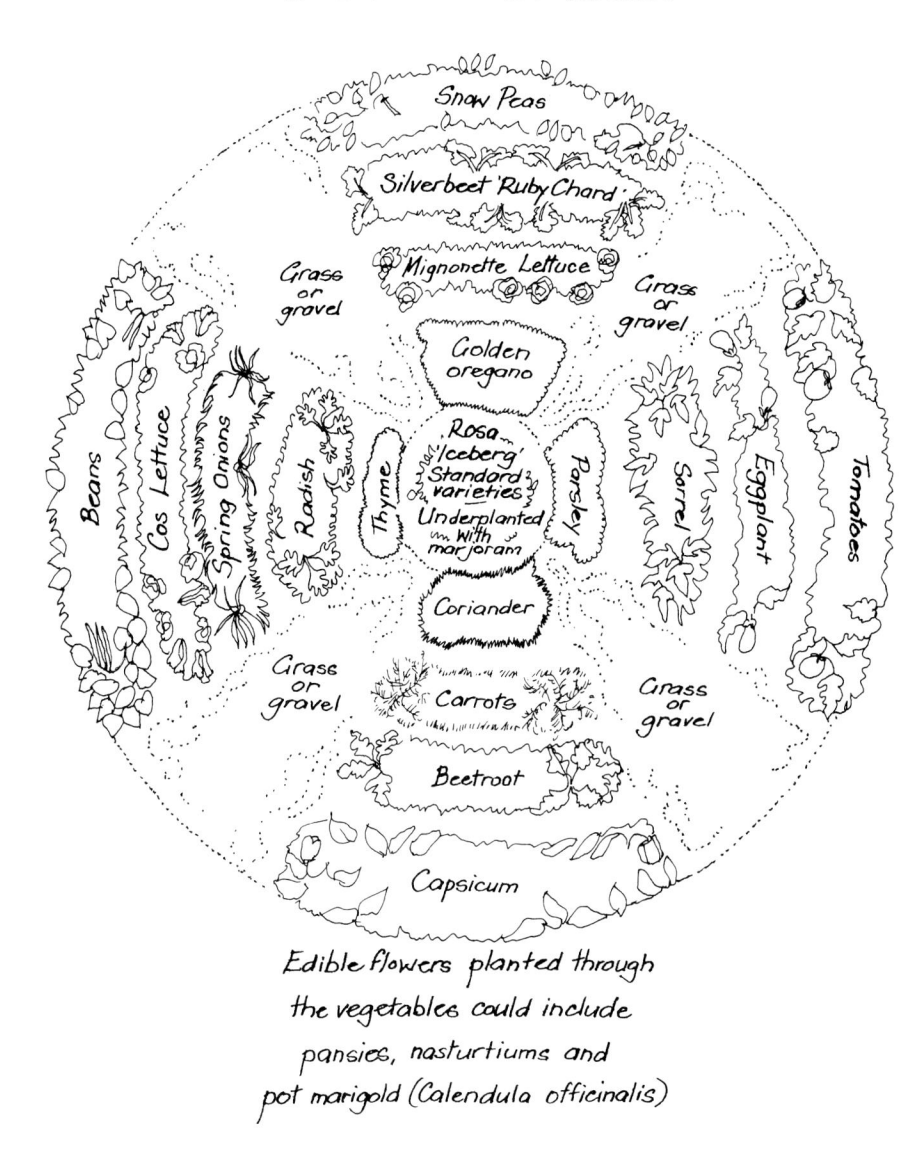

Edible flowers planted through the vegetables could include pansies, nasturtiums and pot marigold (Calendula officinalis)

with the soil type and local climatic conditions, are able to live together and complement each other. In nature this mixture of plants is called a 'natural plant association'. Plants in an association utilise to the fullest extent such environmental factors as light, moisture, and soil. For example, plants that require less light live in the shade of those which have full light. Also the roots of some plants live close to the surface, while those of others penetrate to greater depths. The smell of certain herbs will deter some insects from attacking vegetables, so

Companion plants

Plant	Compatible plants	Non-compatible plants
Asparagus	Tomatoes, parsley	
Beans	Cauliflower, corn, radishes, cucumber, carrots, beetroot	Garlic, onions, shallots
Beetroot	Dwarf beans, onions, kohlrabi	Mustard
Broccoli	Onions, aromatic herbs	Strawberries
Brussels sprout	Onions, herbs	
Cabbage	Beetroot, celery, onions, tomatoes, herbs	Strawberries
Carrots	Peas, lettuce, radish, leeks	Dill
Cauliflower	Onions, herbs, celery	
Celery	Beans, leeks, tomatoes, cauliflower	
Corn	Peas, beans	
Kohlrabi	Beetroot, onion	Tomatoes, pole beans
Lettuce	Carrots, strawberries, radishes, cabbage, beetroot	
Onions	Beetroot, carrots, lettuce, cabbage	
Peas	Radishes, carrots, cucumber, beans, turnips, sweet corn	Onions, garlic
Potatoes	Corn, beans, peas, cabbage	Dill, tomatoes, sunflowers
Radish	Carrots, peas, lettuce, nasturtium	
Tomatoes	Asparagus, parsley, cabbage, marigolds, chives, carrots	Kohlrabi, fennel, potatoes
Turnips	Peas	

that spraying will be unnecessary.

In creating a vegetable garden it is possible to imitate nature's mixed plantings by using plants that are mutually compatible and which make demands on the environment at different times.

Maintaining the vegetable garden

Even where soil has been built up initially with manures or compost, vegetables will still benefit from regular feeding.

Feeding

I usually apply solutions of soluble fertiliser every three weeks to growing vegetables. Although it may seem unnecessary, I find that

Silverbeet and lettuce flourish among irises, roses, poppies and herbs.

fertiliser applied to rich soil will ensure a constant growth rate.

When applying fertiliser, whether it be commercial liquid or commercial dry fertiliser, blood and bone, fish emulsion, seaweed emulsion or manure, always be sure to follow the directions on the package. Too much is usually more dangerous than not enough.

Watering Regular watering is essential for healthy vegetables. Many vegetables consist of almost 90 per cent water and to get a good harvest a continual water supply must be maintained.

Precise instructions on when and how to water are very difficult to give as there are many considerations like weather and soil type.

The main rule for watering is to give a thorough soaking every few days, rather than watering lightly every day.

Some crops require more watering than others. Leaf crops like lettuce, cabbage and

The circular vegetable patch is a feature of this large garden. The lattice fence provides protection from wind and is used to support climbing vegetables.

celery require more frequent watering than root crops.

Mulching

A mulched vegetable garden will produce healthy plants more quickly than an unmulched one. Organic mulches consisting of materials like straw, compost, leaf mould, lawn clippings, peat moss, manures or mushroom compost eventually break down and add their matter to the soil. This in turn improves the soil texture, which will increase the water and nutrient- holding capacity of the soil. Earthworms thrive in the layer of soil just below the mulch, and carry on their work of aerating and enriching the soil. They carry broken-down bits of mulch below the surface, thus increasing the amount of humus around the roots.

The materials used for the mulch will generally depend on local availability of materials.

The best time to mulch is when the soil is completely free from weeds and is well watered. Add to the mulch as it decomposes and after the harvest it can be dug into the garden to provide texture to the soil. A new mulch can be applied with the next planting.

FRUIT AND BERRIES

Landscaping with fruit allows one to combine beauty and practicality. The presence of fruit trees creates an Edenic tone as well as an air of productivity. A few fruit bearing plants will be sufficient to enhance the atmosphere in your garden, particularly if you choose exotic varieties rather than everyday types. I recommend that you consider a range of fruit inspired by culinary requirements.

Fruit trees and berries need not necessarily be planted in beds of their own. Feature them in shrub or perennial borders or drape the climbing types over a pergola to provide summer shade. There are few sights more exotic than a pergola dripping with banana passionfruit.

Most of these luscious crops take up little ground space and provide you with an abundance of fruit. Many berries and vines planted during winter will bear fruit quickly — some during the first season after planting.

A good soil, plenty of sunshine and regular applications of manure, compost or complete plant food are the decisive factors for growing these crops.

Two exotic perennial fruits for a border are naranjilla and cape gooseberry. Naranjilla (*Solanum quitoense*) looks rather like an eggplant and bears large passionfruit-like fruit with a taste similar to a pineapple strawberry. Planted from seed and grown in a frost-free position it will bear fruit in its second and third years. The delightful orange berries of the cape gooseberry (*Physalis peruviana*) are wrapped in a paper-thin, lantern-shaped husk which protects them from insects and soil rot. In warm climates fruit is produced throughout the year.

A very new fruit to Australia is the Nashi pear. Its superb taste resembles a cross between a crisp, crunchy apple and a sweet, juicy pear. Originally from China and Japan, it will thrive in cool to cold climates but can also withstand periods of drought and inundation. Nashi forms quite a large tree but can be kept in bounds by regular pruning or can be espaliered. Nashi pears are becoming available in nurseries and can also be raised from the seeds of bought fruit.

Other unusual and very ornamental trees are the tree tomato (*Cyphomandra betacea*) (or tamarillo as it is often called), lychee (*Nephelium* species) and feijoa or pineapple guava (*Feijoa sellowiana*).

The tree tomato is a small, umbrella-shaped evergreen tree which looks spectacular when it is covered in its red, oval-shaped, pendulous fruits. It will grow in all districts except those with cold climates.

Lychees are large trees reaching 7-8 m in height. They will thrive in the more tropical areas of Australia where the summers are humid, long and hot. The foliage is glossy and the fruits look like large strawberries with a brittle shell enclosing a delicious pulp. Grafted trees produce an abundance of fruit four to five years after planting.

The name 'pineapple guava' is simply a popular name, as the plant and fruit are completely distinct from the strawberry or common guava. Pineapple guava grows wild in Brazil and other South American countries and was introduced to Europe around 1890. Pineapple guava forms a decorative small tree reaching a height of about 4 m and can be used as a specimen or screen tree. The silky-stamened, pompom-like flowers appear in late spring and are followed by the fruit, which has a penetrating aroma and tastes like a blend of pineapple and strawberries.

The name of the African Horned Melon should be sufficient to tempt you to grow it. It makes an interesting addition to fruit salads or sorbets and can be used as an ice-cream top-

256 CREATING YOUR *IDEAL* GARDEN

The small lemon tree makes a wonderful feature in this courtyard garden.

ping. This unusual looking fruit has orange coloured skin which is covered in horns. A member of the cucumber family, it forms a sprawling vine (1-1.5 m) and makes an excellent groundcover. It grows easily from seed in summer when frosts have finished.

For hedges with a difference try the strawberry guava (*Psidium cattleianum*) or the natal plum (*Carissa grandiflora*). Strawberry guava is a large evergreen shrub having red skinned fruit with pinkish-white flesh and a pleasant strawberry flavour. Its vitamin C content is higher than citrus. A bonus is its attractive mottled bark.

The fruit of Natal plums tastes similar to cranberries and is generally used for sauces and jams. The foliage is attractive and spiny and the large white flowers are very fragrant.

Banana passionfruit (*Passiflora molissima*) is a fast-growing evergreen climber which will reach a height of 10 m.
The spectacular, large, pink flowers are followed by soft, banana-like passionfruit in autumn. It deserves to be more widely grown as it is much more disease-resistant than purple passionfruit.

Blueberries are superb when eaten fresh or added to pies and cakes. However you must be prepared to compete with avaricious birds when harvesting this fruit. The main requirements of these extremely hardy small bushes are a rich, acidic soil and a cold climate. Two plants are needed for cross-pollination. Tuck them into a flower border or place them at the back of the vegetable garden. Pruning is not generally required until blueberries are four or five years old and this merely entails cutting back the slender centre stems, which do not bear much fruit.

Currants, which belong to the genus *Ribes*, are ornamental and valued for their fruit, flowers and autumn colour. Like blueberries they prefer cold climates. The blackcurrant forms a caney plant, while red or white currants grow as single-stemmed bushes.

The difference between a raspberry and other bramble fruits is that the former pulls free of its core when you pick it. The exquisite taste of home-grown raspberries can't be equalled by store bought fruit. Raspberries can be grown against a fence or at the back of a garden bed. Pruning encourages an abundance of fruit and is carried out during the winter months by removing all canes that held fruit the previous season. New canes thus produced are left to crop the following season. Boysenberries and loganberries have a similar growth habit to raspberries and fruit just as prolifically. A cold climate is essential for success with these fruits.

The common strawberry is still worth a place in any sized garden. The taste of freshly picked strawberries cannot be surpassed. Strawberries don't require a garden bed of their own. Grow them in pots, hanging baskets, as groundcovers or as border plants. Strawberries are among the easiest fruits to grow, producing a bumper crop several months after planting. A rich soil and frequent watering are their main requirements. Strawberries can grow and make reasonable fruit in the partial shade of other plants but are stronger and more prolific in full sunlight.

The summer shade of a mulberry tree makes a delightful setting for entertaining.

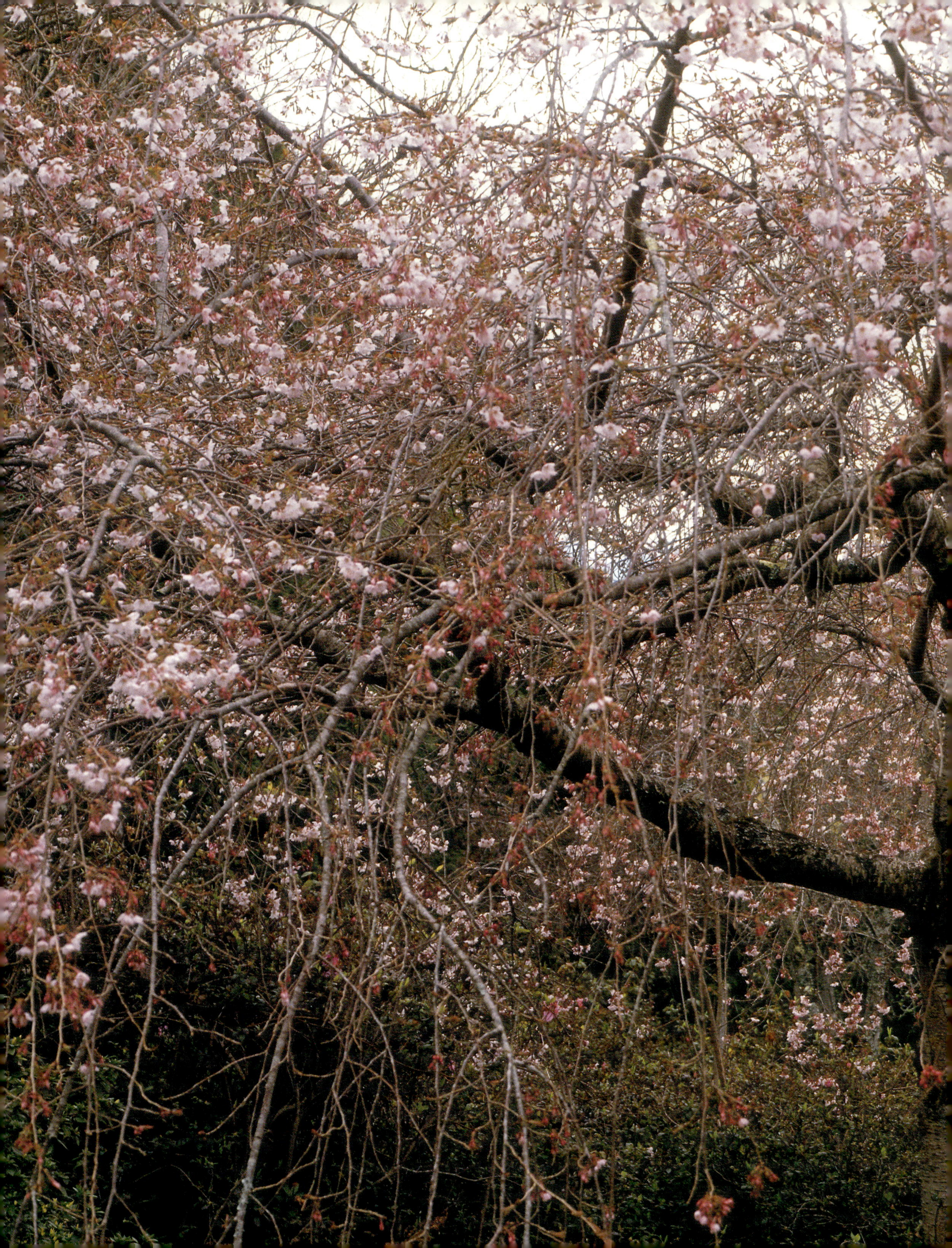

PRACTICALITIES

Maintaining the Effect

The main rule for a healthy garden is to watch your plants and become aware of their needs. A basic knowledge of soil preparation, mulching and feeding will enable you to plan your own maintenance programme.

Soil

Anyone who is interested in gardening quickly learns that the quality of the soil invariably makes the difference between success and failure. One of the secrets of nature is the balance between soil and plants. The soil is the essence of good gardening. It should be teeming with life and as rich and wholesome as soil in a forest.

Taking the time and trouble to understand and prepare the soil initially will save hours of labour and reward you with a healthy garden. Plants will grow more quickly and will be less likely to be affected by pests and diseases.

A good garden should have a topsoil that is at least a metre deep, is reasonably fertile and has a good balance of sand, silt and clay particles. It should have the right amount of air between these particles to promote both good drainage and water retention. It must also have a good acid/alkaline balance for healthy plant growth.

To understand the soil you need to understand certain physical and chemical characteristics. Physical characteristics include the soil's composition, texture and drainage. The main chemical characteristic to be aware of is the pH level.

Components of the soil

Soil consists of inorganic materials, organic matter, water, air and living organisms. Although the proportions may vary, the major components remain the same.

- **Inorganic materials:** the basis of soil components, e.g. sand, silt and clay.
- **Organic matter:** improves the structure of the soil, increases the ability of the soil to hold water, retains nutrients and affects the temperature of the soil.
- **Organisms:** earthworms, fungi and bacteria are examples of organisms which break down the organic matter and increase the nutrients (especially nitrogen) available to plants. Organisms also break down the minerals in the soil and certain fungi assist the plants in the absorption of nutrients.
- **Water:** transports nutrients, keeps the soil temperature down, assists the plants in keeping erect and breaks down minerals.
- **Air:** essential for the growth of plants' roots and helps to break down minerals. Living organisms in the soil require air to live.

Soil texture

The characteristics of soil change greatly from place to place according to climatic and geological conditions. Soil formed from sandstone, for example, is less fertile and more sandy than soil formed from shale. Soil formed in dry climates has totally different characteristics from soil formed in wet climates, just as soil on a slope is different from soil found at the base of it. Because of these variations soil is classified according to its texture and will contain sand, silt, clay or loam in differing proportions and combinations.

The term 'soil texture' can be

A healthy soil is the key to success in any garden.

defined as the quality of a soil resulting from the proportions of sand, silt or clay it contains. A clay soil would therefore be a fine soil as it contains a high proportion of clay and silt particles. On the other hand a sandy soil would be a coarse soil because it contains a high proportion of sand particles. A soil that is roughly intermediate, containing both clay and sand, is termed a loam.

TESTING THE SOIL

If you feel your soil is not of the best quality then there are several simple tests that can be carried out to provide you with rudimentary but helpful information. The easiest method is to test small handfuls of soil from different areas of the garden. Add a little water to make each one slightly moist. Roll this mixture in the palm of your hands until it forms a thread the shape of a small sausage. Compare the consistency with the chart to assess its texture.

REGENERATING THE SOIL

SANDY SOIL

Sandy soil has its advantages as well as its disadvantages. The main disadvantage is that it drains too quickly and nutrients are lost with this free drainage. Sandy soil is easy to improve by adding plenty of organic matter like leaf mould, compost or animal manure. These will increase its water-holding capacity and will supply nutrients to the plants.

LOAM

Most loam soils are easy to work and have good drainage. Adding organic matter into the soil provides nutrients which will be released slowly to plants.

Soil texture	Soil characteristic
Sand	A thread cannot be formed as it becomes a fluid mass when moisture is added.
Sandy loam	Fairly hard to roll into a thread but can be kneaded into a cohesive cylinder that will break easily on bending.
Loam	Threads are not easy to form but can be rolled easily into a cylinder which does not break on gentle bending.
Clay loam	Has a silky feeling and can be rolled into threads which are difficult to bend into a ring.
Clay	Can be rolled into long threads which bend easily.

CLAY

A clay soil has its problems because it retains a high percentage of water. It needs to be watered less often than a sandy soil but it will restrict the normal penetration of the root system because of the slow movement of air and the slow drainage. A clay soil can be balanced by adding large quantities of organic matter like compost, leaf mould or animal manure. Gypsum should also be added as it causes a coagulation of clay particles and this facilitates the drainage and movement of air through the soil. There is a liquid product on the market called an organic claybreaker which, when watered into the soil, will break up the heavy clay. It is claimed that the claybreaker is totally organic and that the treatment will be effective within six to eight weeks of application. It need only be used every four years, but for best results the claybreaker should be used in conjunction with organic matter.

SOIL pH

Soil pH is a measure of the amount of acidity or alkalinity in the soil. The pH of the soil can affect a plant's growth in the following ways: it has an effect on the availability of essential nutrients; it has an effect on soil micro-organisms; and it affects the roots' ability to absorb both water and nutrients.

The pH level of the soil is measured on a scale which runs from zero to fourteen. Zero is on the acid end and fourteen is on the alkaline end. At the middle of the scale, i.e. seven, the soil will be neutral. The soil can be tested by obtaining a pH soil-testing kit from garden centres or nurseries. If you find that the soil is too acidic, this can be corrected easily by adding dolomite or lime. Wood ash is also beneficial to acidic soils. An alkaline soil can be corrected by adding organic matter such as peat, pine leaves or decayed oak leaves.

SOIL ANALYSIS

If you suspect that your soil has any deficiencies — perhaps it is not producing the results you anticipated — a sample can be sent away to a laboratory for soil analysis. This test will tell you if there are any minerals lacking, or if the soil is out of balance. These problems are generally remedied by the addition of the appropriate rock minerals.

A garden with an abundance of plant material and no bare earth in sight will seldom have to be weeded.

Mulching

In a natural environment leaves and other plant materials are constantly falling to the ground to form a mulch. This mulch provides nutrients to the forest plants and makes the ground a suitable host for germinating seeds so that the forest will regenerate. This natural process, which has been emulated in the home garden, is proving to be one of the most popular aspects of garden maintenance.

Mulching benefits

- **Insulation:** Mulching keeps the soil warm in winter and cool in summer
- **Fertiliser:** Manure, compost and leaves release nutrients into the soil as they break down.
- **Moisture:** A layer of mulch will prevent evaporation. This means the garden needs to be watered less often and thus nutrients are not leached too quickly from the soil.
- **Weeding:** A mulched garden prevents, or greatly reduces, the growth of weeds around plants.
- **Plant protection:** Ground-hugging vegetables like cucumbers, strawberries and zucchinis don't rot when they grow on a layer of mulch. They tend to spoil more quickly when they are touching the bare earth.

The best mulches consist of materials like straw, compost, leaf mould, peat moss, manures, pine leaves or mushroom compost. Organic mulches are biodegradable, meaning they eventually break down and add their matter to the soil. Earthworms also thrive in the layer of soil just below the mulch, and carry on their work of aerating and enriching the soil. They carry broken bits of mulch below the surface, thus increasing the amount of humus around the roots.

When to mulch

When starting a new garden mulch thoroughly with manure or compost which is at least 7.5 cm thick. This will help to build up the soil. As the garden becomes full of plants a full mulch should only be needed every couple of years. Shrubs and perennials should be mulched individually around their root systems as a form of feeding in early spring. Be careful not to cover any self-sown seedlings. The easiest method of applying the mulch is to use a garden fork or trowel, spreading the mulch around the base of the plant.

Compost — natural recycling

Recycling is an important aspect of late twentieth-century life. Not all recycling methods are new, however. Composting is a traditional way of using waste organic material and one that is receiving increasing attention as individuals seek to adopt energy efficient practices.

The ordinary compost heap is the site of a remarkable metamorphosis. A regenerative cycle is under way involving the transformation from life to death and back again as the leaves and stalks of dying and dead plants give vitality to the growth of the coming season.

Compost is more than a fertiliser or healing agent for the soil's wounds. In nature it is part of an incessant process. As leaves fall to the ground they slowly decay, supplying fresh food to plants. In the garden, where the process has been interrupted by cultivation, compost must be created by the gardener. It becomes an intensified version of a natural happening.

Organic matter is valuable to the soil only when it is decaying. Even 'finished compost' is only partly decayed. As it continues to break down it creates food for growing populations of micro-organisms. It is also a breeding ground for some of the helpful bacteria and moulds which attack many of the fungi that produce plant diseases.

Compost improves the structure, water-holding capacity and aeration of soils containing excessive amounts of clay or sand.

The range of suitable organic materials is considerable. All types of leaves, hay, waste vegetable matter, vegetable garden refuse, sawdust, wood wastes, grass clippings or any animal manures or weeds can be used. People who balk at the suggestion of adding weeds overlook the fact that a well made compost heap should reach an internal temperature of 42 degrees centigrade, which will kill any weed seeds present.

RULES OF COMPOST-MAKING

There are a few set rules of compost-making. It is not simply a matter of throwing waste vegetable matter into a heap and waiting several months for it to miraculously turn into rich, friable humus. If you follow some guidelines, compost can be made with a minimum of problems.

Inside a compost heap many kinds of bacteria and fungi go to work breaking down or decomposing the various materials in the pile. To do this successfully, the bacteria need a source of energy and a certain amount of moisture. And depending on the type of bacteria, oxygen may be needed.

Aerobic bacteria (those requiring oxygen to live and work) are the most desirable because they are more effective than anaerobic bacteria (those not requiring oxygen). The type of bacteria you have depends entirely on how often you turn the compost heap. Frequent turning of the heap makes it desirable to aerobic bacteria. The more frequently you turn the heap the quicker the process of decomposition will be. Anaerobic bacteria, though slower, will achieve the same result and the heap in which they grow will not require as much of your attention.

Location of the heap is important. A shady location is preferable as sun will dry out the heap too frequently. Avoid placing it in a depression where it might become waterlogged during heavy periods of rain. Although moisture is essential, as it influences the micro-organisms, if the heap is waterlogged the aerobic bacteria will be smothered and the decomposition process will take longer.

BUILDING THE HEAP

Ideally there should always be two piles of compost going simultaneously: the completed pile that is decomposing and one in the process of being built.

It is not absolutely necessary to have an enclosure around the compost heap but an enclosure does make the pile easier to build and maintain. It also prevents any loose materials from being blown around.

The type of bin built can be simple or elaborate — depending on the construction materials available. Bricks or concrete blocks may be used, although spaces must always be left between the bricks to allow air in and excess water to escape. There is no reason why a compost container can't be attractive. In small gardens where the compost can't be hidden bins can be constructed from bush rocks or picket fences. Plastic compost bins and compost tumblers are also handy for gardens where space is limited.

The ideal size for a compost heap is 1.25 m square and 1.5 m high. It can, of course, be larger or smaller depending on the size of the garden. One of the simplest and most effective methods of building a container involves using metal fencing poles and chicken wire. Four stakes are needed for a single heap and six stakes for two heaps. Only three sides of the structure need to be enclosed with chicken wire. The beauty of this type of container is that it allows free air circulation around it.

A SIMPLE COMPOST BIN

Use two bins: one to provide a completed pile, while the other contains decomposing material.

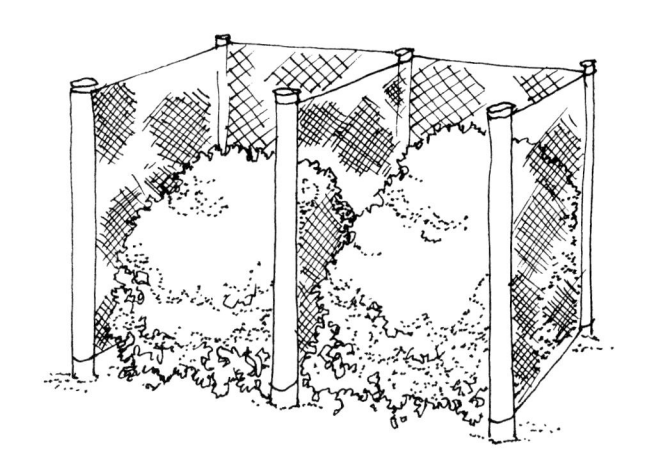

BEGINNING THE HEAP

The most efficient method of making compost is to layer the materials so that decomposition will take place more quickly. Commence by spreading a 20 cm layer of waste material in the bottom of the pit. Then add a layer of manure — if you have it (or a layer of fertiliser). Top this off with 3 cm of topsoil and moisten thoroughly. Lime can be added at this stage if an alkaline compost is required. Repeat the layering process until you reach the desired height. Try to use manure rather than a complete fertiliser if you want an organic heap. However, adding a fertiliser high in nitrogen to each layer will feed the bacteria so they can do their work more efficiently. It will also produce compost with a balanced fertility.

When assembling the materials

Compost can be applied to the garden at any time of the year.

for each layer, try to mix different kinds of materials. Layers consisting of one material, such as grass clippings or leaves, will not decompose quickly.

Adding layers of soil throughout the heap helps to bring in microbes, absorb odours, and hold the compost heap in place.

Managing the heap

As mentioned earlier, as long as there is oxygen within the pile, the aerobic bacteria will swiftly decompose the materials. As soon as the supply of oxygen is exhausted, anaerobic bacteria take over and decomposition takes much longer.

About three weeks after the heap is completed, turn it over thoroughly by forking the outside part of the heap towards the centre. Turning it every three to four weeks will ensure compost is ready for the garden in about three months time.

The bacteria that turn wastes into compost also need moisture. Ideally, the composting material should be spongy, but not soggy. A waterlogged compost heap will block out oxygen preventing the aerobic bacteria from doing their work. Water is also required because of the high temperatures that are generated inside the heap. Such high temperatures can dry out the compost. If it's allowed to dry, the finished compost will burn and be of little value in improving your soil.

Finished compost

Finished compost should be a dark brown colour and have a pleasant earthy smell. It can be used either as a mulch or dug into the soil prior to planting. Compost makes an excellent mulch, both in the vegetable garden and around flowers and shrubs. It also adds texture to the soil.

Compost can be applied at any time of the year. If it is ready to use before you're ready to use it, cover it with plastic or tin to prevent the nutrients from leaching away.

Seaweed in the compost heap

Seaweed will compost easily if it is used with other materials as it contains alginic acid, a bacteria stimulator which makes it an efficient compost accelerator. If it is allowed to dry in the sun, it becomes brittle, making it easy to shred or chop. Add the chopped pieces into the layers of the compost heap.

Quick compost

A quick way of making compost is to shred the ingredients. Compost shredders are available, run by a 5 horsepower, 4-stroke engine. These process all the ingredients including hedge clippings and small branches which are otherwise too solid for the heap. The heap works quickly because the aeration of the mass is greatly improved, as shredded material has less tendency to pack down. Because of this moisture control is better and the heap is much easier to turn.

A shredded heap is not layered. The shredded material is simply piled on the heap and manure or a complete fertiliser is added. The heap should not be any more than 1.25 m high and should be turned three days after it is finished. Thereafter, turn at least twice a week. It is not difficult to turn a shredded heap, as the material is light and fluffy. Compost should be ready for the garden in as little as four weeks. Naturally enough this type of compost is often superior in nutrient value because nutrients have not had time to leach out.

FEEDING

Plants must be fed regularly to keep them growing steadily and free from pests and diseases.

Plants require 16 elements to grow satisfactorily — three of which are the carbon, hydrogen and oxygen found in both air and water. The remaining 13 elements required are divided into two groups — major elements and minor or trace elements.

The major elements are: nitrogen, phosphorus, sulphur, potassium, magnesium and calcium.

The trace elements are: iron, manganese, boron, molybdenum, copper and zinc. Most of these elements are ever-present in the soil but the demands on nitrogen, phosphorus and potassium are such that they need to be replenished more regularly.

NITROGEN

This is the element necessary for the growth of new tissue and, in addition, it promotes vegetative growth. It is also essential in ensuring that plants have a healthy green colour. A nitrogen deficiency is easy to diagnose because the plants appear stunted with yellow or pale green leaves that seem thinner than normal. If the soil in a garden has been properly prepared initially with organic matter like manures and compost, it is unlikely there will be a shortage of nitrogen. Organic fertilisers (rather than the inorganic types like sulphate of ammonia, nitrate of soda and urea) should be applied while the plants are growing, as they are more stable and more easily absorbed, being released at a slower, steadier rate. The most commonly used nitrogen-rich fertilisers are: animal manure (poultry, horse, cow, sheep or rabbit) and seaweed where available.

An overdose of nitrogen in the soil will cause soft, sappy growth with much foliage but very few flowers and fruit.

PHOSPHORUS

This is the element essential for strong roots, healthy growth and fruit development. It also helps plants to resist disease. Plants deficient in phosphorus will appear to be stunted, with poor root growth and little or no fruit. The leaves also tend to become discoloured, turning to a purple, red or bluish-green colour. Organic sources of phosphorus are animal manures and wood ashes. Superphosphate, the inorganic source, should always be used sparingly as it leaches out of the soil slowly and can build up over a period of years.

POTASSIUM

An element required for the development of strong, robust plants. It builds up the firm outer tissues and is responsible for rich-coloured fruits. If the soil is deficient in potassium the plants will have virtually no resistance to heat, cold or disease and the process of photosynthesis will be slowed greatly. The organic sources of potassium include wood ash, straw, and all animal and poultry manures.

Feeding a garden organically, especially a vegetable garden, has proven to be better for one's health than using chemical additives. It also keeps the soil healthy and encourages earthworms.

Manure of any sort is an excellent source of plant food for all

INDICATORS THAT CERTAIN ELEMENTS ARE MISSING FROM THE SOIL

DEFICIENCY	SYMPTOM
Copper	Leaves at the top of the plant wilt and do not recover.
Magnesium	The older leaves turn yellow or red and dry out.
Nitrogen	Leaves turn a yellowish green and the older leaves dry out. Plants appear stunted.
Phosphorus	Leaves turn a very dark green and become red or purple.
Potassium	The leaves develop yellow streaks.
Sulphur	All the leaves turn yellow, starting with the younger ones.
Zinc	The leaves at the top of the plant start to wilt and do not recover. Vegetables have a bitter taste.

plants. It is versatile because it can be spread as a mulch, steadily releasing its nutrients into the soil, or made into a high-powered liquid fertiliser and used as a side dressing around growing plants.

LIQUID MANURE

Liquid manure is easily made by combining one-third manure to two-thirds water in a plastic bucket and letting it steep for about two weeks. Any type of animal manure can be used. Chicken manure works wonders when used on nitrogen-loving vegetables like lettuce, spinach, cabbage, endive, sorrel, mustard and cress.

SEAWEED

Seaweed is a valuable source of plant food. It contains as much nitrogen, half the phosphorus and twice as much potassium as manure, as well as an enormous variety of trace elements and powerful antibiotics. Between 20 and 50 per cent of some seaweeds are minerals. Hose the seaweed down to get rid of the salt before it is used. It can be dug directly into the ground when the garden bed is being prepared, or used as a mulch around plants. Because it is low in phosphorus, add some rock minerals or blood and bone.

WHEN TO FEED

Even if garden beds are mulched regularly with manure or compost I still tend to add supplementary plant food, especially under trees or shrubs where there is considerable root competition. An application of soluble plant food applied in early, mid and late spring and the same times again during summer will give plants in these areas an extra boost.

When applying fertiliser, whether it be commercial liquid or commercial dry fertiliser, blood and bone, fish emulsion, seaweed emulsion or manure, always be sure to follow the directions on the package. Too much is usually more dangerous than not enough.

WATERING

A garden that has been properly mulched and has a healthy soil full of organic matter is able to withstand a great deal of heat before it requires watering. An overwatered garden will weaken a plant's resistance as its roots will stay shallow. The roots of plants in a garden that has not been overwatered will go deeper into the earth looking for water. Unfortunately there are no hard and fast rules regarding when and how to water. It depends on the climate and the type of soil. The main point is to always water thoroughly so that the water seeps right down into the soil.

Healthy soil produces healthy plants which are less prone to insect infestation.

MAINTENANCE TIPS

- Weeds are not a big problem if the garden is packed with plants.
- Hand weeding should always be employed to prevent smaller self-sown seedlings from being disturbed.
- Don't cut off spent perennial and annual flowerheads. Let the seeds disperse through the garden and then cut the dead stalks back.
- Don't remove the leaves and stalks of bulbs before they have died right back. This allows nutrients to return to the bulb, ensuring quality flowers the next year.
- Fibrous-rooting perennials need only be divided every three years. This will encourage better flowers and gives you the chance to increase your perennial supply by replanting the divisions.
- A mulched garden will hold soil moisture and prevent weed growth.

Soil enriched with organic matter is important for the abundant planting of this garden.

CREATING NEW PLANTS

A simple hothouse provides ideal conditions for propagating seeds and cuttings.

GROWING FROM SEED

A seed is the product of a fertilised ovule, consisting of an embryo enclosed by a protective seed coat. It is a young undeveloped plant with a food source.

The process of a seed sprouting roots and leaves is one of the great miracles of nature. Three conditions need to be met before germination occurs: adequate moisture, suitable temperature and sufficient air. Moisture is necessary to soften the seed coat and allow the embryo (the undeveloped plant) to expand and grow. Suitable temperature is needed to break dormancy. Different seeds germinate at different temperatures.

Air is required for seeds to live. If the soil is waterlogged for an extended period or the seeds are started in a heavy potting mix, they will die. Because of this it is essential to have a potting mix that drains well, so that air can enter the soil.

Many people choose to buy seedlings from a nursery rather than start their own plants. The main advantage of starting your own seeds is the large choice of varieties available. Selection of ready-grown seedlings is always limited to a few popular varieties.

PROPAGATING CASES

Propagating cases can be obtained from garden centres and nurseries. The simplest type is a transparent lid or dome that fits over a seed tray. Also available are cases which are similar to miniature greenhouses. These are made of plastic over a wire frame and can be used for seeds or cuttings.

HOTBEDS

Hotbeds are used to start seedlings or cuttings early in the season. Heat is provided below the propagating mixture by an insulated cable laid 10-12 cm below the surface of the topsoil. Automatic temperature control can be obtained by using inexpensive thermostats.

A simple frame construction can be made using 5 cm thick planking. Make the sides 30 cm in length and join them together in a square. The lid, which must contain glass, can be either hinged to the frame or simply placed on top. The top should slope slightly so that water can run off easily. Sink the frame about 5 cm into the soil and fill it with topsoil or seed-raising mixture before planting the seeds.

An alternative method of heating a propagating frame was devised before the days of electricity and cables. Simply dig a pit 70 cm deep and fill it with fresh poultry manure. Place the propagating frame on top. The frame does not have a bottom so the manure will need to completely fill the pit with the frame fitting neatly on top. Water the manure well, then add some seed-raising mixture over the top or sink pots containing seed-raising mixture into it. Plant the seeds and keep the soil moist. The poultry manure generates considerable heat as it breaks down, heating the frame and germinating the seeds. The heat will last for up to three weeks which should be sufficient for the germination of most seeds. Afterwards the rotted manure can be used as a mulch in the salad garden.

COLD FRAMES

A cold frame is exactly the same basic structure as the hotbed, except that it relies on the sun's heat on the glass lid for seed germination. If you don't have a cold frame, improvise with a wooden box covered with a sheet of glass — an old window is ideal. Polystyrene vegetable boxes can also be used. Place in a semi-shaded position and make sure that the soil remains damp at all times.

Seed-raising mixtures

The mixture in which seeds are sown is very important. Seed-raising mixtures can be obtained from nurseries. Choose one that contains vermiculite so the mix will be open enough for the roots to penetrate easily and air to circulate. It should also hold water without becoming soggy. Seed-raising mixtures can be made at home by using the following ingredients:

1 part well-moistened and
  squeezed out peat moss
4 parts vermiculite
4 parts coarse river sand
  or
2 parts coarse river sand
1 part peat moss

Seedlings raised in home-made mixes like the above need to be fed with a soluble plant food diluted to half its normal strength when the plants reach 2.5 cm.

Sowing seeds

Press the seed-raising mixture firmly down to about 1 cm from the top of the tray. Fine seed usually only needs to be pressed down into the surface of the mix. Larger seeds usually need a soil covering of twice their thickness. The depth is usually indicated on the

The majority of perennials can be propagated from division. After division perennials can be swapped with other perennial lovers.

Growing plants from seeds and cuttings is an interesting and easy method of increasing the plants in your garden.

seed packet.

It is essential that while the seed is germinating the mix should be kept moist but not too wet. The easiest method of ensuring this is to place a plastic or glass cover over the container to help retain the moisture. Additional water will not be necessary unless the seeds take longer than three weeks to germinate. Alternatively, place the seed trays in a propagating case or start them in a hotbed or coldframe. Do not water from overhead as the seeds might be washed into congested drifts. If watering is necessary place the tray in a larger container of water and let the seed-raising mixture soak up the moisture from below. Place the seed tray in strong, direct light but not direct sunlight.

Transplanting

After the seedlings have made their second or third leaves, either thin or transplant them. Always water the seedlings prior to transplanting and make sure that the ground into which they will be transplanted is also damp. Thin by removing all but the most promising ones. Take care when removing a seedling from the container not to damage its roots. Lever it out of the container with a small pointed tool. Do not replant at a depth greater than the previous one. When placing the seedling in the ground make sure that the roots are not cramped, then replace the soil gently around it.

During the first week or so after transplanting keep the plants well watered to encourage steady growth.

Direct sowing

Large seeds that are easy to manage can be planted directly into the ground. This saves transplanting and stops any setbacks which can occur when young plants are moved. Always follow the directions on the packet as to the planting depth and distance apart. The soil that covers the seeds should be fine and not lumpy. A seed-raising mixture will give best results. Keep the ground moist after planting until the young seeds emerge from the ground.

Cuttings

Plants propagated vegetatively or asexually reproduce, by means of DNA replication, all the genetic information of the parent plant. This is why the unique characteristics of any single plant are perpetuated in the propagation of a clone. New plants can even be started from a single cell, as any living cell of a plant has all the genetic information needed to regenerate the complete organism.

In propagation by cuttings a piece of stem, root or leaf is cut from the parent plant, after which this piece is placed under certain favourable environmental conditions and induced to form roots and shoots. This produces a new independent plant which, in most cases, is identical to the parent plant.

Stem cuttings are the most common type of cutting and these can be divided into four groups according to the nature of the wood used in making the cuttings: hardwood, semi-hardwood, softwood and herbaceous.

Propagating medium

The correct propagating medium will influence the number of cuttings that will root and the quality of the root system formed. A mixture of 2 parts river sand and 1 part peat moss is most effective.

Plant hormones

Plant hormones are applied to cuttings to encourage the production and even distribution of roots. Hormones also shorten the time taken by the plant to root. The end of the cutting is dipped into the powder before it is placed in the propagating medium.

Semi-hardwood cuttings

Semi-hardwood cuttings are generally used for propagating evergreen plants and are taken just after a flush of growth when the stems have become partially mature. Make the cuttings 8-15 cm long, retaining a couple of leaves at the top of the cutting. If the leaves are very large they should be reduced in size to prevent excessive loss of water. This can be done easily by cutting them in half with a sharp pair of scissors.

The basal cut should be made just below a node. It is necessary that leafy cuttings be rooted under conditions which will keep water loss from the leaves to a minimum. In commercial situations they are placed under intermittent mist sprays. In the home, the pot of cuttings can be placed ei-

Growing vegetables from seed is one of the most satisfying and rewarding aspects of gardening.

Windflower (Anemone japonica) can be divided in early spring.

ther in a propagating case or enclosed in a plastic bag. The plastic bag is not removed, except when watering is necessary, until the cuttings have taken root. Keep the cuttings in a warm, sheltered and shaded position.

Softwood cuttings

This type of cutting is taken from either deciduous or evergreen plants. Take it during early spring when the growth is rapid and the stems are quite flexible. Softwood cuttings generally root more easily and more quickly than the other types but require more attention. The best softwood cutting material has some degree of flexibility, but is mature enough to break when bent sharply. Some of the best cutting material is the lateral or side branches of the stock plant. Cuttings should be 7.5-15 cm long, with two or more nodes and the basal cut made just below a node. The leaves on the lower portion of the cutting are removed, with those on the upper part retained. Large leaves can be cut in half. Keep in a propagating case or seal in a plastic bag until it has rooted.

Herbaceous cuttings

Herbaceous cuttings are taken from succulent plants such as geraniums, chrysanthemums or coleus. Make the cutting 8-12 cm long and prepare the same way as for softwood cuttings.

Division

Plants with multiple stems arising from the base of the plant are usually propagated by division.

Method

- Carefully remove the plant from the ground.
- Shake away some of the soil so the the roots are easily seen.
- The root-ball can now be divided by either pulling it apart with your hands, a spade or a sharp knife.
- Replant the divisions immediately and keep well watered until the new plants are established.

Index

Abelia X *grandiflora* 133, 198, 203
Abutilon species 198, 203
Acacia pycnantha 191
Acacia species 191, 214
Acalypha hispida 198, 203
Acanthus mollis 99, 132, 143
Acer species 75, 130, 198, 208, 210, 214
Achillea species 25, 66, 133, 140, 143, 172, 174, 194, 175
Acidanthera bicolor 179
Aconitum napellus 66, 132, 133, 143
Actinidia kolomikta 165
Actinotus helianthii 194
Adenandra uniflora 203
Aethionema coridifolia 143
African marigold 130
Agapanthus species 43, 99, 133, 179
Ageratum houstonianum 186
Agonis flexuosa 214
Agrostemma githago 'Milas' 134
Ajuga species 99, 143, 170, 174, 175
Akebia quinata 165
Albizzia julibrissim 208, 214
Alcea rosea 66, 84, 132, 133, 143
Alianthus altissima 214
Allamanda cartharica 165
Allium species 131, 179, 225
Alnus species 136, 214
Alpine phlox 16, 107
Alpine strawberry 107
Alpine thyme 107
Alstroemeria aurantiaca 130, 131, 143, 179
Alstroemeria pulchella 141
Alyssum saxatile 130
Alyssum species 66, 186
Amaranth 186
Amaranthus caudatus 186
Amaryllis belladonna 131, 133, 179
American sweet gum 75
Ammi majus 84, 186
Anemone species 25, 60, 66, 99, 129, 132, 133, 141, 143
Anethum graveolens 225
Angel's trumpet 82, 215
Angelica archangelica 225
Angiopteris evecta 58
Anise 226
Anthemis nobilis 56, 132, 107, 143, 175, 225
Anthriscus cerefolium 225
Antigonon leptopus 165
Antirrhinum majus 185, 186

Aquilegia species 17, 24, 66, 71, 84, 129, 132, 143
Arabis albida 143, 175
Aralia chinensis 24
Arbours 119
Arches 120
Arenaria species 66, 108, 114, 143, 172, 175, 194
Aristolochia elegans 165
Armeria maritima 174
Artemisia species 143, 199, 225
Arum lily 24, 53, 70, 89, 181
Ash 75
Aspidistra elatior 99
Asplenium australasicum 98
Asplenium bulbiferum 58, 98
Aster species 132, 144, 194
Astilbe rivularis 132, 133, 144
Aubretia deltoides 144
Aurinia saxatilis 144, 175
Autumn crocus 179
Azalea species 203

Babies' tears 17, 29, 38, 53, 54, 66, 84, 108, 114, 172
Baby blue eyes 188
Baby's breath 141
Balloon flower 147
Bamboo palm 98
Banksia species 192, 214
Basil 226
Bauhinia species 165, 214
Bay 226
Bear's breeches 143
Beaumontia grandiflora 162, 165
Begonias 89
Belladonna lily 179
Bellis perennis 26, 38, 66, 132, 144
Bells of Ireland 187
Bergamot 130, 226
Bergenia cordifolia 99, 132, 144, 174
Betula pendula 57, 75, 135, 210, 214
Bird's nest fern 98
Birdbaths 116
Black locust 75
Black tulepo 75
Black-eyed Susan 169
Blechnum occidentale 98
Bleeding heart 99
Blood lily 180
Blue butterfly bush 29
Bluebells 62, 131, 181
Borago officinalis 133, 225
Boronia species 56, 203
Boston ivy 36, 162,
Bougainvillea species 165

Box 10, 17, 23, 200, 203
Brachychiton acerifolia 130, 214
Brachycome species 66, 108, 132, 144
Brunfelsia latifolia 29, 56, 133, 203
Buddleia davidii 24, 194, 203
Bugle weed 17, 99, 143, 174, 175
Bulbinella floribunda 179
Burning bush 145, 187
Busy Lizzie 10, 28, 66, 70, 89, 182, 187
Buttered eggs 26
Butterfly bush 203
Buxus sempervirens 10, 12, 17, 23, 125, 200, 201, 203

Calendula officinalis 186
Californian poppy 134, 186
Calliandra tweedii 198
Callistemon species 130, 186, 190, 191, 214
Callistephus chinensis 186
Calluna vulgaris 203
Calonyction aculeatum 82
Calothamnus asper 192
Calothamnus rupestris 192
Camassia cusickii 29, 179
Camellia species 133
Camomile 56, 107, 143, 225
Campanula species 16, 17, 29, 66, 132, 133, 141, 144, 172, 174, 175, 186
Campsis grandiflora 165
Canary Island date palm 70
Canary Island ivy 170
Canterbury bells 66, 186
Cantua bicolor 203
Cape cowslip 180
Cape honeysuckle 169
Caraway 225
Carissa grandiflora 237
Carolina jasmine 56, 162, 126, 166
Carum carvi 225
Caryota species 68
Cassia species 198, 215
Castanospermum australe 215
Catalpa bignonioides 215
Ceanothus burkwoodii 29
Cedrela sinensis 215
Celosia cristata 186
Centaurea cyanus 186
Centranthus ruber 144
Cerastium tomentosum 17, 53, 54, 66, 108, 114, 144, 172, 175
Ceratostigma species 133,

144, 203
Cercis silquastrum 208, 215
Cestrum nocturnum 56, 85, 126
Chamaedorea costaricana 68, 98
Chamaerops humilis 68
Chanenomeles japonica 203
Cherianthus cheiri 185, 186
Chervil 225
Chilean bean flower 161
Chilean bell flower 167
Chilean jasmine 36, 162, 167
Chincherinchee 24
Chinese angelica tree 24
Chinese aster 186
Chinese cedar 215
Chinese fan palm 68
Chinese forget-me-not 71
Chinese lantern 203
Chinese pistachio 75
Chinese star jasmine 12, 169
Chionananthus oxycantha 215
Chives 225
Chlorophytum comosum 174
Choisya ternata 24, 133, 198, 204
Chorizema cordatum 204
Christmas rose 43, 62
Chrysalidocarpus lutescens 98
Chrysanthemum species 25, 38, 58, 66, 129, 132, 133, 145
Cineraria 99, 188
Cissus species 36, 162, 165
Cistus laurifolius 198
Cistus purpureus 198, 204
Clematis species 36, 56, 12, 114, 126, 162, 165
Clerodendrum ugandense 133, 165, 198
Clivia miniata 99, 171, 179
Clover 175
Clytostoma calliestegoides 165
Cobaea scandens 84, 161, 166
Colchicum autumnale 179
Coleonema alba 24, 133
Columbines 17, 66, 71, 84, 129, 143
Comfrey 227
Common mignonette 85
Compost 242
Congea tomentosa 166
Convallaria majalis 62, 99, 132, 179
Convolvulus species 108, 174, 204
Cooper's tree fern 98
Coprosma baueri 125
Coprosma repens 198
Coral bells 147

Coral vine 165
Coriander sativum 225
Corn cockle 134
Cornflower 186
Cornus species 75, 133, 198
Coronvilla varia 175
Corylus avellana 'Contorta' 16, 198
Cosmos species 38, 38, 66, 25, 186
Cotinus coggygria 75
Cotoneaster species 125
Cotton lavender 207
Crab apples 208
Crassula multicava 171
Crategeus oxycantha 204, 215
Creeping fig 36, 162, 166
Creeping thyme 107
Crepe myrtle 216
Crinum species 179
Crocus species 179
Crown imperial 180
Cup-and-saucer vine 84, 166
Cupressus sempervirens 'Stricta' 86
Curly palm 68
Cuttings 250, 251, 252
Cyathea cooperi 98
Cynoglossum species 71
Cyphomandra betacea 235
Cyrtanthus o'brienii 179

Daffodils 62, 131, 180
Daphne species 56, 99, 204
Datura cornigera 82, 215
Daucas carota 134
Davallia pyxidata 58
Dawn redwood 75
Dead nettle 174
Delphinium species 66, 84, 132, 133, 140, 145, 184, 186
Deutzia gracilis 204
Dianthus species 132, 145, 194, 186
Dicentra spectabilis 99, 145
Dichondra species 175
Dicksonia antadctica 58, 98
Dictamnus albus 145
Dierama pulcherrimum 179
Digitalis purpurea 38, 66, 84, 129, 132, 145
Dill 225
Dillwynia sericea 194
Dimorphotheca species 185
Diosma 24
Diospyros kaki 75, 215
Dipladenia sanderi 'Rosea' 114, 166
Division 252
Dogwood 75
Dolichos lignosus 84, 161, 166
Doronicum cordatum 146
Dwarf date palm 98

Echinaceae purpurea 146
Echinops ritro 146
Echium fastuosum 133, 146, 204
Elkhorn 99
Elm 217

English daisies 26, 38, 66, 144
English ivy 170
English marigold 186
English yew 125
Enkianthus campanulatus 204
Epacris impressa 204
Erica species 204
Erigeron karvinsckianus 17, 29, 38, 53, 54, 66, 84, 108, 114, 132, 172, 146, 175
Eriostemon species 133
Eryngium giganteum 146
Eschscholtzia species 134, 186
Eucalyptus species 57, 130, 135, 190, 210, 211, 215, 216
Euonymus japonicus 125
Euphorbia wulfenii 146, 198, 204
European fan palm 68
Euryops pectinatus 89, 204
Evening primrose 82
Evening scented stock 85
Evergreen alder 136
Exochordia racemosa 204

Fairy bell 179
False acacia 75
Fatsia japonica 198
Feijoa sellowiana 198, 235
Felecia amelloides 133, 204
Fennel 49, 225
Festuca ovina 'Glauca' 146
Fetter bush 206
Ficus pumila 36, 162, 166
Five-leaf akebia 165
Flame tree 214
Flanders poppy 134, 188
Flannel flower 194
Floss flower 186
Foeniculum vulgare 225
Forget-me-nots 17, 28, 38, 49, 62, 66, 84, 89, 182, 187
Four o'clock plant 84
Foxgloves 38, 66, 84, 129, 145
Fragaria species 107, 174, 194
Frangipani 56
Fraxinus excelsior 'Aurea' 75, 130, 208
Freesia refracta 62, 131, 179, 222
Fringe tree 215
Fringed catchfly 25
Fritillaria imperialis 131, 179
Fuchsia species 89, 162, 166, 205

Galanthus nivalis 62, 131, 179
Galtonia candicans 180
Garden pink 145
Gardenia jasminoides 70, 205
Garlic 225
Garrya elliptica 199
Gazania hybrids 146
Gelsemium sempervirens 56, 126, 162, 166
Geranium species 7, 71, 89, 146
Geum quellyon 146

Ginger lily 99, 145
Gingko biloba 75, 130, 216
Gladiolus species 180
Globe thistle 146
Gloriosa superba 166
Glory lily 166
Glory vine 174
Gold cup vine 161, 169
Golden cane palm 98
Golden rain 209
Golden rod 148
Golden shower tree 215
Gomphrena globosa 187
Granny's bonnets 71
Grape hyacinth 62, 180
Grevillea species 58, 192, 200, 202, 205, 216
Gunnera mannicata 20
Gypsophila species 25, 66, 141, 146, 187

Haemanthus katherinae 180
Hakea salicifolia 198
Hamamelis mollis 198
Hammock fern 98
Hardenbergia species 114, 162, 166, 194
Hare's foot fern 58
Hawthorn 204, 215
Heartsease 84, 189
Hebe species 16, 133, 205
Hedera species 36, 70, 162, 166, 170, 174
Hedychium flavum 99, 146
Helenium autumnale 147
Helianthemum nummularium 147
Helichrysum species 175, 187, 194
Helleborus species 43, 62, 99, 147
Hen and chicken fern 98
Heuchera sanguinea 147
Hibbertia scandens 99, 114, 162, 166
Hibiscus 58, 205
Himalayan blue poppy 99, 147
Hollyhock 66, 84, 143
Honesty 28, 66, 99, 184, 187
Honeysuckle 126, 167
Hosta 99
Howea belmoreana 68
Howea forsteriana 98
Hoya carnosa 56, 166
Hydrangea species 114, 133, 166, 205
Hymenosporum flavum 56, 211
Hypericum calycinum 174, 205
Hyssopus officinalis 226

Iberis umbellata 187
Iceland poppy 188
Ifafa lily 179
Illawarra flame tree 130
Impatiens wallerana 10, 28, 66, 70, 89, 182, 187
Iris species 17, 24, 50, 89, 180

Italian bellflower 174
Italian lavender 16
Ivy 36, 62, 70, 166
Ixia viridflora 180

Jacaranda mimosifolia 133, 216
Japanese anemone 25, 66, 129
Japanese iris 17
Jasminum species 36, 56, 126, 162, 166, 198, 205
Jonquils 62, 131, 180
Judas tree 208, 215
Juniperus 'Grey Owl' 15
Juniperus communis 'Depressa Aurea' 15

Kaffir lily 179
Kalmia latifolia 205
Kangaroo vine 36
Kennedia species 162, 166
Kentia palm 98
Kerria japonica 205
Kidney weed 175
King fern 58, 98
Kniphofia uvaria 180
Kochia trichophylla 187
Koelreuteria paniculata 209
Kunzea ambigua 205

Laburnum vossi 199, 205, 216
Lachenalia aloides 180
Lagerstroemia indica 216
Lagunaria patersonii 216
Lamb's ear 141, 148
Lamium species 62, 170, 174
Lapageria rosea 161, 167
Larkspur 84, 184, 186
Lathyrus species 36, 85, 162, 167, 187
Laurus nobilis 200, 226
Lavandula species 16, 205
Lavender 194, 205
Lavender shower 25, 66, 140, 148
Lemon balm 226
Lenten rose 43
Leonotus leonurus 206
Leptospermum laevigatum 198
Leucojum vernum 62, 131, 180
Leucothoe fontanesiana 206
Liatris spicata 'Floristan White' 25
Lilac 207
Lilium species 129, 131, 180
Lily turf 99
Lily-of-the-Nile 179
Lily-of-the-valley 62, 99
Limonium sinuatum 66, 147, 184
Linaria vulgaris 134, 187
Lippia species 175
Liquidamber styraciflua 75, 216
Liriope spicata 99, 174
Lirodendron tulipifera 216
Little trumpet 108

INDEX

Livistona chinensis 68
Lobelia erinus 29, 99, 114, 187
Lobularia maritima 133, 187
London pride 171, 174
Lonicera species 16, 85, 126, 162, 167
Loropetalum chinense 206
Lotus corniculatus 26
Love-in-a-mist 28, 66, 99
Lovehearts 182, 189
Luculia gratissima 56, 198, 206
Lunaria annua 28, 66, 184, 187
Lupinus species 66, 132, 147, 187
Lychnis coronaria 49, 60, 66, 130, 147
Lycoris radiata 180

Macfadyena unguis-cati 167
Madagascar jasmine 56, 169
Madonna lilies 129
Magnolia species 56, 216
Mahonia species 198
Maidenhair tree 75
Malcomia maritima 187
Malus species 208, 216
Mandevilla laxa 36, 162, 167
Maple 75, 214
Marguerite daisies 38, 144
Marigold 188
Marjoram 226
Mathiola bicornis 85
Mathiola incana 185, 187
Matted pea bush 194
Maurandia barcliana 114
May 207
Mealycup sage 148
Meconopsis betonicifolia 99, 132, 147
Melaleuca species 133, 216
Melia azedarach 216
Melissa officinalis 226
Mentha pulegium 56, 107, 175
Metasequoia glyptostroboides 75
Metrosideros tomentosa 216
Mexican orange blossom 24, 204
Michaelmas daisies 144, 194
Mint 226
Mint bush 206
Mirabilis jalapa 84
Mock orange blossom 24, 206
Molucella laevis 187
Monarda didyma 130, 226
Mondo grass 17, 174
Monkshood 66, 143
Montanoa pipina ifida 206
Moonflower 82
Moss phlox 107, 147
Mother Spleenwort 58
Mountain thyme 107
Murraya exotica 206
Muscari botryoides 62, 131, 133, 180
Myosotis species 38, 49, 133, 182, 187

Narcissus species 62, 131, 180
Nashi pear 235
Nasturtium 99
Native frangipani 211
Native violets 89, 174
Nemesia strumosa 188
Nemophila menziesii 188
Nephelium species 235
Nerine species 181
Nicotiana species 54, 66, 82, 141, 188
Nigella damascena 28, 66, 133, 184, 188
Night-scented jasmine 56, 85, 126
Nyssa sylvatica 75, 217

Oak 75, 217
Obedient plant 147
Ocimum basilicum 226
Oenthera species 82, 141, 147
Ophiopogon japonicus 17, 174
Oregano 226
Oriental poppies 66, 130, 141, 147
Origanum species 226
Ornamental grape 169
Ornamental sage 66
Ornithogalum thyrsoides 24
Oyster plant 99, 143

Paeonia lactiflora 147
Paeonia suffruticosa 206
Pandorea species 58, 114, 167
Pansy 99
Papaver nudicaule 185, 187
Papaver orientale 66, 130, 132, 141, 147
Papaver rhoeas 134, 185, 187
Parrot beak 143
Parrotia persica 75, 217
Parthenocissus species 36, 162, 167
Passiflora species 167, 237
Pearl bush 204
Pelargonium species 206
Pennyroyal 56, 107, 175
Penstemon species 25, 66, 132, 147
Perennial pea 85
Perennial phlox 147
Periwinkle 99, 171
Persimmon 75
Peruvian lily 130, 179
Petrea volubilis 167
Petroselinum crispum 226
Petticoat palm 70
Petunia 133, 188
Phaedranthrus buccinatorius 167
Phaseolus caracalla 36, 84, 162, 166
Philadelphus coronarius 24, 133, 206
Philodendron species 99
Phlox species 16, 54, 107, 132, 133, 147, 175, 188
Phoenix species 70, 98
Phosphorous 245
Photinia species 125, 198

Physalis peruviana 235
Physostegia virginiana 147
Pieris japonica 133, 206
Pimpinella anisum 226
Pincushion flower 184, 188
Pink catchfly 182
Pink evening primrose 141
Pink jasmine 56, 162, 166
Pink shower tree 215
Pink trumpet vine 167
Pinus radiata 20
Pistacia chinensis 75, 217
Pittosporum species 10, 58, 125, 198
Plant hormones 251
Platycerium species 99
Platycodon grandiflorus 147
Plectranthus australis 171, 174
Plumbago capensis 29, 86
Plumeria rubra 217
Podranea ricasoliana 167
Pohutukawa 216
Polyanthus species 44, 99, 132, 148
Polygonatum multiflorum 24, 148
Poplar 75
Poppies 84, 89
Populus species 75
Potassium 245
Potato vine 36, 82
Primula species 99, 132, 133, 148, 188
Princess tree 217
Propagating cases 248
Prostanthera species 24, 133, 197, 206
Protea neriifolia 206
Prunus species 209, 206, 210, 217
Psidium cattleianun 237
Psoralea pinnata 133
Pyrostegia venusta 161, 162, 167

Queen Anne's lace 25, 84, 134, 186
Quercus species 75, 217
Quince 203
Quisqualis indica 167

Rangoon creeper 167
Raphiolepis umbellata 198
Red valerian 144
Red-hot poker 180
Reseda odorata 85, 188
Retaining walls 112
Rhododendron species 20, 197
Robinia pseudoacacia 56, 75, 211
Rock cress 144
Rock rose 204
Romneya coulteri 140, 148, 206
Rondeletia amoena 206
Rosa
  'Apple Blossom' 38
  banksia 78

  'Belle Isis' 78
  'Blackboy' 78
  'Cardinal de Richelieu' 78
  'Cecile Brunner' 78, 82
  'Clair Matin' 78
  'Francis E Lester' 38
  'Frau Karl Druschki' 78
  gallica 78
  'Iceberg' 23
  'Lady Hillingdon' 78
  'La Reine' 78
  'Reine des Violettes' 78
  'Tuscany Superb' 78
Rosa alba 154
  'Celeste' 154
  'Chloris' 154
  'Jacobite' 155
  'Maidens Great Blush' 155
  'Maxima' 155
  'Mme Plantier' 155
  'White Rose of York' 155
Rosa borboniana 155
  'Boule de Neige' 155
  'Gypsy Boy' 155
  'Honorine de Brabant' 155
  'Mme Isaac Péreire' 155
  'Mme Pierre Oger' 155
  'Souvenir de la Malmaison' 156
Rosa centifolia 153
  'Bullata' 153
  'Fantin Latour' 153
  'La Noblesse' 153
  'Old Cabbage Rose' 153
  'Petite de Hollande' 153
  'Reine des Centifeuilles' 153
  'Spong' 153
  'The Bishop' 153
  'Tour de Malakoff' 153
Rosa centifolia muscosa 154
  'A longs Pedoncules' 154
  'Baron de Wassenaer' 154
  'Comptesse de Murinais' 154
  'Golden Moss' 154
  'Henri Martin' 154
  'Lane's Moss' 154
  'Little Gem' 154
  'Mousseux du Japon' 154
  'Old Pink Moss' 154
  'White Moss' 154
Rosa chinensis 155
  'Archduke Charles' 155
  'Comtesse du Cayla' 155
  'Hermosa' 155
  'Louis XIV' 155
  'Old Blush' 155
  'Viridiflora' 155
Rosa (climbing) 158
  'Albertine' 158
  'Blackboy' 158
  'Cecile Brunner' 158
  'Courier' 158
  'Cupid' 158
  'Iceberg' 158
  'Lady Hillingdon' 158
  'Mme Abel Chatenay' 158
  'Mme Gregoire Staechelin' 158

'Paul's Lemon Pillar' 158
'Souvenir de la Malmaison' 158
'Swan Lake' 158
Rosa (Damask) 154
　'Botsaris' 154
　'Celsiana' 154
　'Gloire de Guilan' 154
　'Ispahan' 154
　'Marie Louise' 154
　'Quatre Saisons' 154
Rosa gallica 153
　'Agathe Incarnata' 153
　'Belle Isis' 153
　'Cardinal de Richelieu' 153
　'Charles de Mills' 153
　'Complicata' 153
　'Constance Spry' 153
　'Duc de Guiche' 153
　'Duchesse de Montebello' 153
　'Hippolyte' 153
　'La Belle Sultane' 153
　'Pompom Panachée' 153
　'Rosa Mundi' 153
　'Sissinghurst Castle' 153
　'Tuscany Superb' 153
Rosa (hybrid musk)
　'Autumn Delight' 157
　'Ballerina' 157
　'Buff Beauty' 157
　'Cornelia' 157
　'Eva' 157
　'Francis E Lester' 157
　'Penelope' 157
　'Prosperity' 157
Rosa (rambling)
　'Aglaia' 157
　'Appleblossom' 157
　'Aviator Bleriot' 158
　'Chaplin's pink Climber' 158
　'Dorothy Perkins' 158
　'Felicité et Perpetué' 158
　'Tausendschon' 158
Rosa rugosa 156
　'Belle Poitevine' 156
　'Frau Dagmar Hastrup' 156
　'Lady Curzon' 156
　'Mrs. Anthony Waterer' 156
　'Phoebe's Frilled Pink' 156
　'Rose à parfum de L'Hay' 156
　'Sarah Van Fleet' 157
　'Schneezwerg' 157
Rosa (Tea)
　'Adam' 156
　'Anna Oliver' 156
　'Catherine Mermet' 156
　'Devoniensis' 156
　'General Gallieni' 156

'Lady Hillingdon' 156
'Monsieur Tillier' 156
'Safrano' 156
Rose campion 49, 66, 130, 147
Rosmarinus species 114, 207
Rosemary 206, 207
Rudbeckia laciniata 148

Sage 227
Salad burnet 227
Salpiglossis sinuata 188
Salvia species 25, 66, 148, 188
Sandwort 143, 172
Sanquisorbia bakusanensis 148
Santolina chamaecyparissus 197, 207
Saponaria officinalis 148
Savory 227
Saxifraga umbrosa 132, 148, 174
Scabiosa atropurpurea 184, 188
Scarlet avens 146
Scarlet sage 188
Schizanthus X *wisetonensis* 188
Scilla campanulata 16, 60, 62, 131, 181
Scotch heather 203
Sea campion 148
Sea holly 146
Sea pink 172
Seaweed 246
Senecio X *hybridus* 188
Senegal date palm 70
Shasta daisy 25, 66, 129, 145
Sheep's fescue 146
Silene species 25, 49, 148, 182, 188
Silver birch 57
Silver vein creeper 162
Snail flower 84, 162, 167
Snapdragon 186
Sneeze weed 147
Snow-in-summer 17, 53, 54, 66, 108, 144, 172
Snowdrop 180
Snowflake 62
Soapwort 148
Soft tree fern 58, 98
Soil 240
　analysis 240
　pH 241
　sandy 241
　testing 241
　texture 240
Solandra maxima 161, 169
Solanum species 38, 82, 162, 169, 235

Solidago canadensis 148
Sollya heterophylla 162, 169
Solomon's seal 24, 148
Sorrel 227
Sparaxis tricolor 62, 131, 176, 181
Species geranium 84
Spider plant 174
Spirea cantoniensis 207
Sprekelia formosissima 181
Stachys species 141, 148, 175
Staghorn 99
Star jasmine 126
Statice 66, 132, 147, 184
Statuary 115
Stephanotis floribunda 56, 162, 169
Stigmaphyllon ciliatum 169
Stock 187
Stokesia laevis 148
Strawberry clover 26, 175
Strawflower 187
Streams 122
Summerhouses 118
Sundials 115
Swan River daisy 66, 108
Sweet Alice 66, 99
Sweet alyssum 187
Sweet pea 36, 162, 167, 187
Swimming pools 122
Syringa vulgaris 207
Syzygium luehmanni 191

Tagetes species 188
Tansy 49, 227
Tarragon 225
Tassel flower 186
Taxus baccata 125, 200
Tecomaria capensis 169
Thalictrum dipterocarpum 25, 66, 132, 140, 149
Thread palm 70
Thrift 143, 174, 194
Thunbergia alata 169
Thymus species 56, 107, 114, 132, 149, 172
Tick bush 205
Tiger flower 181
Tigrida pavonia 181
Tilia species 212, 217
Toadflax 99, 134, 187
Tobacco plant 54, 66, 188
Todea barbara 58, 98
Torenia fournieri 184, 189
Tortured hazelnut 15
Trachelospermum jasminoides 12, 56, 126, 169
Tradescantia species 99, 174
Transplanting 250
Tree paeony 206

Trifolium species 175
Tropaeolum majus 189
True snowdrop 62
Trumpet vine 165
Tulbaghia violacea 149, 181
Tulip tree 216
Tulipa species 181

Ulmus species 217
Underplanting 137
Urns 116
Utility areas 101

Vallota species 181
Verbena species 132, 149, 189
Veronica persica 26
Vervain 189
Viburnum species 133, 207
Vinca species 99, 171, 174
Viola species 49, 84, 89, 99, 133, 149, 172, 174, 189
Violets 49, 62,
Viper's bugloss 204
Virgilia capensis 211, 217
Virginia stock 99
Viscari 28, 60, 99, 133, 189
Vitis vinifera 169

Wallflower 186
Wandering jew 174
Washingtonia species 70
Waterfalls 122
Watering 246
Watsonia species 131, 181
Wattle 214
Weeping bottlebrush 130
Weigela floribunda 12, 207
Westringia fruticosa 198
White cedar 216
Wild strawberry 174, 194
Willow myrtle 214
Windflower 99, 143
Wishbone flower 184
Wisteria species 70, 126, 161, 169
Woodland anemone 66, 99, 143

Yarrow 66, 140, 143, 174
Yellow alyssum 130
Yesterday, today and tomorrow 29
Youth and old age 189

Zantedeschia aethiopica 24, 53, 70, 89, 181
Zephyranthes atamasco 181
Zinnia elegans 'Envy' 184, 189
Zoysia species 175